YOU CAN'T CATCH SUNSHINE

YOU
CAN'T
CATCH
SUNSHINE

Don Maynard and Matthew Shepatin

TRIUMPH
BOOKS

Library of Congress Cataloging-in-Publication Data

Maynard, Donald R., 1935–
    You can't catch sunshine / Don Maynard and Matthew Shepatin.
        p. cm.
    ISBN 978-1-60078-375-3
1. Maynard, Donald R., 1935– 2. Football players—United States—
Biography. I. Shepatin, Matthew. II. Title.
    GV939.M2973A3 2010
    796.332092–dc22
    [B]   2010016570

This book is available in quantity at special discounts for your group or organization. For further information, contact:

Triumph Books
542 South Dearborn Street
Suite 750
Chicago, Illinois 60605
(312) 939–3330
Fax (312) 663–3557
www.triumphbooks.com

Printed in U.S.A.
ISBN: 978-1-60078-375-3
Design by Sue Knopf
All images courtesy of Getty Images unless otherwise noted

To my son, Scot;
my daughter, Terry;
and their mom, Marilyn

Contents

Foreword

JOE NAMATH

DON MAYNARD WAS THE MAN OUR OPPONENTS WORRIED ABOUT— the deep threat, the speed guy, the knockout punch—and man, could he fly! He didn't sprint so much as glide past each yard marker with impossibly long, easy strides. He made it look like he was going all out when he ran shoulder to shoulder with the cornerback, then as soon as a high, arcing spiral met his hands, he would accelerate, Road Runner style, leaving the defender behind in a proverbial cloud of dust. Once he got that separation, nobody, not even the fastest defensive backs in the league, ever caught up with him. He was gone—long gone. Namath to Maynard. Touchdown.

But long before there was Namath to Maynard, there was a Hungarian boy from a rugged steel town in Beaver Falls, Pennsylvania, and a skinny kid from the sweltering cotton fields of West Texas. So how did two guys from humble beginnings ascend to the national spotlight and grab those Super Bowl rings? I'm not sure if anybody has the answer to that. But if there is anyone who can explain how the underdog's underdog pulled off the biggest Super Bowl win of the ages, it's my dear friend and former wingman Don Maynard.

Don was there every step of the way—I mean, *every step*. In his rookie year with the New York Giants in 1958, Don learned the finer points of the pro game from none other than Vince Lombardi.

He was there in 1958 for "the Greatest Game Ever Played." Although many people will recall that it featured 15 future Hall of Fame coaches and players, drew a then-unimaginable number of Americans to their TV sets, and changed the face of professional football forever, only the most fervent fan can tell you who the first player was to touch the ball in that history-making first-ever overtime period. Yep, rookie kickoff returner Don Maynard.

In 1959 Don became the very first draft choice of a brand new team, Harry Wismer's New York Titans. He was there in that first Titans season, playing in a defunct stadium to mostly empty stands. He was there when payday occasionally meant sprinting to the bank to cash your check before the account ran dry. He was there through all those hapless defenses and the rotating carousel of quarterbacks. But if you ask Don about those early AFL days, he'll tell you he had the time of his life. That's the way Don is, you see. When everybody else is complaining about the rain, he's looking toward the western horizon for a clear break in the sky.

Of course, the sun did ultimately emerge. Sonny Werblin bought the Titans in 1964, changed their name to the Jets, moved them into Shea Stadium, and committed great sums of his own money to furnish the team with a lot of young talent. And one of those new players was a shaggy-haired quarterback with bad knees out of the University of Alabama.

It was January 1965 and my contract with the Jets was big news in New York. The Jets invited me on a private tour of their shiny new stadium. Of course, the parade of newsmen trailing behind me made it a bit less private. I was led into the empty locker room, the media throng following close behind. There was Maynard, standing in the corner of the room with his back to us, wearing a pair of Levi's, cowboy boots, and a leather belt with the word *Shine* tooled on the back.

As we were introduced, Don looked at me, then around the room, sizing up the newspaper guys in the distance. He spun me around toward his locker and put his arm over my shoulder. "Lookie here, son." (That's how he spoke, you see, in a slow, Texas drawl.) "I know there's a lot of people patting you on the back and shaking your hand right now, but I want you to remember something. This is a cold-blooded business."

I was completely taken aback. All I could think to do was thank him. But I liked him from the get-go. He was a straight shooter. When training camp started six months later, there he was, still looking like he was about to leave on a cattle drive. It seems silly now, but back then football players were supposed to act and dress a particular way, basically in the mold of Johnny Unitas. The problem was, Don was determined to be in the mold of Don Maynard.

When I was just a rookie, Coach Weeb Ewbank told me, "Joe, you are a lucky man. You are going to be working with a great receiver." He was right on the money. If ever I had a question about the passing game, Don was the man to answer it. The more I got to work with him on passing routes, the more I learned to count on him, the more I learned to trust him. It didn't matter what the subject might be, either.

I remember after practice one afternoon when we were in the locker room. I was getting ready to brush my teeth because I had been chewing tobacco. Don was standing beside me, looked over, and said, "Hey, Namath! What are you doing?" I had no idea what he was talking about.

"You don't need all that toothpaste on that toothbrush!" he said. He took my toothbrush and the tube of toothpaste from me and demonstrated. "Lookie here, son. You just put this much on here, and that's all you need. Those people are just trying to get you to use a lot of toothpaste like that. You really don't need it."

Honest to God, I can't tell you how many times over the years that I've thought about Don while I'm putting toothpaste on my toothbrush. And that's how, in his typical Don fashion, he taught me that *frugal* isn't a dirty word.

Don was always coming up with new and interesting ways of doing things. I had heard stories from the veterans about Don's eccentric ways, how he had hooked up some custom-made propane system to his Ford Coupe. Don was ahead of all of us back then. His hybrid car, his sideburns, his Levi's, his custom-made AC units, his strapless helmet, his mesh jersey, his modified shoulder pads.... He paid attention to his body and what went inside it decades before that came into vogue. He invented his own training regimen, and it was a big factor in surviving the physical pounding he took year after year.

Don was around long enough to work with 25 different quarterbacks in his career, and he made most of us better football players. Twelve years after the league's inception, the lean 175-pound receiver was one of only four original AFL players still in the league. How's that for tough?

Don had grit, but he was also sharp as a tack. I think a lot of people saw that country boy exterior and didn't realize what lay beneath. And it was his mind just as much as it was his Texas flash that made him one of the all-time best at his position.

Yet to this day he remains New York City's least recognized sports hero. That's too bad. Because if any player deserves to finally get his due, to be placed in the league of all-time NFL pass catchers, it's Don Maynard.

Don was the first receiver to pass the 10,000 mark in total yards, an accolade that some have equated to running the four-minute mile. That number eventually climbed to 11,834, making him the game's all-time top receiver on the day he hung up his cleats in 1973.

He finished his career with the highest number of receptions—633. He also tied the great Jim Brown for the most touchdowns scored in the 1960s. Only two players in NFL history have had more than 50 100-yard games: Jerry Rice and, yep, Don Maynard. His 18.7-yards-per-catch average is third best among all Hall of Fame receivers.

But as impressive as those statistics are, just as impressive is how he earned them. I can tell you that Don conducted himself as a gentleman at all times, which is rare in a sport known for its violence and brutality. I've seen Don get held, tripped, clipped, and cheap-shotted, but I'll be damned if I remember a single time where he ever lost his cool.

I was struck at first with his speed and his hands, but later it was his character that impressed me most. He had promised his grand-dad a couple of things as a kid and stuck to them over the years. To this very day, his lips have never touched alcohol or a cigarette. If he ever cursed, I never heard him. To me, he's as wholesome as you can be. He's about doing what's right, not what's easy. No one's ever given him anything.

A couple of years ago, he shared something with me that I've shared with my children almost every day since. "Joe, I got something for you. Go get a pencil and paper and write this down," he said.

I learned over the years that when Don asked me to do something, it's actually worthwhile, so I went and got my pencil and paper and said, "Okay, I'm ready."

"Now, I want you to write down these 10 two-letter words." I did, and then I read them back.

If it is to be, it is up to me.

It was the first time I ever thought about my life in those terms, and it hit the nail right on the head. *If it is to be, it is up to me.* If you want it, then you get it done. I like that attitude.

It's because of the values he lived by but never preached—strength, integrity, and the courage of conviction—that he's become more than New York's greatest big-time receiver. He's been a great friend to me for more than 45 years.

Because Don Maynard has always been the same easygoing country boy who never cared about fame or recognition, his personal tale has been largely overlooked. I guess that makes me among the lucky ones, for to know Don is to encounter his down-home wit, his wily and wondrous worldview. After doing that, you can't help but feel that anything is possible, whether it's in sports or in life. It's like he said to me, all you have to do is write down these 10 two-letter words: *If it is to be, it is up to me.*

Of that, Don is living proof.

–Joe Namath

No Rest

Donkeys may kick and snort, but their reaction to stimuli is vastly different from that of horses. The horse is an animal of flight; when it is threatened, it runs. The donkey, on the other hand, tends to use its brain to outsmart danger. The mule retains this incredible sense of self-preservation through intelligence, and its methodical approach to life comes from its well-developed sense of self-preservation—a trait that keeps it from getting into as much trouble as a horse. If, for example, a mule is caught in a fence (which rarely happens) it will usually stand quietly, waiting for help. Most horses, by contrast, will panic, thrash around, try to break free, and often wind up with serious injuries. Most muleteers will tell you that, while a horse may be bullied into doing something, a mule will not do anything until it accepts the activity being proposed, knows that it is safe, and feels good and ready to proceed.

DRAFT HORSES AND MULES: HARNESSING EQUINE POWER FOR FARM & SHOW
BY GAIL DAMEROW AND ALINA RICE

MOST KIDS RODE A HORSE TO SCHOOL, but I rode a mule named Kate. She belonged to my granddad, Ralph Sharpe, who had a 600-acre homestead in Frederick, seven miles south of Carnegie, in what was then the Oklahoma Territory. Granddad Sharpe used to walk behind her while she and a horse pulled a two-row cultivator through his crop fields. Seeing that it was six miles from my granddad's farm to the schoolhouse, I was allowed to ride Kate there and back. My granddad would come outside at 7:00 in the morning and hoist me onto her. I was in first grade and barely four feet tall on my tippy-toes. Kate, on the other hand, was 18 hands high, making her one of the biggest mules around.

From there, it was one mile to the main gravel road and five more to the school. In the winter, Kate would clomp through the snow—why, in Oklahoma, you could get up to five inches—while my small feet dangled above the frozen, wet ground. When I reached the schoolhouse, getting off the mule was no problem. The challenge came at the end of the day, when I was ready to come home and I had to get back on the mule. I used to see the other kids walk their horses over to the fence beside the school. They'd scale up the fence and leap backwards awkwardly, onto their horse.

One day I walked Kate down yonder to the outhouses behind the school. The other kids looked at me curiously. Both the boys' and girls' outhouse had an L-shaped partition made up of seven-foot vertical boards, which hid the entrance of the toilet from any spectators. I climbed up the beams until I got high up on the wall. From there, I jumped over on the mule's back with ease. As soon as the other kids saw me doing this, they started getting on their horses in the same way.

Five years old might seem like an early age to start riding horses, but in farming towns like Frederick, kids were taught to ride even earlier than that. When I was three, Grandad Sharpe would sit me in his lap while he rode Kate. We'd ride a quarter of mile down to the stock tank and round up the cattle, then drive them back to the barn. Along the way, Granddad showed me how to work the reins. *Still hands and a light touch.* Good advice for riding a mule—or for catching a Joe Namath bullet pass.

I was different because I rode a mule and the other kids rode horses. Maybe their granddads didn't own mules, but mine did, so that's what I rode. There are some people who think mules are temperamental and thus a bad choice of transportation. The truth is, a mule isn't so much stubborn as careful. Kate was so good-natured that she'd do anything my granddad asked her to do—including give me a ride to school. I also rode Kate bareback, something the other kids didn't do with their horses. I never rode in a saddle—I didn't even own one. My family didn't have the money. It didn't matter much to me. The only reason you got on a horse—or a mule—was to go down a short distance to the pasture to bring in the cattle. Otherwise, you were walking behind her while she plowed the field. I was a freshman in high school before I ever rode in a saddle; and even then, the horse and saddle belonged to my friend. I rode it a couple of times, and that was it. I never owned a saddle in my life. But like I said, Kate was a gentle mule. She never once gave me any trouble.

Frederick, Oklahoma, was where my mom and dad met. Ten years earlier, my dad had heard that there was cotton to be ginned up in Oklahoma, so he drove all the way from Paris, Texas, to the cotton compress in Frederick. When he arrived at the plant he met my mom, who was working as a secretary in the office. They fell in love, got married, and had my brother, Thurman, and my sister, Marilyn. Not long after they were born, my dad got an opportunity to manage the cotton gin down in Crosbyton, Texas. So that was that—they moved.

I was born on January 25, 1935, in Crosbyton, which is 36 miles east of Lubbock, 1,800 miles southwest of New York City, and a million miles from Canton, Ohio. My mom was 42 years old when I was born. Mom and Dad were more like grandparents to me. I used to kid my Mom, "I know I'm not supposed to be around here, but

I love you anyway." My mother never responded to the comment—it doesn't mean it was good or bad or anything else.

When I was four, my momma was sent to a tuberculosis sanatorium, which is how I ended up living with her parents. My mom's brood had been among the first 50 families to settle in Ohio. When, in 1862, the government passed the Homestead Act, offering free land to anyone willing to put down roots in the new territories, my granddad put in his application. He received 160 acres of land in Frederick, and in return, he agreed to work that land for five years. If, in that time, he built a house, grew crops, raised livestock—and managed not to get shot or scalped—then he could file for a deed of title. Which, when the time came, is exactly what he did.

My dad would have cared for me, but he was off managing cotton gins around West Texas. His name was Tom. He was a plain guy. Worked ever since the day he was born. He didn't make it past the third grade. I respected my dad. In a way, I was very scared of my dad. He wasn't a big guy—maybe 5'9", slender build—but when Dad called my name, I didn't just turn my head, I got up and walked closer. I knew he probably wanted me to do something. Before he finished the sentence, I said, "Yes sir." Same went with my mom: "Yes, ma'am." I didn't get up from that dinner table until I ate everything on my plate. When there was something there I didn't like, I'd sit there for half an hour. But you have to understand that most working-class parents raised their kids a certain way.

Like most kids who came from a farming town, I went to a one-room schoolhouse. The name of the school was Lone Star, which was odd because it was in Oklahoma. My teacher's name was Mary Jo Roderick. As far as I know, she was a good teacher. Naturally, she never had any discipline problems with me or any of the other kids. You came to school, you sat in your row, you kept quiet, and you did your work. Graduating to the next grade was easy: you just moved down a row. You knew you had graduated from sixth grade when you bumped into the big potbelly stove in the back of the room.

The arrival of the cotton harvest every fall meant that school would be closed for three weeks so that all the kids could work in the fields all day, picking cotton. To make up for the days missed, we attended classes on Saturday once a month throughout the year. I'd follow my older brother, Thurman—he was 12, I was 5—out to the fields where he showed me the right way to pick the hulls. Just like Dad, Thurman was big on doing things the right way. He was an Eagle Scout. A real straight shooter. He never drank or smoked. He'd grow up to be an Army paratrooper, and then 13 years later he became an FBI agent. My brother is a class individual—he has been his entire life. When he finished his homework, he would help me with mine. And I knew if I didn't study, or if I did anything wrong, he'd get on my case about it. But then, he didn't have to. There wasn't much trouble to get into unless you were going to try to conjure it up yourself. But why get in trouble when it was easier to be a good person?

I enjoyed living with my grandparents. Except for P.E. class, there wasn't much in the way of organized sports for kids my age, but you could run free on a farm. You got to be around animals—horses and cattle and dogs. You could go fishing in the streams or cottontail hunting in the woods. Beats me how I got into football. Youth football leagues sure didn't exist back then, and neither did Little League baseball. Probably some kid got a football for Christmas and we'd go down to a vacant lot and toss the ball around.

For two and a half years, my grandparents raised me as their own child. I like to say, they raised us with love through discipline and then disciplined with love. As a result, you didn't do anything wrong. Maybe there wasn't much to do wrong, anyway. There sure wasn't much time to do wrong between going to school and doing chores around the farm, between picking cotton in the fall and growing your own vegetables and milking your own cows. On a farm, believe me, there's always something to be done.

When my mom came out of the TB sanatorium, my dad moved our family down to Pettit, Texas. Leaving my grandparents was hard. I didn't want to go, but I didn't have a choice. Pettit was where the cotton was, and where the cotton was, is where we had to go.

I never knew the extent of my mom's sickness. All I knew was that she had gone to stay at this "sanitation" place. And then one day she was back. I didn't question anything. She lived to be 86, so what didn't get her then never did.

Because my father had to move us around so much for work, my family always rented. In his whole life, my father never owned a house. My mother didn't own one until she was 65 years old. When we arrived in Pettit in 1941, our family rented a two-bedroom house a couple of miles outside of town. My mom and dad slept in one room, and we kids slept in the other. Back then, there was no such thing as a living room. Nearly everybody had a big kitchen with a table against the wall, and that's where everything went on. It's where my mom canned jars of fruit from the garden so that we wouldn't go hungry in the winter or sewed patches on our clothes so that we wouldn't get cold. In the middle of the night, I'd get dressed in front of the fire before walking outside and scampering to the outhouse. That got cold. Real cold. It wasn't until fourth grade that we finally had indoor plumbing.

Pettit was a farming town in Hockley County with a population of less than 500. It had a church, a general store, a post office, two filling stations, and that's about it. The town used to be named Lookout until a railroad was built through the town. The railroad forced the locals to change it because their passengers kept freaking out every time the conductor yelled out, "Next stop, Lookout!"

My dad was a perfectionist. It didn't matter if you were taking out the trash or writing a letter or building a doghouse; you did it right the first time so you didn't have to go back and do it over again. When he told me to go out to the vegetable garden and chop all the weeds, I made sure to chop every last one of them. I'd make sure to get down really low, down on my hands and knees, where a weed couldn't hide from me behind a stalk. I knew, let that weed live there next to the carrot, and that weed would sop up the moisture that carrot needed in order to grow. As a result, that carrot would grow 5 inches long instead of 10 inches long. Worse, it might not grow at all. And that would be one less carrot my mom had to can, one less carrot our family had to eat.

It didn't matter the size or importance of the chore, our mom and dad never had to tell us kids to so something twice. My dad would send me out to the woodpile with a five-gallon bucket. I'd fill that bucket until it was overflowing with timber—some pieces the size of my arm, even some the size of my leg from the knee down. Then I'd always get a couple of big logs—as big around as a coffee can—to burn on through the night to keep the kitchen and bedrooms warm. This went on day after day. I was 12 before I realized my name wasn't "Git Wood."

What was the toughest financial period for my family? I don't know. Every day. The thing was, everybody I knew was poor, including us. It's just that none of us knew it. That was just our way of life. Nobody felt like they were lacking. I never thought about being poor, and I never thought about being rich. In a way, we felt rich just being alive and getting three meals on the table each day.

The unhappiness came every time we had to move from one town to the next. We might spend only six months in one place before the movers came and packed up all our belongings. I barely had time to say good-bye to my friends, the boys I'd gone fishing with down by the stream or played football with in the vacant lots. Six months would pass in a new town, or another year, and it would be the same thing all over again. I had to leave my good friends behind, and I hated it. Every time, I'd ask my mom the same thing: "Why do we have to move?"

Constantly moving to new towns meant that I was always looking for new friends. This is why I was such a big fan of going to Sunday school. I'd arrive at the new church and meet two or three all right guys who didn't live too far away. Who knows, maybe one of them had a football. Or they would ask me if I wanted to go fishing. *You want to go, Don? You bet.* I might not even have a cane pole or a float, but I would go along with them to the stream and find out that they had brought an extra one for me to use. I would be fishing with my new friends and before long that sad feeling would disappear.

Because our family was always moving around, we attended a lot of different Protestant churches. Some of them were a lot more Baptist than others. My mother was more religious than my dad, I suppose, but they were both religious in their own quiet way. The number of times his kids went to church wasn't nearly as important to my dad as making sure that we were good people and that we did good things and that we did our chores and errands without being told twice. I'd watch how my older brother and sister would act— good and kind and polite—and I just followed their example. They didn't smoke or drink, and neither did I.

I had made a promise to my Grandad Sharpe at age five that I would never touch beer or alcohol. To be honest, the stuff held little interest to my buddies and me. And anyway, it wasn't like it was widely available; the six-pack wasn't even invented yet. Naturally, it would have been nice if somebody told me that, in the future, Super Bowl champions would celebrate their victory by drinking champagne—that is, before I swore to Grandad Sharpe that alcohol would never touch my lips. In addition to learning the importance of staying clear of alcohol, I also grew up learning not to waste money. Just because you have some extra money, that doesn't mean you have to run out and spend it. Take some of your earnings and put it aside for a rainy day or perhaps for a special occasion. In our family, Sunday dinner was such a time. My mom would make chicken with all the trimmings. During the week, dessert consisted of applesauce, but on Sunday Mom would bake an apple pie or a peach cobbler.

At Christmastime, Thurman, Marilyn, and I would make a list of the things we wanted. We were each given a piece of paper with three columns on it. Column 1 would be expensive items; Column 2 would be less expensive items; and Column 3 would be the cheapest items you could buy. You might have felt that you really needed something in Column 1, but you knew it was wishful thinking.

Now, some people in my life have called me frugal, even cheap, but the way I see it, everything has a value. The question is, do you want to waste it, or do you want to maximize it? We all have things we want, but if you ask yourself, *Do I really need this?*, then you can help regulate those desires. One time, I saved up enough to buy a foxhole shovel. Do you know how much easier it is to build a foxhole with a foxhole shovel? Well, I did, but the other kids didn't.

In the summer, I made extra money mowing lawns. I could make a quarter mowing the front yard, maybe 50 cents on a bigger yard. Occasionally, I'd also put in a few hours at the store, sacking groceries. By the end of every summer, I'd saved up a little money. It was the only time all year I had extra spending cash. The first thing I'd do was go into town and buy five pairs of Levi's to get me through the school year. After that, there wasn't much money leftover. For years I saved up for a bicycle. It wasn't until I was in the eighth grade that I got one, and even then my dad paid for half of it. I wanted to ride it to school, but it was 13 miles away. Thirteen miles might not have been too far for Kate, but it was for me.

Then, at age nine, we moved to Levelland, Texas, and I started a newspaper route. For the first time in my life, I had extra spending money in my pocket. I went out and bought myself a flashlight. My friend, who also had a newspaper route, bought himself a cap pistol instead. I hooked the flashlight to my belt and, after finishing my deliveries, I used it like a headlight as I rode home in the dark. It was handy being able to see where I was going. To this day, I keep a flashlight by my bed, one over on the dresser, one in the bathroom, and one by the front door. I also have three spotlights I can trigger. I guess you could say I've always had guidelines regarding the usage of lights: use them when needed; don't use them when not needed. It's a practice I like to call common sense and reality. As for that kid with the cap pistol, he probably ended up riding through the pastures all night, delivering newspapers to goats.

Levelland, Texas, was a cotton town west of Lubbock that earned national notoriety in 1957 when it became the site of a series of unexplainable UFO sightings. High school football was a big deal in Levelland, just like it was in most small towns in Texas. And they had a great football team, went as far as the regional championships. It wasn't much of an interest to my parents, though. My dad was too busy working at the oil refinery to go to football games, even if my older sister, Marilyn, was a Levelland cheerleader. Thurman wasn't on the team, but he would take me with him to the games. I didn't care that my brother didn't play sports. I wanted to be just like him, all the same.

With football ruled out again because of ineligibility, I had to find other sources of entertainment in Levelland, which you might say were a bit limited. I wound up following in my brother's footsteps, joining the Boy Scouts. Thurman was my senior patrol leader.

He was twice as tough on me as he was the next guy because he wanted me to be my best. I didn't make Eagle Scout like him, but I did well enough and had a lot of fun.

I didn't have a television and neither did anyone else I knew. It was nonexistent. Sometimes on Saturdays I'd go into town with my brother or a couple of pals and pay nine cents to see a movie on the big screen. If people wanted to catch a football game, they flipped on their radio sets. Back then, the NFL wasn't even a blip on the radar. If you lived in West Texas, all you cared about were teams in the Southwest Conference. The rivalry between the league's two powerhouses—SMU and Texas—was always intense, but it went into overdrive during those years because standing on opposite sides of the fight were Doak Walker and Bobby Layne, two of the very best players in the country. Adding another twist to the tale, Walker, SMU's great running back, and Layne, Texas's great quarterback, were best friends from childhood.

When I got into middle school, I'd travel 600 miles on a bus to work for my uncle in South Oklahoma for the summer. As always, you went where you could get work. How far you had to travel didn't matter. My uncle had a painting business, mostly painting cotton gins but also water towers and smokestacks. You'd go to one little town, paint a cotton gin, and then move on to the next location, which might be 50 miles away. It was a good-paying job and it kept me busy. I liked it fine.

My uncle was a guy by the name of Howard Sharpe. He had been a great athlete at Oklahoma University, a track star. After he graduated, he started the painting business. He worked hard in his profession. He painted the entire Evansville Bridge in Oklahoma at least once. His three boys, all much older than me, worked for him. In some cases, being kinfolk means you don't have to work as hard as the next guy, but to people like my uncle, being kinfolk means you have to work even harder. My uncle believed in working hard but he treated me fairly.

Most of the small schools had track teams because meets didn't cost much to put on. You just line people up to start in one place and finish in another. I started running track in the fourth grade and competed in the only two events they had: the 50- and 100-yard dash. For three years straight, I finished in first place.

In 1948, I was 13 years old. That summer, as usual, I'd gone to work for my uncle, traveling from town to town painting cotton gins, smokestacks, and water towers. My uncle had a five-man paint-ing crew. I was painter No. 6. We might work two days in Lubbock, than a couple of days in Levelland, and then head over to Waco for a few more. One summer, we painted all the light poles at Texas Tech. Then when we got done there, we painted the light poles at Oklahoma A&M. And then we traveled down to Oklahoma University, where my uncle had been a track star years back, and painted the light poles there.

One day my uncle and I were painting a water tower over in Morton. Once you got high up on those towers, you melted faster than a snowball in a furnace. He said to me, "You know, Don, anybody can be a sprinter, but not everybody can be a hurdler." I glanced over at him. He paused, wiped the sweat from his brow, and went back to painting.

After we were done for the day and my cousins had packed up their gear and drove off in their pickup trucks, my uncle and I stayed behind at the cotton gin yard. The yard, which was a lot like the parking lot of a football field, was where the farmers brought their trailers—which were 25 feet long and 10 feet tall and filled with cot-ton. Day and night, the trailers were lined up one after the other, like cars at a drive-in theater, waiting to get their cotton weighed.

My uncle took two sawhorses and hammered them into the ground three feet apart. He then took a stick and laid it across the other two sawhorses. He then looked at me and said, "There's your hurdle, Don."

After work, from time to time, I would practice the low hurdles in the gin yard with my uncle looking on. Naturally, I struggled at first. "You don't jump the hurdle, you hurdle the hurdle," said Uncle Howard. "Why do you think they call it a hurdle?"

He showed me I had to step over the hurdle with my lead leg and let my back leg drag behind it. That took care of the "getting over" part. Then, of course, the quicker you could get over the hurdle the better you would be in the race. Another thing my uncle emphasized was "running smooth." The smoother you run, the less effort it takes to move your body, and the faster you'll go. Over time, I got the hang of it.

Now, I'm not going to tell you that I practiced every day. Some days we would be working real late and it would be dark by the time we were finished. Those days, I wasn't going out there and jumping hurdles. I went to eat supper and shower. But I knew from working on my granddad's farm and from watching my brother climb his way to Eagle Scout that by working harder, I could achieve better and better results.

Next, we moved to Stegall, Texas. The fall of my freshman year, I attended Three Way High School (made up of students from several small communities that might have had nothing more than a grocery store, filling station, and a cotton gin). It was then I went out for the football team. Because of the small size of the school, they played what was called six-man football. In six-man, you have a center, two ends, a quarterback, a left half, and a right half. I was a backup quarterback. The QB could throw it to one of his ends or pitch it to one of his halfbacks. Everybody on the team was eligible to catch the pass except the quarterback. It's kind of funny that the first time I ever played organized football, the only person not allowed to catch a pass was me. Not only that, I couldn't run with the ball under the rules of six-man, either, so I couldn't even show off my speed.

There was a kid on our six-man team named Charles Smith. He wore No. 13. On the opening kickoff of the season, he broke his leg. Most everybody attributed his bad break to the fact he wore No. 13. After that, nobody would get within shouting distance of his uniform. Give it to me, I told them. I'll wear the darn thing.

At midterm of freshman year, our family moved to Portales, New Mexico. Football season was over already, and basketball season was starting up. I joined the freshman basketball team that winter.

My dad lost his job every Christmas, and there wasn't a thing he could do about it, either. Winter is when farmers plow and dig up the stalks in preparation for the start of the planting season in the spring. You have no cotton; you have no cotton to gin. So one day, Dad picked up a set of books on carpentry and, over time, he taught himself a new trade. I don't know how he read all those books—he only went to school up to the third grade—but I guess he found a way. Every winter, from then on, Dad drove to the city to do carpentry work, and the money he made carried us over until it was time to gin cotton again. You do what you have to do to get by.

The cotton season was over, and before you knew it so was the school year. At the end of summer of ninth grade, we moved to Lamesa, pronounced *Lameesa*, where my dad was hired by a small local construction company that built houses.

Mom, why do we have to move again?

I went out for high school football, but after a week I decided I didn't want to play on the team. I didn't play any sports that year. Who knows why? I didn't do anything but go to school. I guess I didn't care much for the coach, but the main thing was being able to work a little after school so I had some spending money. Maybe buy an extra pair of boots—or a pair of boots, period.

Last semester of sophomore year, my parents told me we were moving yet again, this time to San Angelo, Texas, where my dad got a job as a manager at the local cotton compress. We lived off Chadbourne and 19th Street. The number on the house was 13 West 19th Street. Another one of those 13s that kept popping in my life. My dad's birthday was on the 13th, my sister's birthday was on the 13th, and my brother had two 13s in his army serial number.

I had a friend from school who lived across the street and he had a pickup truck. We would pile in there and drive out to Concho River on the weekend. Maybe I mowed the lawn in the morning and I would get permission to go fishing out there on the river, which fed into Lake Nasworthy. We could catch a bunch of fish—a small fish the size of your hand called blue-gill. Seemed like there was always a bunch of them in a school. If you could catch one, you could catch a whole bunch in the same area of the river. I also played some B-team basketball (JV) and ran track.

As much as I loved San Angelo and fishing for blue-gill, Dad had gotten an offer to run the compress up in Colorado City. It was a full-time job, meaning he didn't have to do any more carpentry work.

Mom, why do we have to move again?

Because we moved to Colorado City in early summer, I had an opportunity to meet some of the guys on the football team through Sunday school, which meant I felt more relaxed about joining the team. I met my best friend, Corbell—but everyone called him Corby. He was the quarterback junior year and then moved over to tailback senior year. As time went on, we became close friends, worked out our pass patterns in the summer, and on other days we'd go fishing on Lake Colorado City. I would play pranks on him and the others.

I used to put cake coloring in my hair—one day it would be purple, another day it would be red. I did it before Dennis Rodman was born.

Colorado City (in Texas that's pronounced *Colorada*) was known as the Mother City of West Texas because it was the first town between Fort Worth and El Paso, which was a stretch of about 600 miles—and it was a stopover as they moved the cattle herds from South Texas or Mexico up to the Midwest. They had a parade that year to celebrate the town's centennial. I suggested dressing up as Davy Crockett and riding a float. Ol' Davy fought back in the Alamo. He was one of the guys, along with Sam Houston and Jim Bowie, who were outnumbered and who nobody really gave a chance. There were just 180 men against 10,000 soldiers. And they held them off for 13 days or more. I liked that spirit, keep fighting. I went all summer without a haircut. It was long, although it wouldn't be called long today—maybe down the back of my neck. I had colored my hair orange for amusement's sake—I did some odd things and that was just one of them—and so I made a perfect Davy Crockett with my hair tinted the color of orange crepe paper. I put a little baby oil on it, which gave it a glisten, and borrowed a coonskin cap and a fringe leather jacket. You couldn't miss me.

I was fortunate that the Wolves had a real fine football coach named J.J. Buxkemper. In addition to being an easy guy to get along with, I was impressed that he had played with the great Bobby Layne at Texas, which at the time was one of the top teams in the nation. He knew football real well. We ran a formation called "the wing-T" in high school, and most the teams back then ran it that way. You'd have a flanker to the right and you'd call it wing-T right or wing-T left. Buxkemper was a young coach but real good, real dedicated, and he went on and had quite an interesting career himself. That year there was a national polio epidemic—school stopped all physical activity for one week and canceled all games. The school discussed giving all of us the Salk vaccine but never did. I missed the first two weeks of football practice at the start of my junior year. I had the chance to help my uncle paint on his route—cotton gins in Lamesa, Post, Turkey, and Paducah, Texas; a water tower in Loving, New Mexico; and back to Texas again for a gin up near Morton. When I got back, Buxkemper allowed me to play on defense, although technically I wasn't eligible. I still had yet to ever start a game on offense before.

Later, in my junior year in Colorado City, I played on the B team in basketball and then ran track. (You only had to live in town for eight weeks to become eligible to participate in track.) Buxkemper coached track and football, so he saw how fast I was on the track field. His thought was, *I'm sure we could use this kid on defense. He'll learn enough to figure out the rest.*

Finally, in my senior year at Colorado City, I was eligible to play varsity football for the first time. I looked forward to taking the field as a starter for the first time in my life. Despite my lack of experience, I was named the starting halfback on offense and safety on defense. Back then you went both ways because you had only about 23 players on what they call the varsity, or what they call in Texas the A team. Some guys had been playing ever since grade school. But I had something they didn't: speed. The speed to chase down receivers, the speed to recover, the speed to leave the opponent's secondary in the dust. Being fast always helps in any sport, but in football it helps even more—especially when you're playing on both offense and defense. Being able to outrun the defender makes all the difference in the world. You might play an entire ballgame and not throw the ball but four or five times. But I made sure that I made heads turn those four or five times.

I never thought about becoming a professional football player or going to college. There was a proper way to run track, and that's the way I tried to run. It's just like there was a proper way to write a letter or paint a water tower or pick cotton or weed a garden. Once you knew the proper way to do something, then it was just a matter of practicing it until you got better. Do something, do it properly—that's how my parents raised me. Later in life, I'd see some of these guys signing autographs and you couldn't even read their names. I guarantee that you can read every letter I write in my name.

In 1953 I was a senior in high school. That year, I made it past the regionals in the hurdles and qualified for the state tournament in Austin. Over three days in Austin, I made it past the biregional, then district, then sectional, and finally I ended up in the final championship race in the low and high hurdles. My uncle was 800 miles away in Oklahoma, painting with his boys, so he didn't see it, but I won both races.

My parents didn't make it either. They couldn't go to a track meet 580 miles away. When I got home, I showed my dad the gold medal. He congratulated me. Later, he framed a write-up from the local newspaper and hung it on the wall. When I thought back on all the places we had lived, from that one-bedroom house in Pettit to that three-bedroom in Colorado City, it occurred to me that every time my dad moved us to another town—until I'd been to 13 schools, five high schools—our lives got a little better. He'd get a raise, and, as a result, we'd get an extra pair of pants that year. Later in life, I understood things better. I understood my dad better. I finally had an answer to that question that I had asked my mom so many times growing up.

Yes, Dad, I know why we had to move.

No Eligibility

I GRADUATED HIGH SCHOOL WITH A PERFECT ATTENDANCE RECORD. Since the day I first rode Kate to that one-room schoolhouse in Lone Star, I had not missed one day of school. For that matter, no tardies, either. There was no reason to be late. I knew the distances I had to walk to school. My whole life, I left the house 30 minutes early. That way, I had nothing to worry about. Getting handed that "perfect attendance" certificate at the end of each school year was something to be proud of—or at least I thought so. I might not be able to get straight As, but I could earn perfect marks for attendance and for conduct. Besides, if you could do something the best—in this case, the best was perfect attendance—why wouldn't you try? The streak served no larger purpose in my head. I was happy to get my diploma. I hadn't thought too far beyond that.

Winning the Texas state title in the low and high hurdles spun my life in a direction that I couldn't have anticipated. Soon enough, the head coaches from all the Southwest Conference universities arrived at my doorstep, offering me a full scholarship to attend their school: the University of Texas, Texas A&M, Texas Tech, Baylor, SMU, TCU, and Hardin-Simmons—they all showed up to recruit me. I can't say I'd ever been much interested in college. I didn't really think about it, one way or another. I knew I was going to work with my uncle that summer; the only difference was that come fall I wouldn't need to buy five pairs of Levi's for the school year.

My parents had an opinion about me going to college, one they weren't shy in expressing. They said to me, "Here comes this rare opportunity to get an education, because of what you've achieved on the track—why pass it up?" My dad never actually said, "Go to college so you can have the advantages that I never did." He didn't have to. I knew my dad's feelings on how a man should live his life. You took it.

Naturally, my dad wasn't around when the coaches came by the house to recruit me. He was off working. So, I'd meet them alone. Sometimes, Corbell and I would take a trip to see a school's campus and check things out, if it wasn't too far away. One time, we took a train to tiny Texas Western College, situated on the northern bank of the Rio Grande in El Paso. It was founded back in 1914 as a mining school. The State School of Mines and Metallurgy, as it was once called, became Texas Western College in 1949. It changed its name for a third time in 1967 to the University of Texas at El Paso.

When we arrived in El Paso, Wayne Hansen was waiting to greet us at the train station. You've heard of a guy named Dick Butkus, right? Well, Wayne Hansen was the Bears linebacker that came before Butkus. He was also one of the greatest players to have ever come out of Texas Western. He ended up playing nine seasons in Chicago, during which time he became the team captain. In the off-season, Hansen ran a car rental business in El Paso. As a favor to the Texas Western head coach, he'd pick up recruits at the train station and give them a personal tour of the school, hoping to help entice them to come play for the Miners. He helped out during spring training, as well. When fall arrived, he'd go back to Chicago and rejoin the Bears.

When Corbell and I met Hansen, he was in his fourth season in Chicago. The first thing we noticed upon seeing Wayne Hansen was his size. He was big guy: 6'2", about 235 pounds. His hands were massive. Following him around the campus, our minds couldn't help but get to thinking, *Here's this West Texas boy just like us. And now he's the linebacker for the Chicago Bears.* For a couple of guys still in high school, we couldn't help but be impressed.

Decades later, I was at a golf charity event and some guy was talking about the Bears linebacker at the time. (Hint: he's now the coach of the 49ers.) I listened to this guy go on and on and then I said, "He's no Wayne Hansen." And he said, "*Who?*" I just chuckled.

We followed Hansen up to Kidd Field. On our way there, we passed an old mine shaft, a small reminder of the school's humble origins. Once we reached the field house, we went inside and met with the Miners' head coach, Mike Brumbelow. Years back, Brumbelow had been an outstanding running back at TCU. He took over the Texas Western football program in 1950. Within four years, he'd guided the Miners to consecutive Sun Bowl victories. Back then, there were only six bowl games played, but what made this feat even more impressive was the fact that Texas Western was a tiny Division II college competing in the same conference as big-time Division I universities including Texas Tech, Arizona, and Arizona State. This was a school that had specialized in mining and metallurgy just a year before his arrival!

Coach Brumbelow believed that the key to victory was a great defense, and this mindset was reflected in how the team was built. You might assume that, as a speed receiver, I had a problem with Brumbelow's "defense first" ethos. Not so. In fact, one of the reasons I was excited about the possibility of joining Texas Western was the chance to play both ways. See, I never preferred to be an offensive player, neither did I think I was any better at halfback than I was at safety. Whether it was offense or defense, I was going to make sure I was the top player.

We returned to Colorado City. A couple of weeks later Corbell let me know he had decided to enroll at Texas Western. I told him I thought it was great. But I had been doing some thinking and decided on going to Rice University in Houston. Naturally, he was surprised. I don't blame him. But, right or wrong, I felt that if the reason my parents wanted me to go to college was to get a degree, I should pick the school with the best academic reputation. When the coach from Rice University came a knocking, I realized I had a shot at attending one of the top academic universities in the nation. The way I saw it, if I graduated with a degree from Rice, I could get a job anywhere. So I paid no mind when they sent the baseball coach to recruit me for the track and football teams.

I hated taking off and leaving behind my family and friends—and I'm sure it was especially hard on my mom to see her youngest leave—but I said good-bye to her and to my dad. Then I said good-bye to Barbara, who was my girlfriend at the time. She had been my first love in high school. I went to the bus station, bought a ticket for $9.90, and boarded the Greyhound bus to Houston. Because there were no freeways back then, the trip took nearly 18 hours.

A couple days after moving into my dorm, I went out for my first football practice at Rice. As soon as I arrived on the field, along with the other 35 players, the football coach made us do wind sprints—which made zero sense to me. The right way to do wind sprints is *after* practice. The reason being, you've had a chance to loosen up your muscles. Performing gassers cold is a great idea, if your goal is to pull a hammy. This head coach saw it differently. So, for two weeks I did wind sprints his way. After that, I walked into the athletics department and I told them if they wanted to keep me on scholarship for track, fine, but I wouldn't be playing football anymore. They agreed, because after all, track was the main reason they recruited me.

The next day I quit the football team. I guess you could say I was being stubborn. On the other hand, I didn't miss a single football practice or game in high school. I also didn't miss a single practice or game in college. I didn't miss a single practice or game during my final five years as a Jets player. I didn't miss a pass in my last eight years as a Jet. I also didn't run wind sprints before practice.

Nobody in my family cared that I quit the football team as long as I stayed in school and got an education. So, I went to classes like everybody else, like a regular college student. At the time, I wanted to be a petroleum engineer. As a result, I spent a lot of time in the labs. I also began tuning up for the track season, although it didn't start for another three months.

As for Barbara, we tried to carry on our relationship, but that was hard to do from 585 miles away. I didn't have the money to spend on phone calls (there was no app for that), so I'd just write her letters and she would write letters back to me. Coming home at Thanksgiving and again at Christmas was nice because we could spend some time together. But in the end, the distance became too much. So I moved on. I'm not even sure if she went to college or not.

I don't remember the first time I rode a Greyhound bus from Houston back to Colorado City with the intention of staying home for good. All I know is that it took roughly 17 hours to get there. I wasn't home three days before my brother arrived from Abilene, 67 miles away, to put me on the Greyhound returning to Rice.

"You got to get back on that bus," said Thurman.

"I don't like it there. It's god-awful humid."

"You got to finish school," he said

I knew he was right, so I got back on that Greyhound bus and traveled those 585 winding miles back to Houston. A short time later, I took another Greyhound bus home. When Thurman heard the news, he drove down again from Abilene. He met me at the bus station, but this time he said, "You're so determined to come home. Fine. Why don't you transfer to Texas Western? That way you can go to college with your buddy Corbell. Hopefully, then you'll be happy."

I called Corbell to ask him what he thought. He said I should go for it. But, I told him over the phone, there was a fly in the ointment. If I went to Texas Western I'd lose my scholarship. How would I pay for room and board?

A couple of days later Corbell called me up to tell me that he had gone to see Coach Brumbelow. He asked him if he would give me a scholarship to play, even though I wouldn't be eligible to play until the following year. Brumbelow okayed the deal. What a load that was off my mind. Right then and there, I was convinced to hightail it to Texas Western and continue my education there—and then after I graduated, who knows, become a teacher or maybe even a coach.

Although I'd decided to transfer midyear to Texas Western, that wouldn't be the last Greyhound bus to show up in Colorado City with me on it. I left Rice a couple more times—five times all together—or roughly 150 traveling hours by bus. But every time I came home, my brother drove down from Abilene to set me straight. "You're going back on that bus," he would say. "You're going to stay in school and make your grades. I don't care how humid it gets. You're going to gut it out so you can transfer your hours to Texas Western."

It didn't occur to me not to listen to my brother, and before long, I'd take my seat on the back of the Greyhound and complete that 17-hour drive back to Houston. On February 1, 1954, I arrived on the Texas Western campus in El Paso. Naturally, I brought with me my Levi's, my flat-heeled cowboy boots, and my extra-long sideburns. But I also came with something else: my course hours from Rice.

I liked Texas Western just fine. It had only 1,200 students—half as many as Rice. I wound up getting to room with Corbell in the athletic dorm. That worked out great. He helped me with lots of things—picking classes, meeting people, finding my way around campus. We took a lot of the same classes, and I helped him with his studies. Also, it was a 480-mile drive home for holiday break, so it was good to have another guy to split the gas money.

Being a red-shirt player meant having to sit out a full season. I suppose I should have been in the dumps. But gee whiz, there I was back in West Texas, back with my buddy, and then I found out there was a whole group of guys at Texas Western who grew up near my hometown. After meeting all the players on the team, I discovered that six guys were from Abilene and another eight from Odessa and a couple more from Snyder. Back then, everyone had a nickname. One player, who was also on the track team with me, they called "Greyhound," for the way he ran. As for Jim Bevers, well, we just called him "Beaver."

It turned out that Brumbelow would purposely recruit at least two players from the same town or several players from the same area so that they had things in common. These were people who had grown up in towns like mine. I could relate to them. They understood me. I knew I had their back and they had mine. Back in Houston, I never felt that I belonged. There wasn't a day in El Paso when I didn't feel like I was home.

At Texas Western, I no longer felt like I was playing football to fulfill the requirements of some scholarship. I might be prohibited from playing in the games, but I could practice with the team—and nobody had more fun practicing than I did. I felt like a horse that had been let loose from his reins and allowed to run free in the pasture. After hours of leaping and diving for ball after ball, my face was caked with dirt and my uniform stained with grass. I trotted off the field, soaked with sweat, with a big grin on my face. Being back in El Paso reminded me of a simple fact: football, like any other sport, is best played for the joy of it.

Before practice, we players would get changed at their lockers and then convene in the meeting room. Everybody made sure to be in his seat 5 to 10 minutes early. Truthfully, I never saw anybody come in late in those four years. When Brumbelow stepped into the room he would go straight to the blackboard and start explaining the plays we were going to run. Brumbelow mapped out his practices like a military campaign.

As soon as we stepped out onto the field, it was all business. There wasn't a single minute of activity that wasn't organized. You had your offensive day and then you had your defensive day, and then you had your day split in half between offense and defense. You had your individual workout day and your day where everybody worked on special teams. On those individual days, I might be running pass drills while the offensive line is over somewhere practicing drive blocks on a dummy. On Fridays, Brumbelow would run a short practice, but we made sure to loosen up real good and be as ready as a man could be for the next day's big game.

Brumbelow was strict, but he was also good about giving a guy a pat on the back when he deserved it. If a guy fumbled, even in practice, Brumbelow would make him carry a football around everywhere he went for a week straight—classes, the cafeteria, the dorms. He had to hold onto that ball in his sleep. Brumbelow might chew you out at practice, but after that, you weren't likely to make that same mistake again. You probably wouldn't make it again for the rest of your career.

Brumbelow worked our team hard, but after coming from Rice, the way he ran his practices, the crispness and the focus, was a welcome burden. He never chewed me out, but then I didn't give him a reason to. My brother, sister, and I were raised to listen to our elders, and we didn't even think about stepping out of line or dare to talk back. So I suppose I had an advantage over some other guys in playing for Brumbelow; I found his way to be enjoyable. It's what I'd been used to my whole life. Discipline with love and love with discipline.

Brumbelow was all business on the field, but afterward, say, in the dining hall, he was easy to approach. I remember him waiting in the dinner line just like everybody else. I think he wanted his players to realize that he was just like them. It was a respect thing. The players would always step aside and tell him to go ahead. I suppose that was a respect thing, too. Years later people would ask me what it was like playing for Vince Lombardi and I tell them that I had already played for Lombardi—his name was Mike Brumbelow.

Having to wait a year to contribute to our team was tough. The one benefit of being a red-shirt player that maybe the next guy didn't have was having the extra time to think about how I could turn myself into a better receiver. Sitting out that season, I began to see ways to train more efficiently. During one practice, I heard a guy comment to another, "What the heck is Maynard doing now?"

The guy answered, "It looks like he's trying to catch passes with one eye closed."

Here's the thing: too many players start running before they make the catch, and as a result, they drop the pass. But by catching the ball with one eye closed, I would lose my depth perception, forcing me to look at the ball a little bit longer and to wait for it. By training myself to look the ball in a split-second longer, I made the chance of a dropped pass that much less likely. Also, when you're a receiver and you're looking back over your shoulder or streaking across the middle, you're seeing the ball with only one eye, anyway. Or, certainly, you're seeing less than you think you are. I guess if you want to improve your vision, first you have to realize that the things you think you see with two eyes, you're only really seeing with one. Limit what you see—or what you think you see—and things start coming into focus.

I also had an exercise where I would face forward—I called that 12:00—and see how far I could twist my upper torso. Well, when I started doing that, I could turn my head and shoulders a couple of inches so that I was facing 3:00. Over time, I got flexible enough to face 4:00. Heck, after doing that for a bunch of years, my range of motion was darn near that of an owl. By becoming so limber, I could turn back farther to see more balls thrown to me. Just like the 31 sit-ups I had been doing in bed since I was in eighth grade, this was just another simple way to gain extra movement that maybe somebody else—like my opponent—wouldn't have. I didn't know it at the time, but I would need every last bit of my power of elasticity if I was going to make what was the biggest catch of my life with nothing less than a trip to Super Bowl III riding on it.

After workouts, Corbell would stay on the field with me so I could practice catching. As long as he could make it back by supper at 6:30, we could stay out there. Corbell threw me every type of pass, from long spirals to quick slants. He would throw me five high ones over my right shoulder, then he'd throw me five high ones over my left shoulder. After doing that, he'd throw me five low passes to my right, and then five low passes to my left. I would make sure to catch every ball Corbell threw my way. Our drills were simple and repetitive, but what we were doing was reproducing every pass that could possibly occur in a real game. We hoped when the time came for us to take the field together, it would be automatic.

Over time, I began transferring the know-how for running track to the football field. That meant I did a lot of extra stretching that the other football players didn't do. Prior to the start of team calisthenics, I would be over on the side working my limbs and joints until I was a human spring cord with the balance of a stiletto hammer. As I gained more flexibility, the less pressure I put on my muscles, especially my hamstrings. Well, an ounce of prevention is worth a pound of cure. You don't go outside in the winter without a coat, and I wasn't going out on the field without my muscles firing on all cylinders.

By running pass-outs with Corbell, I also realized how to gain an extra stride on deep passes, enabling me to catch a ball that was just out of reach. The secret was to keep my hands working like a sprinter, pumping my arms and hands, and not turn back to the ball or reach my hands out until the last split second. By never breaking stride until the last possible moment, I could increase my step maybe half a stride, which was all I needed to catch the ball that would otherwise have sailed just beyond my fingertips.

My track coach at the time was a guy by the name of Ross Moore. He had been a great basketball and football player at Texas Western, then returned after he graduated to become an ends coach. By the time I got there, he had become the track coach and was also the equipment trainer for the football team. I told Moore that my goal was to someday become a full-time athletic trainer and that, considering I was ineligible to play, I could assist him. He said, "I could use some help in here. Come on."

We soon discovered that we shared a belief that the equipment players used could be a heck of a lot better with a little innovation and common sense. One of the first things we did was to shorten my cleats to give me better traction on the rock-hard Southern ground. Moore also invented a special mouthpiece for me, which he called the "feather-bite" mouthpiece. He designed it to be molded to your teeth, a more effective form of protection than a uniform plate. When I went to play with the Giants, I was the only one who wore a mouthpiece. I was also the first player at Texas Western to wear a face bar. I asked Moore to put one on my helmet so that ain't nobody going to give me a shot to the chops with their elbow or fist. He also invented a little fiberglass heel cup to protect a bruised heel. During a hurdle jump, my left leg would drag behind me, and the metal bar would tear the hide out of that ankle. The first time it would tear a hole in your sock the size of a silver dollar. Three or four times after that, and you're practically down to the bone. So, another thing I got him to make was a four-inch fiberglass shield to fit over the inside of my left ankle bone. That made all the difference in the world for me because I was no longer gun-shy about dragging my leg and getting it all cut up. I don't know if hurdlers used things like that later on, but if I were them, I sure would. I still have that fiberglass shield somewhere around the house.

Also, I knew the flesh of my forearm had a more gripping texture than a slick satin jersey, and that catching the ball against my exposed skin would give me a better feel for the ball. One of Brumbelow's rules, however, was that nobody could cut the sleeves on his uniform. Well, if that's the rule, okay. There's a way to fix that. I'll just roll them up above the elbow and go on about the ball game. I didn't give it a second thought. Of course, suddenly, Beaver is wearing his sleeves rolled up above the elbow. And then you see Greyhound is wearing his sleeves rolled up above the elbow. Well, before you know it, all the receivers and cornerbacks are wearing their sleeves rolled up above their elbows. I got a laugh out of that. As for my shortened cleats, Brumbelow probably didn't even know about them.

Ross Moore was the greatest guy in the world. During that year of ineligibility, I had a great time taping ankles and wrapping bandages and tending to charley horses. He also let me aid him when he put on clinics for all the local high school trainers. At these clinics, Moore would show them how to make his molded mouthpiece. I also traveled with him to the regional training clinics around Texas. Then there was the big event of the year, the Texas state convention of trainers. A company like Johnson & Johnson would supply the tape and the pads while the top trainers in the state traded new ideas and techniques. It's here I got to meet all the other head trainers from the Southwest Conference. There was the great head athletic trainer at Rice, Eddie Wojecki, who had been the head trainer for the U.S. Olympic Team in Helsinki, Finland, in 1952. Then there were Delmer and Elmer—Delmer was the head trainer at East Texas State, and Elmer was the head trainer at TCU. It was great to be around such talent.

Every Monday after workout, the redshirts and ineligible guys would take on the second- and third-stringers in a scrimmage. After a week of not getting to play, I was pretty wound up. The guys who got to play in the game would come out after practice to watch the scrimmage and, naturally, Brumbelow and all the coaches were right in the middle of it. Actually, Brumbelow would have Ross Moore take one team and another of his coaches take the other and he would stand on the sidelines and watch. I was the quarterback on the red-shirt team and felt like this was my time to be a star.

I figured, as long as I was going to participate in football, I was going to do whatever it took to get better. At the same time, I ran around and threw passes on Kidd Field with the same carefree feeling as I did back in those vacant gin lots growing up. Brumbelow and his assistant coaches and all my teammates started taking notice of all the great plays I was making during scrimmages. One day, in front of everybody, Jim Bevers yelled out to me, "You're like the sun. You shine all the time!" Wouldn't you know it, after that, the guys started calling me "Sunshine." Then Sunshine got shortened to just "Shine."

There was no Sunshine when the season got under way against North Texas. That's because Sunshine was on the bench. I could only sit and watch helplessly from the sidelines as my team settled for a 7–7 tie. For our second game of the season, we traveled to Albuquerque, New Mexico, to battle the University of New Mexico. The night before we played, a bunch of us went down to the restaurant in the hotel where we were staying. As my buddies and I were walking through the lobby, I saw a beautiful blonde in her majorette uniform standing over with a girl I knew from high school. The majorette was wearing an ankle-length wool skirt, saddle shoes, and high dress socks; she was also holding a little stuffed monkey. I walked over and said to her, "Do you have a name for that monkey?" She said, "No, I just got it." I said, "Well, why don't you call it Sunshine?"

My friends busted out with laughter. She didn't understand what was so funny. As I walked away, I could hear the girl I knew telling her friend, "He's a nice guy." The next night we went out and beat New Mexico 34–0. While the rest of the team celebrated on the bus ride home, all I could think about was the majorette. We didn't get back to Colorado City until late that Saturday night. Once I got home, I called the girl I knew and asked her about her friend. She told me her name was Marilyn Weaver and that she was a senior at one of the high schools in El Paso. Then she said, "I'll fix ya'll up," and that's how she and I ended up going out on our first date. We met at the drugstore for a Coke—unfortunately, this other girl came along with us. On the next date, it was just the two of us. We had a better time.

We dated all through football season, and it was great. However, we had a problem: her mom, Frances, didn't like me. Her dad, also named Francis but spelled with an *I*, was an easygoing guy, so I don't think he minded. As for her mom, she didn't look upon me as being good enough for her daughter. In her eyes, I was just an old country boy who wore Levis and cowboy boots. One day, I went over to Marilyn's house to pick her up, and Frances told me that Marilyn wasn't going to be seeing me anymore. She told me not to come by the house ever again and not to call.

Marilyn had lived in El Paso all her life. At the time we were dating, I lived over in the dorm with Corbell; Marilyn lived with her parents, not far from Austin High School, where she was the head majorette. If her mom didn't want me coming around the house, I would respect her wishes. I didn't want to cause any problems. On the other hand, she didn't say anything about my football buddy Beaver coming by the house and picking her up (on a supposed date), or him driving down the road a bit where I'd be waiting to meet her. Marilyn would then get into my car and Beaver's date, who had been waiting with me the whole time, would get into his car, and then we'd all go out somewhere. I would take Marilyn home later that night after her mom and dad had gone to bed. We snuck around like this once a week for more than a year. Neither Frances or Francis Weaver ever had a clue.

When the summer came, I went back to Colorado City to work at an oil refinery, just as my dad had done a decade earlier. If I went to work for my uncle, painting light posts and smokestacks, I'd have to travel thousands of miles around Texas and Oklahoma. At the refinery, I could walk outside the front door and go down a short distance to work. Staying in town also meant I could see a lot more of Marilyn.

What we had between us was special. I might not have been the kind of guy to write love poems, but it was love at first sight. That summer, I drove down to El Paso to see her every couple of weeks. When Marilyn was home, she'd occasionally sneak off somewhere in the house where her mom couldn't hear her and call me, but we had to keep our conversations brief for fear of being discovered. In September she enrolled at Texas Western. We were happy to finally be together; at the same time Marilyn was tired of hiding our relationship from her parents. I was too. So I said to Marilyn, "Well, let's just get married and then we don't have to put up with anything from your mother."

That November, I drove down to El Paso to see Francis alone. I told him about the sneaking around and everything else. Then I said to him, "If it's all right with you, I'd like to marry your daughter." He said it was okay by him. A little while later, we told her mother. That didn't go quite as smoothly. The thing was, she could express all the disapproval she wanted—we were getting married whether she liked it or not. Had her mom been more understanding, would we have still gotten married? Maybe eventually. But not then. Not with Brumbelow's new rule.

No Wives

FOUR WEEKS OF SPRING TRAINING, 12 weeks of the regular season. As a sophomore, another four weeks of spring training. After all that waiting, I would finally get to suit up and play football. I was as ready as a coiled rattler.

In the '50s, the Border Conference was tough and everybody knew it—at least everybody west of the Mississippi. If you planned on winning the conference and playing in the Sun Bowl, first you had to travel a brutal road going through the likes of Texas Tech, Arizona, Arizona State, University of New Mexico, and Hardin-Simmons. Of all the schools in the conference, North Texas and Texas Western were by far the smallest. Truth was, we weren't even classified Division 1. None of that mattered. Somehow we had to find a way to compete.

I would describe our team's style as hit 'em quick and run 'em to death. I say this because we had only two guys who weighed more than 200 pounds. The only way to stop bigger defensive lines from overpowering our offensive line was for our linemen to hit them quick, before they could get leverage and exert their force. You played to your strengths. We might have been undersized, but we were a well-coached unit of fast, lean, rangy Texans.

The way I saw it, the size of the team we faced didn't matter because—when all was said and done—they could put only 11 players on the field at one time, same as you. If you could find 11 hardworking, fearless, rough-and-tumble men, it didn't matter how many blue-chippers you had on your side of the field. As it turned out, we only had two—the Forest twins, Bob and Dick, of Carlsbad, Texas. The rest of us were just ordinary guys from small towns in Texas and Oklahoma.

My position had been quarterback all through my freshman year of ineligibility and into spring training of my sophomore year. When I finally became eligible to play, Mike Brumbelow brought me into his office and told me he wanted me to back up Jesse Whittenton. I was a good quarterback, but I was also a sophomore who wasn't going to try to beat out a senior, not when that senior was the greatest athlete I had ever seen. So versatile was Jesse Whittenton that he had played halfback as a freshman, then was equally great playing fullback as a sophomore and then played quarterback his junior year—and made all-conference. But Jesse Whittenton saved his best for last, putting on a show against Florida State in the Sun Bowl that would go down in college football lore. Throwing for three touchdowns, running for two, and kicking five extra points, he was responsible for 35 of 47 points our team scored against the Seminoles that day on Kidd Field—a Sun Bowl record that has survived the last 55 years. So let's just say, I knew that if I played second-string behind Jesse Whittenton, my butt would be sore from riding the bench so much.

I told Brumbelow that I felt that I could be more useful out on the field than twiddling my fingers on the sideline. I needed to be out there, playing every down. To my relief, Brumbelow decided to start me at halfback. Of course, I also started at safety. Back then, everybody played both ways. In addition to his quarterback duties, Whittenton played cornerback. Our other halfback, Bob Laraba, also played linebacker. When you made that goal-line stand, you didn't have time to exchange a bunch of high-fives. You went directly into the huddle and tried to figure out how the heck to move the ball 99 yards the other way.

My sophomore year I averaged 7.5 yards a run, which ranked second in the nation behind Jim Swink, a punishing two-time All-American running back from TCU. Hailing from Rusk, Texas, "The Rusk Rambler" led the Horned Frogs to consecutive Cotton Bowls in '55 and '56. At the end of that '55 season, he was runner-up in Heisman voting to Howard Cassady of Ohio State. After football, he went down to live in Fort Worth, Texas, earning a reputation as a great surgeon. When Swink turned his shoulders north-south, he was impossible to stop, but I felt I had a couple of weapons maybe he couldn't match: speed and versatility. Not only could I run the ball but I was also a great receiver out of the backfield. And I returned kicks and booted extra points. In other words, I did everything Brumbelow asked me to do.

The game of football has changed as the world has changed— back then, there was no color TV and the closest anybody got to the moon was firing a rifle in the air. Back then, not many footballs had been launched through the air, either. Over the three years I played at Texas Western, we averaged only around five passes per game; therefore, the ball might be thrown to me only once a game. Well, that better be the time I'm on the same page as my quarterback. Running extra passing drills with Corbell was about staying sharp for that moment in the game when the quarterback took his shot down the field—because in those seven seconds the game would likely be won or lost—and it was up to me to make the grab and run it in for the winning score. I might have caught only seven passes that season, but I averaged 23.6 yards a catch. The next season I caught eight passes, bumping my average up to 34.4 yards a catch—best in the entire nation. So you could say this: when I made a catch, I made it count.

In my first year playing for the Miners, our team finished with an outstanding mark of 6-2-2. But after having led Texas Western to back-to-back Sun Bowl victories, Brumbelow was as angry as a hornet. Just as anything less than a division title and a Super Bowl wasn't good enough for Vince Lombardi, anything less than a Border Conference title and a Sun Bowl wasn't good enough for Brumbelow.

As it so happened, several of the players on that team were married. The coach decided that this situation was becoming harmful to the squad. He worried that he would have a hard time keeping his married players in school, focused on football, and that he would have to find jobs for all their wives. So, Brumbelow laid down a new law: get married, lose your scholarship.

After I got wind of Brumbelow's decree, I went to see him at his office. I sat down across the table and told him I had plans to get married. He quietly stood up from his desk, went to the blackboard behind him, and started quickly scribbling with the chalk. At first I thought he was writing up a pass play, but then I could see it was a bunch of numbers.

You know how much money you'll have to raise if you're off scholarship? You got your tuition, rent, textbooks, transportation, food, and other various living expenses.

Yes, sir.

Let's assume you get a part-time job. Well, I'm adding up the numbers here. You got a tough situation, any way you look at it.

Yes, sir.

The rule is the rule, Maynard. No married football players on scholarship.

Yes, sir.

So if I see you check into camp and pick up your equipment next fall, then I'll know you're playing. If I don't, well, then I'll know you chose to do something else.

And with that, I left his office and went home. I explained the rule to Marilyn, and we decided to get married anyway.

I didn't get down on one knee or anything to propose. One night, I just asked her. We were sitting in a car on a date—and that's the way that went. I'd say that going ahead with the marriage, even after Brumbelow announced the new rule, was more my doing than it was hers. Love is blind sometimes.

Soon word got around campus about how I was the first player to lose his scholarship as a result of getting hitched. Nobody on the team said anything to me. Not even Corbell. It was really nobody else's business. It was what she and I wanted to do, and so we did it—and we had to live with it.

Actually, love is blind a lot of the time.

After Marilyn and I got married, we didn't have enough money to live on campus, so we desperately began looking for a place to rent nearby. One day, I was walking around when I passed by a house with a sign in the front yard that read "Room for Rent." Living in the house was an older Mexican couple. The husband, a tailor who had once made clothes for Poncho Villa, and his wife showed us the rental space; it turned out to be nothing more than the bedroom on the back of their house.

The place was small, of course, but not as small as the trailer-size bathroom attached to it. There was a little gas stove about two feet square that had three burners and the smallest ice box you'd ever seen. Next to the stove, you had a little old bitty kitchen table about three feet long with two chairs, one on each end. When you cooked a TV dinner and the oven door was down, you couldn't get between the stove and the kitchen table. So the true comment was "room" for rent, and we lived in it.

I still had no idea how I would afford the $45 rent in addition to paying for school, but I felt fortunate that at least our place was only 20 blocks from campus. I wouldn't have to take a mule there, so that was good. The only other bit of good news was that every football player, scholarship or not, received $10 a month for laundry. Also, the athletic dorm had a full library, meaning I wouldn't have to buy textbooks. Other than that, I was on my own.

Finally, I picked up a job washing dishes in the athletic dorm for $29 a month. I was one of six guys who worked in the kitchen, two of whom were from the basketball team. Basketball players lived in the athletic dorm as did the track guys and even a few tennis guys. As a result, I became close friends with everybody, not just the football players. Anyway, the six of us would show up before the students arrived and eat dinner together in the empty dining hall. Then we'd go back into the kitchen and wait for the students to start bringing us up their trays. I'd knock the leftovers, like the biscuit crumbs, against a rubber thingy, and they'd fall into a barrel. I'd swing around, put the dish on the rack, and run it through the washer. After the dishes came out of the washer, a couple of guys would be there to dry and stack them. As my teammates came up to the window with their trays, I'd say hello to them, and they would say hello to me. No football player is going to miss a free meal, so I ended up saying hello to all 35 guys, three times a day, seven days a week for three years. I washed a lot of dishes.

I ate three big meals a day and still never gained any weight. One time, I went with my friend to the doctor's office to get his inflamed tonsils removed. While I was there, the doctor said to me, "You ought to get your tonsils taken out; you'll gain 20 to 25 pounds." And I said, *Really?* And he said, "Well, yeah."

All of a sudden, I'm thinking, *If I was 25 pounds bigger I could really be a rompin', stompin' halfback*. Later that week, a couple of players and I went back to the doctor to get our tonsils out. Afterward, the two other guys went back to the dorms while I went over to Marilyn's parents' house. I'd been vomiting up blood for a good while so her dad brought me up to the hospital. At 2:00 at night, I was taken into surgery. The doctor comes in the room and I smell alcohol on his breath. I'm scared to death.

The doctor gave me three stitches on one side of my mouth and two stitches on the other side, and then I went back to Marilyn's house and stayed over night. The next day all I could eat was Jell-O and ice cream, but at least the bleeding had stopped. I got my strength back a few days later. Here's the kicker: I never gained a pound. That's one of those things that if I had to do it all over, I probably wouldn't have the surgery.

At the time we got married, Marilyn was a full-time student at Texas Western and a majorette in the band. She loved being a majorette, a coveted role that went to only three girls out of the whole college. After we got married money grew tight, so to help out Marilyn quit school. She got a part-time job at the El Paso Natural Gas Company, which pumped gas up from the Gulf of Mexico all the way up through Canada. Marilyn still came to the games to watch me play, but no longer could I look over at the band and see her standing there in her majorette uniform, smiling at me and twirling her baton. From then on, she sat up in the stands with the other wives. And that's how that went.

I got a second job teaching P.E. class where I made $1.15 an hour. Then one day, I saw a flyer on campus offering money to be a model for an art class. There were a few stunned faces the first time I strolled into the art room dressed like a cowboy with my Levi's and my rawhide boots. I did whatever the art teacher needed me to do while the students sat around the room, drawing me. Stand up, sit down, lean over—it didn't matter to me so long as I got paid and the boots stayed on, along with the rest of my clothes. She wanted me to hold a vase, I held a vase. She wanted me to sit at a table like I was studying, I did that. The way I saw it, three hours of paid work was three hours of paid work.

Marilyn and I got married in December 1955. I started that day washing dishes in the morning, then went to my 8:00 class, and then to my 9:00 class. I cut my 10:00 class so I could get to the church on time. After the ceremony, we went over to a little reception Francis and Frances put on. The reception went until 1:00. Then I drove to campus, changed out of my wedding gear and into my football gear and participated in football practice. At night, I washed dishes in the dorm. After work, I went home to our little bedroom to be with Marilyn. And that was it.

In the fall of 1956, I showed up at Kidd Field as a nonscholarship player. I checked into the athletic facility and collected my football equipment. As I jogged onto the field, I passed by Coach Brumbelow. I looked at him, and he looked back at me. He didn't say anything so I continued out to the field. And that was that. He knew I was still on the team.

The 33 players on the team milled around the field, warming up, tossing the ball on the side. Most of us hadn't seen each other since the previous spring, and so nobody knew what anybody else had been up to for months. Corbell and I were stretching on the 10-yard line as the sun baked the dusty turf below our feet. That's when Bibb Wilcox came over to us and said, "Hey, you hear Jim Bevers got married?" By the time we started running drills, it was floating around that along with Jim Bevers, Hugh Harmon, Ray Morgan, and Keith Wharton had also got hitched (naturally, not to each other). Later during workouts, Corbell came up to me and said, "Did you hear Dick Forrest also got married? And then his twin brother Bob announced in the huddle that he got married. Well, by the time practice was over, I'd learned that eight other guys besides me had tied the knot. As a result, each one had his scholarship stripped.

I don't think Brumbelow had counted on so many players coming back married. Nor do I imagine he was too pleased by this development. At the same time, he wasn't going to run anybody off the field. Like I said, he was tough but fair.

After a couple of weeks of grueling competition, Brumbelow settled on his first string. I stepped in as starting left halfback and safety. As I looked around the field, I started counting the number of married players that had made first string. One, two, three, four... well, wouldn't you know it. Out of the nine players to defy the marriage rule, every one of us had made the starting lineup.

Let's face it. You had to be a little soft in the head to go to college, play on the football team, work part-time, and be married. Oh, it was probably coincidence that all nine married guys made first string, but it's also possible that throwing a bunch of just-married 19- and 20-year-old college students into the position of having to not only survive school, but also suddenly pay for it, forced us to be hungrier and more disciplined than we could ever imagine. Getting married forced me to grow up quick, and maybe that's what happened to the other guys, too.

While the single guys hung out after practice playing cards and pinnacle in the dorm, I'd come straight home to see my wife. A couple of hours later, I'd go to my dishwashing job at the dorm. By the time I got home it was late at night, but I still had to study in that back bedroom while Marilyn slept beside me. With so little free time in my day, I had to focus that much harder to stay on top of my classes. I never cut a class; I was never late for a class. Funny enough, my grades actually raised up a little bit. As for those single guys on the team, they could goof off and party. They had that luxury. We didn't. We had been a close team before, but in a strange way, Brumbelow's marriage rule had brought us even closer. I doubt Brumbelow had planned it that way, but that's how it worked out.

Some coaches have playbooks that are longer than *War and Peace*. I'm sure they make for an outstanding doorstop. Brumbelow had a great coaching mind, especially for defense, but that didn't mean he was interested in writing a thesis. His approach with most things was, keep it simple. When training camp started, he would run two-a-days and, oftentimes, he would make us spend the whole morning running one play. To the right, 12 Quickie. To the left, 13 Quickie. For the next 30 minutes you run it over and over again. To the right, 12 Quickie. To the left, 13 Quickie. According to Brumbelow, if after 30 minutes of running the same stinking play, you still haven't learned it, then you ought to find another game. That afternoon, Brumbelow would have us run one pass play. 62 to the right, 61 to the left. We ran that play for 30 minutes, at the end of which, you better have it down pat. 62 to the right, 61 to the left. How in the world can a mature, dedicated athlete make a mistake? Heh. Heh.

The quarterback would call the play loud enough to hear it. When you're in the huddle, he's a foot away from you. It was possible for you as a player to be beat physically—after all, some of the players on the other side are bigger—but there was no excuse for making a mental mistake. That's the first thing I learned under Brumbelow and later under Lombardi. There's no excuse for a mental mistake.

Just before the start of the season, Brumbelow called me into his office and told me the starting quarterback job was mine if I wanted it. Well, of course, I wanted it. But I knew by accepting the position, I'd be taking that spot away from Corbell. I told Brumbelow I wasn't going to be in competition with my high school friend. And that's the way I wanted it. Well, Brumbelow more or less accepted my wishes. You could call it courtesy, but my main deal was keeping our friendship.

I came back to the room and told Corbell what Brumbelow had asked me to do. He said, "Well, that's your choice. We're going to be friends either way."

The season started with a game on the road against powerhouse Texas Tech, who had won the last seven out of nine Border Conference titles. In his college football preview, *Sports Illustrated's* Herman Hickman predicted Texas Tech would win its fourth straight conference championship with Arizona State second and Hardin-Simmons third. Out of the six teams in the Border Conference, we were picked to finish fourth. Riding up to the stadium in Lubbock, I looked up at the top of the light posts—the same light posts that my uncle and I had painted many summers ago.

Corbell started the game under center. I stood ready beside him in the backfield, ready to break up the field. After all those years practicing our deep passes and short passes, flat routes and corner routes, slant patterns and swing patterns, we were ready to put on a show. I don't remember if it was on the first play or the first quarter, but a defender planted Corbell into the ground. He suffered a concussion. The team doctor said a recurrence could cause irreparable harm to his brain, and so he wasn't going to let him play. He wasn't going to take the chance of him—who knows—getting killed.

With Corbell out of the game and our offense struggling, beating Texas Tech fell squarely on the shoulders of our defense. We played three deep in the secondary. I covered between the hash marks, meaning I was responsible for covering the deep middle. Beaver would take care of the left side. Even without our top defender, Jesse Whittenton, on the right side—he's been drafted by the Los Angeles Rams—we were as tough to get around as a razor fence. We held the Red Raiders to one touchdown to secure a 17-13 victory. It would be the last time in history that the Miners beat a Big 12 team on the road.

Our defense pitched shutouts against our next two opponents, routing Abilene Christian 20-0 and New Mexico 34-0. Next, we faced Arizona in our third consecutive home game. Our offense busted out for 28 points while our defense continued to freeze out their feared running back Art Luppino, holding him and the Wildcats to a measly 6 points.

On October 20 we took our perfect 4-0 record into North Texas to play our first road game in a month. North Texas was the other tiniest school in the conference, but we knew they would battle as hard as we did. Once again, our defense was stout, holding North Texas to 13 points, but our offense sputtered all afternoon. We ended up losing 13-6. Although we were devastated by the loss, we were just as determined not to lose again.

We beat our next opponent, New Mexico State, 51-7, then we had to go up against Hardin-Simmons College, which was coached by the legendary Sammy Baugh. We knew from studying game film they had a great team and that whenever we got together it would be a whippet-quick, freewheeling desert country football game. Baugh, not surprisingly, loved to throw the ball—I mean, really loved it—and in Ken Ford he had a quarterback who could carry out his aerial high-wire act, with its dizzying array of spread formations. Baugh torched countless defenses with his ingenious passing attack, taking his Cowboys to the 1958 Sun Bowl. Naturally, we respected their players and their players respected us. Brumbelow and Baugh were great friends off the field, and each coach respected the other. They were only one of two teams we lost to the previous year—barely missing on a 23-21 defeat in Abilene. But things were different this time—we put up 51 points on their defense while the great Ken Ford managed only 13 points.

Our next game was on the road against undefeated Arizona State, ranked one of the top 10 teams in the nation at the time. When we played them the prior season, I scored the first touchdown on a 22-yard run in the second quarter, but with the game on the line in the fourth, one of the Sun Devil defenders stripped the ball from Whittenton at our own 12-yard line, sealing their 20–13 triumph.

We knew they had world-class coach Dan Devine. They also had bigger, more physical players than we did. If we were going to give Devine and his boys a fight, our defense would have to come up big, but more crucially, we would have to force them to make mistakes. Our first score was all our quarterback Bob Laraba. First, he kicked a punt that stopped on their 1-yard line. After getting the ball back in great field position, he drove us within the 10-yard line, keeping the ball and diving into the end zone on a quarterback sneak. They spent the rest of the night trying in vain to catch our halfback trio—Jim Bevers, Bob Coleman, and me. With our explosive speed, we weaved and dodged past their big defensive line as they tackled the air behind us. Their offense repeatedly marched deep into our territory but we refused to let them score. The closest they came to crossing the goal line was in the second quarter when they moved the chains down to the 1-yard line. On the crucial play, they handed the ball to their bruising fullback Joe Belland. He barreled ahead. As he dove into the end zone, we popped the ball from his grip. Fumble. We recovered the ball. As the game wore on, their mistakes mounted, including three interceptions. By continuing to apply defensive pressure, attack them with our speed, and pounce on a few mistakes, we not only knocked off the national power, but we also shut them out 28–0. We knew we could play with them, but we also knew it would take an inspired game to actually defeat them. Luckily, we did our job.

That would be Dan Devine and Arizona State's only defeat over a two-year span as they would go on to a perfect 10–0 mark in 1957.

Although that would be Devine's final season in Tempe, he went on to win a national title in 1977 with a pretty good young quarterback by the name of Joe Montana. In the movie *Rudy*, they made Devine out to be the villain, pedaling the notion that he tried preventing Rudy from playing in his final game. I understand that this silly concoction makes it a more inspirational story, but maybe Devine deserved a less comical fate after being an outstanding head coach for 25 years.

After our huge upset over Arizona State, we rode the bus back to the motel and had a small celebration by the pool. There was no drinking or anything, but we were having a good time. The players huddled up and called one last play. We broke the huddle and ran a play where we threw all the coaches in the swimming pool. Ross Moore and the other trainers got tossed in, too. Everybody got thrown in—except maybe the cheerleaders. We got back on a pair of Greyhound buses and headed back to El Paso. Believe me, it was the shortest 400 miles my teammates and I had ever traveled.

A couple of weeks after we got back, I bought a 1940 Ford sedan from my classmate Jerry Campbell for $250—and I thought I owned the world. I learned a lot of mechanic work from my brother and dad but luckily the most I had to do in college was change a spark plug. Only upperclassmen had cars, so out of the 35 guys on the football team, I was only one of six or seven guys who had one. I didn't drive anywhere much farther than the Dairy Queen to take Marilyn for a hamburger. You want know what we did for entertainment in El Paso? Well, that was it, or we would go out to the drive-in theater. Once a week, a bunch of us would cruise to the Fiesta Drive-In with our dates. Football players got a special pass where your ticket was free, and all you had to pay was the 10-cent tax. My friends and I would also hang out at the student union on campus, listening to the jukebox and snacking on subs from the Sub Hub. After coming back from a road game, we'd often meet up at the student union. They didn't serve alcohol but they would give us soft drinks and sandwiches.

Naturally, when the doctor told Corbell that he could never play quarterback again, he took it hard. Anytime something you care about is taken away from you it hurts. Corbell had been playing quarterback all his life, so this was a great disappointment to him. The great part was that because of Corbell's all-round ability he became our punter and field-goal kicker, becoming part of the reason we had a successful season. He got his letter in football just like the rest of us. So that worked out real fine.

Even though Corbell was no longer allowed to play quarterback for the team, he would continue to throw balls to me after practice. That was just the kind of guy he was. We always had fun running through our passing drills, so there didn't seem a good reason to stop. Sure, what happened to Corbell could happen to me. I could get clipped in the back or suffer some other kind of cheap shot. With that said, I was going to be in top shape, and I hoped that would keep me injury free, as well as supply me with the speed and stamina to whip any corner that I faced. Heck, at Texas Western, I played three years as a starter and never missed a game on offense or defense. More important, I never missed a practice, not in high school and not in college.

Once, during the '56 season, my brother showed up to one of my games. To my surprise, he had brought our father with him. It turned out Thurman had driven all the way from Abilene to Odessa in his station wagon, picked up my dad and my mom, and drove them out to Texas Western to see me play in a football game. This wasn't just the first football game my dad had ever seen me play. It was the first football game he had ever seen, period. I don't remember which team we faced or how I played in that game. It was just a nice gesture on my brother's part.

Our regular season ended with a 54-0 drubbing over Trinity University, our defense's fourth shutout of the season. That North Texas game was, indeed, the last time we would lose in the regular season. Our offense put up more than 50 points against three of our last five opponents; our defense allowed only two more touchdowns in the rest of the season. All in all, we skunked four teams. We were named Border Conference champions with our 9-1 record, and earned a spot in the Sun Bowl against Southern Conference champion George Washington University on New Year's Eve day.

That afternoon on Kidd Field, our defense held the Colonials to just one touchdown. Unfortunately, no matter what we tried, we couldn't do anything against them on offense. The final result was 13-0 Colonials over Miners.

Naturally, we were disappointed to lose the game. But if you think we were going to let that one defeat take away one iota of the pride we felt as a team, think again. That loss didn't change the fact that our defense managed to hold our opponents that season to a total of 78 points, which worked out to about one touchdown per game. Darn North Texas would be the only team to score more than one touchdown on us all year. It didn't change the fact that for the next 32 years, no UTEP team would equal our nine victories in a season. (Not until 1988, when UTEP, then playing two more games in their season, finished with a 10-3 record.) That team—did I mention the two extra games?—and ours are the only ones in the 96-year history of the school to win nine or more games in a season. It certainly didn't change the fact that, to this day, we're still the only school in the history of the Border Conference to beat all of the other members of the conference in the same season. To have the kind of year that our team did—the nine wins, four shutouts, the perfect conference record, the win over Arizona State, the Border Conference title, the Sun Bowl bid—was something special. I'm not sure how many college teams in history have accomplished so much with an undersized starting lineup consisting of only two scholarship players. I reckon not many.

As for us nine married guys, any one of us could have called it quits after losing our scholarships because of it, and nobody would have judged him. But not one of us did. It's true that when I got out of college I realized I owed my folks money. I owed my brother money. I owed Marilyn's grandparents thousands of dollars that we had borrowed so that I could stay in school. We even moved in with her grandmother so that we wouldn't have to pay any more rent. So, I had a tough time. If I had to do it over I would have waited to get married. I wouldn't have gone through what I went through.

Maybe we all showed up at that first practice out of bull-headed Texas pride, but we continued to show up, out of devotion to each other. While you never heard anybody complain about Brumbelow or about the marriage rule costing them their scholarship, there was something about being in a huddle and looking around at the dirty faces breathing the same cold air, and knowing exactly the hell that each one of them had gone through to be there. Beaver. Tomahawk. Greyhound. Birdy. Flapjack. Knowing that they were in the same financial firefight as you, it made you run a little faster, hit a little harder. And when the game was over, there was no doubt you and all your teammates had left everything you had on the field. How many guys did they have defending the Alamo? That's the same mentality we had. It's better to have 11 talented guys willing to fight than 100 gutless wonders.

Those 33 guys on that ballclub were as tight as any group you'll ever find. We lived together, went to class together, ate together, studied together. It's a different world today because of the money but also because we were all such good friends—and whether we lost or we won, we did it together.

I'm sure a lot more people know the name Lombardi than they do Brumbelow, but both of them had been great, dedicated ballplayers long before they became coaches, and I think that's how we all saw them. And maybe that's how they saw themselves, more than they did as powerful authority figures. I think that's why those two coaches didn't have to punish guys as much as you'd think. Their men worked their butts off and played their hearts out, not out of fear, but out of devotion.

That Sun Bowl would be Brumbelow's last. Although he only coached at Texas–El Paso from 1950 to 1956, that seven-season stretch would go down as the most successful in school history. In the half-century since Brumbelow has coached, no UTEP coach has ever equaled his astounding winning percentage or taken his teams to three bowl appearances (and Brumbelow's included those back-to-back victories in 1954 and '55). With only two blue-chippers, the Forrest twins from Carlsbad, Brumbelow squeezed out every drop of talent we had inside of us. Every one of those nine victories was sown through his fondness for working us hard, until the fundamentals were beat into our heads. His coaching guile turned mediocre players into great players, great players into unbelievable players, and the Miners into a team to be reckoned with. I think that's about the highest compliment you can pay a coach.

Our 1957 team, under new coach Ben Collins, wouldn't be able to duplicate the magic of the previous year, but we did end up with a solid 6–3 record and played another memorable game against Texas Tech. Earlier that day Texas Tech had officially withdrawn from the Border Conference. As it so happened, our game was scheduled that night, so we would be the first team to play them since they spurned the league for greener pastures. During the game, Bob Laraba connected with me on a 15-yard catch and score. It would be the only touchdown reception of the game as we ended up beating them

26–14. Our victory was big talk around West Texas. We had brought pride to the little Border Conference. Meanwhile, Texas Tech joined the Southwest Conference and later the Big 12. After their loss, the Red Raiders wouldn't win another conference championship for the next two decades. Fifty-three years later, we are still the last Miners team to beat a Big 12 opponent.

By the time I graduated, I'd collected several Border Conference hurdle titles. A decade later, a Miner by the name of Bob Beamon would come along and shatter the long jump world record, accomplishing one of the greatest athletic feats of all time. In the three years our secondary played together, nobody ever caught a deep pass on us, and nobody in the nation could beat me deep. Part of it was my speed—I was clocked in 9.5 seconds for the 100-yard dash—but the other part was thinking one step ahead of the receiver. A guy could catch 10 passes in front of me, but there's nobody in America who was going to catch one behind me. By playing cornerback I learned what a defensive player was supposed to do on a certain play. While I caught only around 30 passes my entire college career, I averaged more than 28 yards a catch. Years later in the pros, I would be able to recognize a mistake the corner was making, or one he was about to make, and take advantage of it. In the NFL, if you can beat a guy with a fake and get one step on him, he's dead. My philosophy was, *they're never catching Sunshine.*

At season's end, I was picked to play in the East-West Shrine game in California. While I was happy to be selected, I wasn't thrilled about the prospect of having to travel that far distance. Then one day I got a call from the athletic director at Texas Western. He told me that Sammy Baugh wanted me to play for him at the Blue-Gray Game in Montgomery, Alabama. For a great star like Sammy Baugh to make this request was a great honor to me. I'd been reading about him in sports magazines since I was in seventh grade, about his playing days in Sweetwater, which was only 25 miles from where I grew up, and then, of course, about his legendary exploits as a three-way threat with the Redskins. He was named All-Pro in three different positions; he led the league in passing, interceptions, and punting yards. To this day, he's the only man to accomplish that feat. His versatility was something I admired and spent my life trying to duplicate. I might not turn into Sammy Baugh, but I could still salute the person I saw in the mirror every day.

Knowing I was one of the 23 best players in the entire nation to be selected to play in the Blue-Gray game was a thrill. Not to mention, I would be playing with Baugh's great quarterback at Hardin-Simmons, Ken Ford, and I knew about Baugh's radical style—his offenses passed! I figured he would be throwing the ball a lot. I had a chance when I got out of high school to go play for Baugh at Hardin-Simmons but my parents wanted me to get the best education possible so I chose to go to Rice and get an engineering degree. You can always second-guess your decisions, but I never did—even in spite of those five long trips back to Colorado City on the Greyhound bus.

Playing in the Blue-Gray game was one of the highlights of my life. I flew into Montgomery a week before the December 28 matchup. I was assigned a room at the hotel with a running back from the University of Georgia named Jimmy Orr, who would later be named Rookie of the Year with the Pittsburgh Steelers and then be traded to the Baltimore Colts. As we sat talking in our hotel room, I could never have guessed that 11 years from then I would face him in Super Bowl III.

At Texas Western, I had been playing against Baugh's high-powered passing attack for three years, so I knew his offense. Baugh had me playing strictly at the wide receiver position because he had Jimmy Orr and Phil King in the backfield. He was the first coach to use me only on offense in this specialized role. Back at Texas

Western I would line up at halfback, receiver, and defensive safety. I guess it was a sign of things to come. After three years coaching against me at Hardin-Simmons, he'd seen me blow past enough of his cornerbacks to know that my speed, combined with Ford's big arm, made for a deadly combination. Still, Ken Ford and I had only a week to work on pass plays and develop our rhythm and timing. It was a time to have fun, but the game was still a serious deal. We practiced right through Christmas.

None of my kinfolk were in the stands at the Cramton Bowl, and I couldn't afford to have Marilyn come with me. After the game got under way, Ford threw me a quick out pattern about seven yards down the field. I caught it and turned up the field. The defensive back came up to tackle me. I lowered my shoulder and shook him off. And then I was off to the races. I sprinted 20 yards to the end zone. I had scored the first touchdown of the game. There were no high-fives or Funky Chickens. If the sold-out crowd of 25,000 went wild, I didn't really notice. Back then, you just did your job. You did what you were supposed to do. Besides, I didn't have time to celebrate because I had to go line up and kick the extra point. It went through the uprights. I kicked two more extra points that day, the last point being the difference in the game, which we won 21–20. Toward the end of the game, they announced that Ken Ford and I won the game's co-MVP honors. My brother had watched the game on television. It was always nice for me to see him do well, and so I'm sure it was nice for him to see me do well.

After the game, Ford and I each got a blue and gray football. I felt grateful to Ford. We had been working pass patterns all week long, but it was his unforgettable performance in the game that allowed me to share the MVP award with him. The main thing was that I had performed well for Baugh, who had given me my chance. I owe him a big thanks for the opportunity.

Our football team at UTEP started with 36 players from the class of 1956. On graduation day I looked around and realized that only eight of us were left. As for those who didn't make it, they transferred or flunked out or just decided they didn't want to be in college. Maybe they had a sick parent back home they had to take care of. One guy's father was killed, and he had to go back and help out his mother. Who knows where everyone went? But looking around, I felt glad that I had made it and that so had Corbell. I know for a fact that, of the guys on the starting lineup, only one didn't get his degree—and he got a great job with an oil company and didn't need the three more hours. Nobody flunked out or got arrested for dope. These were just hardworking guys from good, hardworking families. In the three years I played Miners football, our team lost a total of seven games.

Before the co-MVP honors at the Blue-Gray game, I had been named All-Border Conference my junior and senior years. So it seemed to me that the decision not to compete with my friend for the first-string quarterback job worked out okay. The best part was that Corbell and I remained good friends throughout college. And today, at 75 years of age, we still are.

Some guys are going to be sad if they can't play football for a living, but I don't think that was ever me. I didn't go to Texas Western to play football. I went there to get an education, hoping that as a result I'd have a little bit easier time in life. I still might have ended up in construction working a backhoe or a tractor or a crane. I've always said that I'll drive anything that has wheels on it. Maybe I would have become a great athletic trainer like Ross Moore. I think I would have been happy doing that. Of course, then I got drafted and that became my path. Even so, I kept up my athletic trainer credentials during my 13 years with the Jets.

At the graduation ceremony, they handed me that diploma and then, well, I stuck it under my big belt buckle. And then I turned around so that my friends, my teammates, and everybody else could read the words on the back of my belt: "Shine." In 1974, UTEP, formerly Texas Western, named the athletic building after Mike Brumbelow. He is still the winningest coach in school history. He didn't allow mistakes in football, and I didn't make any. I never fumbled the ball as a running back or a punt returner. I missed one pass in college—but it was out of bounds. So it wouldn't have counted anyway. Now that I think about it, it doesn't even need to be commented on.

No Sideburns

IN DECEMBER OF MY JUNIOR YEAR, I received a letter in the mail. Oddly enough, it was from the New York Giants. They were writing to let me know that they'd selected me in the NFL Draft a month earlier, behind No. 1 overall pick and Notre Dame's Heisman-winning superstar Paul Hornung. Well, actually, *108* players behind him.

The truth was, coming from an itsy, bitsy school from the old Border Conference that a short time before had been named the College of Mines and Metallurgy, I felt darn lucky to have been drafted at all. Plus, getting picked in the ninth round beat getting picked in the 10th round.

Although I was the only player from El Paso to be drafted in 1957, lots of other great ballplayers from the Southwest got their shot at the big time. In the second round, the Chicago Bears took TCU's Jim Swink—the one guy in the nation who bested my junior-year yards-per-carry average. In the third round, the Philadelphia Eagles took Oklahoma's All-American wide receiver Tommy McDonald (and later in the draft, they snagged a pretty good QB from Wilmington, North Carolina, by the name of Sonny Jurgensen.) In addition to me, the Giants drafted TCU quarterback Chuck Curtis, also in the later rounds. Also taken, in the '58 draft, was my Blue-Gray co-MVP Ken "Model T" Ford, who was selected in the 13th round by the Washington Redskins.

I'm sure I wasn't the best player to come out of the draft that year, not among names like Hornung, Jim Brown, and Len Dawson. Heck, I might not even have been as good as Jim Swink. But I can tell you this: I was better than Don Bruhns of Drake College and Gary Gustafson of Gustavus Adolphus. Those were the two guys picked after me. The other thing I know for sure: of the nearly 300 players drafted in the middle of the seventh round or later, I would be the only one to end up in Canton.

At the time, I didn't know much about the New York Giants. I've kidded that after they drafted me I had to look up New York City in *National Geographic* to find out where it was, but the truth is that I had never been outside of West Texas for any long duration of time. I bought a few sports magazines to get more familiar with the team. I recognized a few names, but there was one that stood out: Kyle Rote. I'd followed Kyle's career from back in his days as a tailback at Southern Methodist.

Every Texas kid knew the story about how, in 1949, SMU's superstar running back Doak Walker went down with an injury before the biggest game of the year, against the most celebrated program in the country, the top-ranked Irish of Notre Dame. With Kyle Rote, a junior, subbing for Walker, nobody gave SMU a snowball's chance. In fact, they came into the contest a 27½-point underdog. But that afternoon, Rote wreaked havoc on Notre Dame's defense as a rusher, a passer, and even a kicker, scoring all three of SMU's touchdowns. Notre Dame escaped with a narrow win, but Rote would forever be remembered as the guy who almost single-handedly beat Notre Dame. In 1951 the Giants made him the No. 1 overall pick in the draft, but at his first training camp with the Giants, at a workout on a high school field, he stepped into a gopher hole and destroyed his knee. Rote would never come back all the way, forcing the Giants to convert him from halfback to receiver. While Kyle was deprived the chance to show his full talent as a rusher in the pros, he never quit, and eventually he turned himself into a perennial Pro-Bowler, as well as captain of the Giants for 10 years. Not too shabby for a guy who, as Frank Gifford used to say, "played on one leg."

To imagine that I might be Kyle Rote's teammate in the pros was thrilling. Naturally, my first priority in college had been my degree. After I got that, a front-office executive from the Giants showed up with a contract for me to sign. I told him that I wanted a guarantee in writing that if I made the ballclub I'd get to wear No. 13. He said, "Well, we don't have a No. 13. As a matter of fact, there isn't a No. 13 in the entire NFL."

I said to him, "If I can't get my number, I ain't going to play."

The executive took my lone request back to New York. A short time later, the Giants agreed to let me wear No. 13. I said, "Make sure you put it in the contract." Supposing they hadn't? Well, I wouldn't have played for the Giants.

Signing a contract with the Giants didn't put any money in my pocket, though; that would come only if I made the team. So seeing that I still needed a salary, that summer I went to work in the maintenance yard of El Paso Natural Gas. The company had just opened the new Blue Flame Building. Their motto was, "If the flame is blue, no change in the weather is due. When the flame is gold, then cold is foretold. When the flame is red, warmer weather ahead." Sometimes in West Texas the wind would whip the dirt and dust into the air to the point where the sky would grow dark and people would have to drive with their high beams on in the middle of the day. Years later I was on a local Texas talk show and I said, "I've got another motto for you on that Blue Flame Building: 'And when the flame ain't showing it means the sands are blowing.'" It was nothing strange to play a football game in El Paso with 45 mph wind gusts. No wonder we threw the ball only five times a game. If I didn't catch the football, there's a chance somebody in the upper stands would.

I was working in a yard instead of running for yards, but I was making a living for my family. As far as I was concerned, that was the important thing. Not that playing for the New York Giants wouldn't have been a dream come true. But just because I had some letter saying that I'd been drafted by the Giants, it was no guarantee I was going to play for them. I would try out for the team and see what happened.

Arriving at the training camp of the famed New York Giants was something else. I had never been that far from El Paso in my life. There I was, a lanky 23-year-old kid from Colorado City, traveling 50 hours on a train to Salem, Oregon, where I would be mixing and mingling with some of the greatest ballplayers in the world: superstars like Frank Gifford, the versatile speedster of the Giants' dream backfield; Sam Huff, the roving terror in the middle who anchored an all but impenetrable defensive corps; and future Hall of Famer Emlen Tunnell, a big, strong safety who led the Giants' notorious umbrella defense.

After arriving in Salem, I walked from the train station to the dorm, carrying two bags on each shoulder and a couple more under my arms. I was the first rookie to arrive at camp. By showing up a day early, before the rooms had been assigned, I wound up on the second floor with all of the veterans. All of the other rookies got assigned to the first floor.

The first guy I met in the dorm was Emlen Tunnell. He lived in the room straight across the hall. Later, I learned that he'd gone to Iowa, served in the Coast Guard, and then hitchhiked to New York with $1.50 in his pockets. He showed up at the Giants' headquarters, walked into the office of owner Wellington Mara, and asked him for a job. Mara told him, "Well, since you had the nerve to come in and ask for a tryout, we might as well give you one." And that's how he became the first black man ever to play for the New York Giants. In fact, he was one of the first black players in the NFL, period. Only Em had the million-dollar charm to pull that one off!

Em and I hit it off from day one. I think he got a kick out of the fact I walked in wearing cowboy boots and Levi's with my hair shaggy and my sideburns long. Right off, he started calling me "Tex." From then on, he always sort of looked after me. A player would get fined for being late, and Em always made sure that I was where I was supposed to be. "Come on, rookie, it's time to eat," he'd shout from across the hall. Or he'd say to me, "Don't forget, Tex. We got a defensive meeting in an hour." It seemed like as soon as Emlen flashed me that big smile of his, I'd feel a bunch more relaxed. I'm sure it was the same smile he gave Wellington Mara the day he showed up at his office looking for a tryout.

In his 11th year with the Giants, Em held just about every defensive record in the pros that a cornerback could. I came into camp thinking I knew how to play safety—and then Em started working with me during tryouts. He detailed the art of playing the position that he had revolutionized himself: how to read a quarterback's eyes, how to anticipate a route. He taught me how I could capitalize on my closing speed. Patiently, he showed me the techniques that top NFL defenders like him used. I'd never seen anything like it before. When I was having a little trouble understanding, Em would explain it to me with ease. In those two weeks of camp, Em taught me more about football than I'd picked up in two years of college.

You have to understand—veterans hung with veterans and rookies hung with rookies. The few times a veteran might actually interact with rookies were at the chow hall or during workouts. Em certainly wasn't going to invite me to come out for beers with him and the boys. One of my fellow rookies, Jack Kemp—who would go on to be a great quarterback in San Diego and Buffalo and later run for president—said that the man he backed up, our veteran quarterback Charlie Conerly, didn't speak a single word to him in his entire rookie season. For Em to take me under his wing like he did was a really fine deal on his part.

There I was, living on the same floor as all these great players I'd read about in sports magazines, eating the same chow, and then I got out on the practice field and suddenly I was working out beside these great talents. A part of me just wanted to go around collecting autographs. Another big moment in camp was when Kyle Rote came over and introduced himself. He said to me, "Glad to have another Texas boy around here." I couldn't believe he knew I existed. A couple days later, after he had watched me in workouts, he said, "You know, the Giants are adding an extra two players on the squad this year. So I think you've got a great chance of making the ballclub." That might not seem like much, but it gave me a lot of inspiration.

Before I had arrived in Salem, I had never really heard of either of our coordinators. That changed quickly as I overheard players talking about each man with great respect. They spoke about our defensive coordinator, Tom Landry, and how he'd been a great lineman for the Giants; they also talked about our offensive coordinator, Vince Lombardi, and how he had served as an assistant to legendary Colonel "Red" Blaik at West Point in the '40s.

Right off, I was impressed with Coach Lombardi. At our first workout, he jogged out on the field in gray sweatpants and led the team in calisthenics. In all my life, I'd never seen a coach do that. My goal since I was in grade school was to be into the best physical shape possible, and here comes this trim, hard-nosed guy—my coach, my leader—and he's matching my dedication push-up for push-up and squat for squat. Lombardi made you feel like, you never know, he might just suit up and go play. He also made one thing clear right away: he would teach you what he wanted you to know, but he wasn't going to tolerate any mental mistakes.

Unfortunately, I didn't hit it off quite as well with our head coach, Jim Lee Howell. The first day I showed up for workouts, he approached me in the locker room and said, "You're with the Giants now. You don't walk around here in cowboy boots and jeans. And you get those sideburns shaved."

I nodded silently and he walked off.

The next day I showed up to workouts dressed exactly as I was the day before. And I went on about my business. Well, I probably made an effort to stay out of Jim Lee Howell's way that day, so to speak. Looking back now, I suppose the smart move when I came to the Giants would have been to try to blend in, maybe pick up a suit at Macy's, but I didn't see the big deal about doing things my own way. Some guys wore tennis shoes, some people wore basketball shoes; I just happened to wear leather cowboy boots with No. 13 on them. Some guys wore suits; I wore big belt buckles. Some guys wore white button-down dress shirts; I wore Western shirts with pockets on the sides and snap buttons so I could put it on and take it off faster. Some guys wore fedoras; I wore a cowboy hat. Some guys had crew-cuts—okay, most guys had crew-cuts—my hair was a little longer and I sported long sideburns. But what was it to him? A couple of strips of hair on my face weren't going to slow me down any in a game.

With training camp over, the team flew back to New York the day before our first exhibition game. Our bus pulled up to the Concourse Plaza Hotel in the Bronx. It crossed near 161st Street, about two blocks up from Yankee Stadium, which the Giants shared with the Bronx Bombers. The Giants had been playing there for only two years, but they started off with a bang, winning their first title in almost 20 years in 1956. Many of the Giants veterans had lived at the Concourse Plaza for years, as had several of the Yankees players, including greats like Babe Ruth and Mickey Mantle. To this day, Huff and Gifford argue over which one shared the same locker with "the Mick."

As I stepped off the bus, I craned my neck upward at the Concourse Plaza. It was a sight to behold, an old red-brick hotel that rose up to the heavens. I leaned my head to Em and said, "That building has more bricks than some of the towns I've lived in." He just laughed. Later, I'd come to find out that 400 people lived there, which was more than the entire population of Lone Star, Oklahoma, where I lived as a boy with my grandparents.

By the time we rookies arrived in New York, our wives and kids had already moved into our new apartments at the Concourse Plaza. I checked in at the front desk and went up to my room. As a rookie, I didn't exactly get the continental suite. There was a couch that could be made into a bed, a bathroom, and a kitchenette. Though I guess it was an upgrade from living in the back of a Mexican tailor's house.

When I walked into the room, Marilyn came over and gave me a big hug. It was the first time I'd seen her since leaving for training camp. It was also the first time I got to lay eyes on my newborn daughter, Terry Lynn.

My daughter had been born in El Paso while I was in training camp in Salem. I'd heard stories of players today missing a game to be at their child's birth. But at the time, there was no way I could fly round-trip from Salem, Oregon, to El Paso, Texas. I didn't have the money. When Marilyn went into labor, I kept calling the hospital to make sure she was okay. If I couldn't talk directly to her, I would check in with her father. He kept me informed the best he could.

No, I didn't enjoy being across the country when my daughter was born, but that's the way it was.

Back then, teams played six exhibition games in the preseason. Each week, another round of players were cut. Among the unlucky men who were sent packing was Don Sutherlin. He had been a kicker for the Ohio State Buckeyes, who, in the 1958 Rose Bowl, booted the game-winning field goal to beat Oregon. Sutherlin and I had become good friends during tryouts, so I was sorry to see him go. I also felt bad that he suddenly had no source of income. The NFL commissioner, Bert Bell, delivered a speech to us rookies about how we shouldn't expect to make a living playing pro football, so don't quit your day job. That was very true. At the same time, the joy you got from playing football was stripped away from you. As soon as you're cast off from the NFL, there are few places a man can go to make a living as a football player. In Sutherlin's case, he went up to Canada in search of work. He managed to hook up with the Hamilton Tiger-Cats of the CFL.

Day after day, players around me kept disappearing. I knew that I could wake up one morning and, the next thing you know, I'd have to start packing my own bags. With that said, I had a few advantages over some of the other players who were fighting for the same job. For one, there wasn't anybody on the field who could get down it as fast as I could. Also, I shared a special quality with Frank Gifford—versatility. I could fill in at halfback, flanker, and even at defensive back. At the same time, I was emerging as the front-runner for the team's return specialist.

On the Monday morning after the last exhibition game, everybody reported to the team meeting. Moments later, Howell went down the list of the 35 guys who were on the ballclub. Almost every name Howell called out that day had been a holdover from that great 1956 championship team. I looked around the room and realized that of the 27 players the Giants had drafted in 1957, there was only one left standing. And let's just say, he was wearing cowboy boots.

That night I went back to my room at the Grand Concourse Hotel. I could have sworn I heard Em's voice from down the hall, *Way to go, Tex.*

• • •

It took some time to adjust to living in New York. I'd see people walking down the street going 90 miles a minute. It reminded me of how, back in Texas, if you stomped on an anthill, the ants would go scurrying off in all directions. I thought to myself, *Gee whiz, where's everybody going?* You'd think that somebody was giving out free lunches somewhere.

Getting held up at knifepoint wasn't something we worried about in Colorado City, but once you get dropped smack-dab into the middle of the urban jungle, it crosses your mind. My dad always used to tell me to be home by dark. So when I was out on the city streets, I learned to walk close to the parking meters—close to the curb, where I wasn't worried about outrunning anyone. I always walked down the curb.

Although I might have been more cautious walking around at night than some of the older guys, I enjoyed seeing the bright lights of the city. We didn't really go out during the week, only on special occasions. We might go downtown to see a movie, where on any given night you could see Gregory Peck riding a horse in *The Big Country* or ballplayers singing and dancing in *Damn Yankees* or Paul Newman and Elizabeth Taylor steaming up the screen in *Cat on a Hot Tin Roof*. We also caught a couple of plays. My favorite, naturally, was *Oklahoma!*

We enjoyed the city, even if it was in different ways. Just because Marilyn and I didn't go saloon-hopping with the Websters or nightclubbing in Harlem with Emlen Tunnell didn't mean there was ever a shortage of things for us to do or places for us to go. Although Frank's idea of a good time was a night of cocktails and good conversation at Toots Shor's, a well-known sports-celebrity hangout and Em was holding court at the swinging Red Rooster nightclub in Harlem, I was more likely to find enjoyment in taking Marilyn downtown for a great-tasting burger and then to the movies.

If I had a day off, we'd go to the tip of lower Manhattan and catch the Staten Island Ferry to Governor's Island or the Statue of Liberty. Or we might spend the afternoon taking a ferry around the entire island of Manhattan. Once a year, a bunch of us players would take our families to the sensational Bronx Zoo.

Sam Huff was another guy who looked after me as a rookie. He came from similarly humble roots—a four-room mining house in West Virginia. He told me where I should go in New York, where to eat, and things like that. On any given Saturday night, six or eight of us married couples might ride the D train together from the Bronx en route to different restaurants or cocktail bars. You might run into the Huffs or the Giffords or the Websters on the subway train, dressed to the nines and heading for a night out on the town.

Every Sunday after home games, the team would ride the D train to Henry Stampler's Filet Mignon, a restaurant at 61st Street and Central Park West. It was one of the few times the rookies got to hang with the veterans.

As a rookie, you were low man on the totem pole and nobody on the team—not the coaches or the veteran players—would let you forget it. You dared not stand out for any reason—best to just fall in behind the older guys and keep your mouth shut. You didn't even think about taking over a conversation. The veterans were always making jokes at each other's expense but you knew not to cut on anybody. As a newbie, you just kept quiet and were happy you were still there.

The one exception was Frank Youso, a huge rookie tackle who for some insane reason wasn't intimidated by anybody, not the veterans, not even Vince Lombardi, whose wrath was something a rookie avoided at all costs. Once at practice, Youso did something wrong in a drill, setting off Lombardi, who burst out, "You big, blind, dumb tackle." Youso fired back, "Well, Coach, I may be blind, but I'm not dumb."

If Youso wanted to stand up to Vince Lombardi, that was his business. All I was interested in was doing my job and being accepted. It was, *Yes, Sir. No, Sir.* If a veteran asked me to get him a Coke out of the freezer, I got him a Coke from the freezer. Every week, when Ballantine, the Giants' beer sponsor, came into the locker room with a case of beer for each player, I gave my case to Alex Webster, nicknamed "Big Red." I wasn't drinking it anyway, and I figured maybe in return I could draw on Big Red's experience reading defenses. Sure enough, he would sit down next to me in film sessions and help me break down our opponents.

As a rookie, I knew the only way to be accepted by my teammates was to prove myself as a ballplayer, and the only way to do that was on the field. But as backup to Frank Gifford—only the best halfback in the game—the only playing time I was going to see was in my dreams. At Texas Western, I was All-Conference. I shined on both offense and defense, and there wasn't a ball I didn't catch or a defender I couldn't outrun. As soon as I got to the pros, I was a too-thin, too-small halfback, just another rookie grunt who couldn't get a whiff of the starting lineup.

Playing pro football was a job, like any other. Though sometimes I would wonder why I was getting paid $7,500 to sit on a bench inside a huge stadium when I could be back in El Paso working as a master plumber for $8,500. It seemed silly, is all. I'd never given any thought to playing pro ball in New York City. No rookie expected fame or accolades, least of all me. The games weren't even televised in certain regions of the country. But then, that would all change a few months later.

Making a pro ball salary didn't change my spending habits one bit. I didn't grow up with much, so having money to buy a few more things was nice, but I still was careful to live within my means. A family was hard on the wallet, but my only big expenses that season were my rent at the Concourse Plaza and payments on my car.

The Giants were known as a class organization, from owners Jack and Wellington Mara to the front office on down to the maintenance crew. For me, just walking into the Giants' dressing room was a great honor. I was one of three rookies assigned as backup rushers, and as a result, we formed a camaraderie. Phil King was the backup to fullback Mel Triplett, Billy Lott backed up halfback Alex Webster, and I was the backup to Frank Gifford. Of course, Frank was such a great player that being second-string to him felt to me like being first-string on any other team in the NFL.

After six years in the league, Gifford did everything so well, from running draws to faking handoffs to returning punts, that all I had to do was to watch him in workouts and in games and then try to copy him. To give you an idea of what an amazing all-around player Frank was, he ended up making All-Pro at three different positions—first as a defensive back, then as a halfback, and later as a flanker. The press called him a glamour boy, which is fine—he was a good-looking guy and they needed to sell papers. But for me, I just saw him as a great and dedicated player who happened to make some movies in the off-season. People work different professions when they're not playing football, that's all. I had never been introduced to the world of surfing, sunshine, and movie stars. Frank had grown up around that stuff and so maybe that's where he felt comfortable, whereas I preferred to be fishing with my buddies on Rattlesnake Lake.

In addition to being the Giants backup halfback and safety, I was the featured punt and kickoff returner. If playing that position in college had taught me anything, it was that I needed the right footwear. As it so happened, before joining the Giants organization, I had read about the famous "Sneaker Game" in Yankee Stadium. On the day of the 1956 championship game against George Halas' imposing Chicago Bears, the Giants players changed out of their normal cleats and put on sneakers—actually basketball shoes—supplied by teammate Andy Robustelli, who owned a sporting goods store in Connecticut. The Giants players, like Gifford and Rote and Webster, were able to get better traction on the icy, frozen field than the Bears, and as a result they whooped them. I'll tell you what, getting the winner's share from the title game is a lot better than getting the loser's share. The point is, I knew about Yankee Stadium and how the ground was hard and would get harder as the season wore on, and about how the grass would die out. So when I came to the Giants, I brought my special cleats from college. The spikes were shorter than everybody else's, but I didn't care. I knew what I could do in them.

When the field got muddy, a lot of players wore mud cleats that had even longer spikes than their regular cleats. I never did. I had disciplined myself to take shorter steps and run with my body in a more straight-up position when the field became a quagmire.

As in college, I also asked the Giants' equipment manager to make some special alterations to my uniform to improve my performance. It always aggravated me to have my jersey up around my throat, so the first thing I asked him to do was to make my jersey with a V-neck, which no players in the NFL wore at that time. I also had the manufacturer add six inches to my jersey so that the tail went down below my butt. This wasn't so much performance related—I just didn't want the dirt from the infield to get all down my pants. Any player before my time could have asked for a V-neck or a longer tail, but I guess they just never thought of it. When the equipment guy gave them their jerseys and pads and shoes, the only thing they cared about was making sure they were the right size.

• • •

Because we lived together at the Concourse Plaza, a lot of the Giants and Yankees players struck up friendships. There was definitely a mutual admiration among players on both teams; we would go to the stadium to see their games, and they would come to our contests. In September the football and baseball seasons in New York overlapped. When it came to games at the stadium, the Yankees had priority over the Giants. As a result, the Giants played lots of road games in the first month of the season. Sometimes our games would be going on at the exact same time as theirs.

One Yankee player I became good friends with was Mickey Mantle. Years before we'd met, I'd heard stories about his heroics at Oklahoma and then with the Yankees. So, I was already a fan. Then we started hanging out, and I thought he was just the greatest guy in the world. Mickey might have enjoyed going out and drinking—that didn't interest me—but what he did was his business, and what I did was mine. People are people and friends are friends. One off-season, Mickey and I were teammates at the American Airlines Golf Classic in Arizona; they paired one football player with one baseball player. Wouldn't you know it, the Mick and I won the tournament. I was sad when he passed away.

Just like on the Yankees at the time, talent permeated the '58 Giants roster from top to bottom. The running attack was dynamite throughout the season. Lombardi paired Frank Gifford, an elusive halfback, with Alex Webster, a strong fullback, to create an over-powering one-two punch. The sweeps that Lombardi devised were not complicated, but to execute them well took a special breed of player. You had to find not one but two running backs who were equal parts smart (the rusher had to decide in a split-second when to hit the right hole) and mobile (he had to be able to cut it inside or swing it outside on a dime).

When I learned Lombardi had coached at Army, I wasn't sur-prised. I had grown up idolizing former track star Doc Blanchard, who ran a similar package at Army. Blanchard's strength up the middle combined with Glenn Davis' outside speed, gave them a devastating ground attack. If the inside-outside sweep started with Blanchard and Davis, then it was perfected with Gifford and Webster. Of course, Lombardi used that play in Green Bay with the great Paul Hornung and Jim Taylor, not only resurrecting a team in ruins but also bringing a tremendous sense of pride to a city. Yet Lombardi would be the first to admit there was nothing spectacular about the play. Most of the time the defense knew the sweep was coming. Stopping the play when run to perfection—and Lombardi made sure it was—was a whole other story.

Lombardi always told you up front in team meetings what he expected from you as a player on the field and as a person off the field—which, put simply, was your best. He believed a player's top priority was always to make sure he had his affairs in order with the man upstairs. Number two was family, the team was number three, and you always put yourself last.

A lot has been made of Lombardi being a short-tempered dicta-tor. As far as I'm concerned, you can throw all that in the trash can. First, he'd never ask anything from you that he hadn't at some point asked of himself during his time on earth. Sure, he'd chew a guy out once or twice a day at practice. But when Lombardi cursed out some player, he never did it to embarrass the player but rather to get his point across. He sure did that. But Lombardi treated everybody fairly. In his eyes, there were no white ballplayers and no black ballplayers. There were only smart players and dumb players.

When Em, a recognized star in New York, went with Lombardi to Green Bay, he had a hard time finding a hotel that would admit him due to his race. So, Lombardi put him up at the first-class Northland Hotel and secretly footed his bill. It wasn't a big deal; it just showed the respect he had for Emlen's intelligence and his appreciation for what he could do on the field.

Around 9:30 in the morning one Tuesday, Lombardi was going over game film with the entire team. As it so happened, I had filled in a little at safety during Sunday's game. So, Lombardi showed some play where the running back busted through the middle of the line, and I came up as safety, and I didn't hit the guy. *Heck, he was already being tackled,* I figured. *Why pile on?*

Lombardi replayed it three times in a row and then, in the dark, he said, "What's the matter, Maynard? Aintcha *hungry?*"

I said, "No, sir. I had a big breakfast before I came over."

The projector went off and the room went dead silent. You could hear a pin drop. All of a sudden, you hear a booming laugh in the dark that could have come only from Lombardi. Then, the whole ball team cracked up. As much as every man in that meeting room looked up to Lombardi, respected him, and lived to earn his praise, in those moments you couldn't help but feel like he was just one of the guys.

As for Jim Lee Howell, he was a good enough head coach when it came to running practices or giving halftime speeches. But sometimes the best thing he could do on the day of the game was stay at home. I didn't have much respect for him as a football mind; I didn't think he knew that much. Lombardi and Landry ran the offense and the defense. Huff used to joke that Howell was in charge of making sure the balls were inflated.

Of course, no coach could teach me what I learned from watching Gifford and Kyle play. To my surprise, Kyle came up to me one time before practice and said, "You just watch what I do." After the Giants moved Kyle to receiver, he was determined to excel in his new role. When Kyle set his mind to something, there wasn't much he couldn't do. Besides playing football, he was also an accomplished songwriter, poet, and painter. By creating his own moves and adding wrinkles to existing moves, eventually Kyle evolved into one of the top receivers in the NFL. Naturally, he didn't have to tell me to watch him. I had every intention of watching how he did everything from lacing up his shoes to running a post pattern, and then I'd try to do the same.

Heck, I learned more in one week from watching those guys than some people learn in a career. For example, I noticed that Kyle and Frank rounded their pass routes instead of cutting left or right. It clicked in my head. You take a car around a corner at 40 miles per hour to make a tight 90-degree turn, and you have no choice but to slow down, unless you want to crash over the edge. But by curving through the turn, you can maintain your speed. The same thing applied to football. Round the pass pattern, gain an extra step on the defender. If I do that, nobody in America is catching me—I don't care who it is. I'd eat Deion Sanders up for lunch. Naturally, I could never test out my theory about rounding routes with the Giants. One, I hardly ever got to play. Two, why in the world would you rely on a passing attack when you had Frank Gifford, Alex Webster, and Mel Triplett in the backfield? You'd be crazy. Of course, I knew I could really turn it into a weapon if I had a quarterback who could throw me the ball as early as it took me to get open on the route.

But for that, I'd have to wait a couple of years. Well, actually, a little more than a couple years.

As the '58 season progressed, the Giants continued winning. Meanwhile, I sat on the bench, thinking how I could be fixing the pipes in the locker room. Then suddenly, in the fourth week of the season, Frank went down with an injury in the second quarter. Finally, it was time to go to work.

The Giants ran an offensive package with Frank at left halfback and Kyle Rote at the split end position. So when I filled in for Frank, my job was to cross behind the quarterback like he was going to give me the handoff and then swing up the field where quarterback Charlie Conerly would shovel me the pass out wide. Conerly was the veteran leader of the Giants' outstanding run-control offense. In 1956 he guided the team to an NFL title. Before serving as a marine corporal in World War II, he had been a great quarterback at Ole Miss under new head coach John Vaught, a respected offensive mind, who taught everything he knew to Mike Brumbelow.

I always thought Charlie was one of the greatest quarterbacks to play the game. He was as smart as they come, ran the fake as well as any signal-caller I've ever seen, and retained a toughness—which probably came from his days fighting in the jungles of Guam. He didn't have a particularly strong arm but he didn't need it. He always threw the ball to the exact, perfect spot on your route, and with a soft touch that made it easy to catch. Later, Conerly became the "Marlboro Man," as images of him in cigarette advertisements became iconic to a whole new generation. But I knew him as Charlie, one heck of a quarterback.

The first time we ran the play, I crossed behind Conerly, but I cut up the field so quickly on the fake that the defensive linebacker wasn't fooled one bit. Under pressure, Conerly had no choice but to get rid of it. As a result, he hit me in the back with the ball. When

I ducked my head back into the huddle, Conerly looked me dead in the eyes, "Hey, rookie, you're supposed to swing out wide." That was my first mistake as a pro. I never forgot it. I was never going to make a mistake like that again.

As usual, the running game took center stage as the game progressed. But every so often, Conerly would toss the ball to me in the backfield. The next time, I made the catch and ran it for 16 yards. Charlie hit me again and I scooted up the field for 31 yards. When you have NFL defenders trying to knock your head off a swivel, you try to juke the defensive guy so he doesn't get a straight-on shot at you. I had enough sense not to run straight into a guy like Gino Marchetti or Chuck Bednarik. I'd always cut to the right or the left so that when the guy does tackle me, it's not a direct shot. As a result, most of the hits I took were glancing blows, and many didn't hurt as bad as they sometimes looked.

I played three quarters that day and was scared for all three of them. Scared of blowing a play. Scared of dropping a ball. Scared of costing my team a score. But, in the end, I didn't make any more mistakes. I played to the best of my abilities, and although we ended up losing to the Cardinals, I finished the day with five catches for 85 yards.

Following the game, Lombardi told me to go down to Toot Shor's on Monday morning where a big-time sportswriter was going to interview me. Come Monday, I woke up and took the train downtown. I came out of the subway. Toots was supposed to be nearby. I went two blocks north, then turned back and went two south, then two blocks east and two blocks west, and I couldn't find it. But I wasn't about to get too far away from that hole in the ground, so I'd know how to get back. When I didn't see the restaurant, I got on the subway and went back up to the hotel. The next day when I showed up to the athletic facility, there was a note on my locker to go see Coach Lombardi. I went into his office and Lombardi said, "You had an interview downtown with a sportswriter. Why didn't you go?"

I replied, "I did go there, Coach. I went this way and that way but I couldn't find the place."

And he said, "Well, I don't know how you can miss it. Toots is one of the most famous places in New York."

"Well, Coach," I said. "Have you ever heard of Hadocol Corner?"

"Hadocol Corner?" asked Lombardi.

"Yes, sir. It's in Odessa, Texas. Once it rained. Once it snowed. And once the wind almost blowed Hadocol Corner off the Road."

Lombardi didn't say anything. He fined me $50, which to me was like $500. I carried balls out on the field for him for the rest of the season, and at the end of the year he gave me back my $50.

How could a New York Giant not know where Toots's was? Gifford wondered to himself. Then it sort of dawned on him. *Because Don's the kind of Giant who never left the small town inside of him.*

No Giant

IN THE WEEKS THAT FOLLOWED THE GAME, I filled in for Frank at halfback and I studied harder than ever. In film sessions, I sat in the dark beside Big Red watching the black-and-white images of the game projected on the screen, the silhouette of Lombardi just off to the side, the light flickering off his horn-rimmed glasses. I listened to him, transfixed on every word, like he was delivering a sermon in the desert, wearing long robes, holding a couple of stone tablets. At workouts, Em continued to teach me the finer points of defensive coverage. He told me, "You might get beat, but the important thing is that you don't get beat badly, that you're still able to make the tackle." Sometimes, I'd ask him or Sam Huff to explain why we ran a particular play. On offense it was the same thing. If it wasn't Kyle showing me the proper techniques, it might be Frank or Big Red giving me a pointer or two.

Dealing with New York reporters was one area where I could have used a few more keen suggestions from Frank and Kyle. They were both smooth operators wading in the media fishbowl of Yankee Stadium, and I was a small-town kid who grew up with no TV. The biggest newspaper that ever talked to me was the *El Paso Times*. When the New York reporters asked me a question, I gave them an honest, straightforward answer. At first, they called me a split end, which I knew I wasn't, so at workouts one day I explained to a group of them that I was only the split end if we ran the play to the left side, but if the play went to the right side then I was a flanker. I said, "To make it easy for you, why don't you just call me a wide receiver. That's my position, and that's how you folks need to refer to me." That's how sportswriters started using the term *wide receiver*.

Of course, the reporters from New York ended up calling me a lot of other things, all of which a farmer could use to help fertilize his soil. "Looks like Wyatt Earp just came into town," I overheard one writer say.

If I seemed to have a knack for getting on the wrong side of the New York reporters, the Giants had just as easy a time forming bitter rivalries, none greater than their blood feuds with the Eagles and the Browns. The Philadelphia Eagles had dominated the league in the late 1940s with their 7-4 defense, led by tough-as-nails line-backer "Concrete Charlie," aka Chuck Bednarik. There was always strong animosity between the Giants and the Eagles, but it became all-out war as stories about the Giants' sudden success was increasingly splashed across national headlines in the early '50s. Up to that point, no team had an answer for beating the Eagles' great defense. That was, until Lombardi showed up in New York and devised an offense that hadn't been seen before—not by the Eagles, not by any-body. It took a grand total of two years for Lombardi to help the Giants supplant the Eagles as the elite of the NFL, as they trounced George Halas' mighty Chicago Bears 47–7 in the 1956 title game.

Matching the intensity of our battles with the Eagles were those against the Cleveland Browns. Everybody knew that if you wanted to stop Cleveland, you first had to stop Jim Brown. Well, good luck. The man was 232 pounds of solid steel. No back in the NFL could

Posing at my eighth grade graduation from Three-Way. The next year, I'd play my first six-man football game. PHOTO COURTESY OF THE AUTHOR.

My senior class picture at Colorado City, Texas. PHOTO COURTESY OF THE AUTHOR.

Brumbelow's boys: the 1956 Texas Western University football team. (Inset) Me wearing my No. 13 jersey. PHOTOS COURTESY OF THE AUTHOR.

Texas Western coach Mike
Brumbelow. PHOTO COURTESY OF THE
AUTHOR.

Marilyn and me on our wedding day. PHOTO COURTESY OF THE AUTHOR.

The best part about playing for the Giants was learning from Vince Lombardi and great players like Frank Gifford.

Playing in "the Greatest Game Ever Played" is one of my most cherished football memories.

Right: I was the first player on the AFL's new New York franchise, the Titans.
PHOTO COURTESY OF AP IMAGES.

Below: Sonny Werblin was a brilliant businessman. As soon as he took over (and renamed) the team, the Jets took off.
PHOTO COURTESY OF AP IMAGES.

Sammy Baugh (left) was an incredible influence on my playing career. He's shown here with Harry Wismer, owner of the Titans. PHOTO COURTESY OF AP IMAGES.

Allie Sherman told me to shorten my stride. Thank goodness I didn't listen to that advice. PHOTO COURTESY OF AP IMAGES.

Neither did I listen to people who told me to get a haircut.

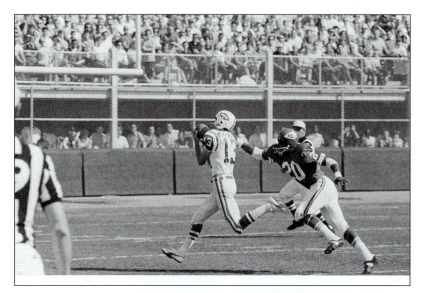

Get me in the open field, and I'm gone. PHOTO COURTESY OF AP IMAGES.

When a young kid out of Alabama arrived in 1965, it was the beginning of a beautiful friendship. PHOTO COURTESY OF THE AUTHOR.

match the size of Sam Huff—that is, except Jim Brown. He would literally *run over* defenders.

We ended up playing the Browns three times in my rookie year—and each game was a true clash of titans. The spirit of those all-out confrontations was captured in the one-on-one battle between Huff and Brown. A tall, quiet guy from Mission, Texas, defensive coordinator Tom Landry staggered three linebackers behind his four linemen, creating his famed 4-3 defense. The key to this alignment was middle linebacker Huff, who had a unique set of abilities. He could cover the middle on the runs, or he could drop back in the middle and defend against the pass. At the same time, Sam was as good as anybody ever in chasing the sweeps to the left or right.

At around 235 pounds, Sam was bigger than most of the backs. (I was sure glad that, at 60 pounds lighter than he was, I didn't have to face him myself.) He had an engine that ran only in fifth gear. He had a well-known reputation around the league for delivering serious hits, but there was nothing dirty about the way he played. He just played hard and with tons of heart.

The first game between the Giants and Browns that season was played in Cleveland. Tom Landry had defensive ends Jim Katcavage and Dick Modzelewski pinch the guards to give Sam Huff a clear lane to Brown. Landry told Huff, "Wherever Brown goes, I want you to be right there with him. If he goes to the restroom, you go with him. From now on, you're his shadow. You hit him on every play, whether he touches the ball or not." Brown rushed for more than 100 yards, but Landry's defense was able to contain him. We won the game by four points.

Our year came down to the final game of the season, a rematch with the rival Browns in Yankee Stadium. A win would secure a tie with them for the division title, forcing a playoff game one week later; a loss would send us home.

It was one of those frozen-outfield-grass, see-your-own-breath December days in New York. By that point in the season, there wasn't a defense that Jim Brown hadn't busted up. Coming into the game, he brought with him 1,300 rushing yards, 16 touchdowns, and a silent message of intimidation. I'll never forget it: on the second play of the game, Jim Brown burst up the field like some Roman gladiator and churned ahead for a 65-yard touchdown, silencing the crowd. That play could have devastated our defense, but Landry met his men on the sidelines, telling them to keep fighting. Then again, he didn't have to tell men like Sam Huff, Harland Svare, Rosey Grier, Emlen Tunnell, and Andy Robustelli to keep fighting. There was no quit in that bunch.

For the rest of that afternoon, with snow swirling over the stadium, our defense shut down offensive guru Paul Brown and his high-powered offense. They held Jim Brown to just 83 yards after his touchdown run. With our team trailing by a touchdown in the fourth quarter, Conerly led us on a tremendous drive to tie the score, 10–10. With two minutes left, the defense forced one more three-and-out. Now it was up to our offense to try and score. If we failed, Cleveland would be heading to the championship game and I'd be heading to Rattlesnake Lake.

After a short punt from Cleveland, we started with great field position. Sure enough, Lombardi sent me in on first down. In the middle of a snowstorm, Conerly took the snap. I cut around the corner, managing to get open for a second. Conerly raised his arm and threw me the ball. I saw the pass coming through the snow and, at the last second, I leaped up to grab it. The ball sailed high, just out of my reach. Lombardi called another pass play on second down. Conerly threw a deep spiral to Alex Webster, who had it slip from his grasp. Lombardi decided to throw it for a third time, probably thinking it was four-down territory. After all, you'd have to be out of your mind to go for a kick from that distance in a windy blizzard.

On third down, Conerly threw a short pass to Gifford. If anybody could make something happen at that moment, it was our best playmaker. But as soon as Frank caught the ball, Cleveland linebacker Galen Fiss hit him, knocking the ball to the ground.

By then, the wind and snow had darkened the afternoon sky to the point where the lights had to be turned on in the stadium. Summerall was a great kicker, but that one was just plain out of his range. Not to mention you couldn't even make out the line markers, on account of all the snow. When Howell sent Summerall onto the field, there were more than a few sideway glances exchanged on the sidelines. Lombardi looked like his head was going to pop off.

Apparently, when Summerall poked his head into the huddle, Charlie Conerly said, "What the hell are you doing in here?"

"I'm going to try and kick a field goal," responded Summerall.

A moment before the ball was snapped you could have heard a pin drop in Yankee Stadium. The crowd was dead silent. So were both benches. Kyle Rote claimed that from where he was standing on the sideline he was sure it was 52 yards away. Ray Wietecha snapped the ball. Through the blinding snow, you could barely make out the ball as Conerly, who was also our holder, placed the ball nose down. Amid the chaos of diving and colliding players, Summerall's foot made contact with the ball. All at once, those of us standing on the Giants sideline turned our heads to follow the path of the ball through the snow and lights.

"I remember watching as it got closer to the goal post; it was breaking back and forth like a knuckler," said Summerall. "I wasn't sure it was going to go in."

Well, it did. Final score: Giants 13, Cleveland 10. As the players congratulated Summerall on the field, we erupted on the sideline, cheering and back-slapping each other. As Summerall got to the sideline, Lombardi grabbed him by the front of his jersey. He barked in his thick Brooklyn accent, "You know, you SOB, you can't kick it that far."

Just one week later we were back in Yankee Stadium to take on the Browns again. *For the third time that season.* The first two had been epic nail-biters, and now the entire season came down to this one game. There had been title games where the stakes didn't feel this high, the drama so personal.

In the first quarter, the Giants drove the ball down to the Cleveland 19-yard line. Everybody was expecting Lombardi to call another one of his patented sweeps with Gifford and Webster. As usual, Conerly handed it off to Webster, who then gave the ball to Gifford, who then ran it around the corner. But around the 9-yard line, Gifford did something shocking. He lateraled the ball back to our slow-footed 37-year-old quarterback. Of course, nobody was covering Charlie Conerly. They were all focused on stopping Gifford. As a result, Conerly rushed into the end zone for the score. With that bit of wild misdirection, Vince Lombardi had outsmarted Cleveland's head coach, Paul Brown, considered the greatest football mind of his time, and by doing so the Giants scored the only points they would need all day.

It was late in the third quarter, and the Giants were holding onto a 10-0 lead. I was back to receive the punt. I mishandled the football. Before I knew it, I was hit. The ball was loose on the ground. Cleveland recovered in our territory. I'd been taught to put a bad play behind me, so I didn't give it any more thought. It didn't cost the Giants the game. It didn't even cost them a touchdown.

In New York, that game would go down in lore, as our defense skunked Cleveland's great offense. They might as well have parted the Red Sea! But truly, if you want to know how great our defense played, you just need to look at Jim Brown's stats in their defeat. Over the years, there have been countless barroom arguments from Euclid Avenue to Delancey Street about who came out on top in those famous Huff-Brown heavyweight fights. As for Sam, he would simply say, "Seven carries, eight yards."

I don't know if anybody else besides Sam Huff could have stopped Jim Brown—if even just for four quarters. If there was, I wasn't made aware of it. In the end, maybe our offense is what drew the crowds to the stadium, but it was our defense that put us in a championship game that would be celebrated in this country for the next 52 years.

The next day I opened up the newspaper, looking forward to reading about our historic victory over Cleveland. Instead I got a bunch of stories about how rookie Don Maynard fumbled the game away. First of all, the terminology wasn't even right. I thought, *don't they know the difference between a fumble and a muff?* A fumble means you first had control of the football before you lost it, while a muff is when you mishandle the ball without ever having possession of it.

Over the next couple of weeks, I tried over and over again to explain to the New York sportswriters that I hadn't fumbled the ball, I had muffed it. But they just kept referring to the play as a fumble. Before you know it, they had made me out to be the greatest fumbler in the history of pro football.

In a classic battle of two great defenses, we beat Cleveland 10 to zip, and so you can throw all that negative stuff about Don Maynard costing the Giants in the East River where it belongs. As for my coaches and teammates, they had nothing bad to say to me. It was the press that was 100 percent responsible for turning it into something bigger than it was. I didn't think the negative press coverage would affect how fans treated me, but some of them booed me at games. Being helpless to change their opinion about me was horrible, but I'll tell the worst part about the press labeling me fumble-prone: it stuck.

You can be sure, it doesn't feel good messing up in front of 60,000 New York fans. But you can't imagine anything more humbling than reading all the negative comments that followed. I knew the New York press would have something to say about my flub against Cleveland, but that they would jump on me like a pack of starving hyenas, tearing away at my carcass until there was nothing left but my dry bones? Well, butter my butt and call me a biscuit. (I mentioned we won that game, right?)

It felt important in that moment to realize that I was human and then to reevaluate what I could do better. At the same time, I had to get ready for our championship game against the spectacular Baltimore Colts in one week. My best was required, and I knew I couldn't give my best if I let regrets linger and doubts grow. After physical talent, a pro athlete's ability to move on from personal failure is the most important quality he needs to possess. When I say move on, I don't mean from one game to the next. I mean from one play to the next.

Our preparation for the Colts in the week leading up to the championship game was no different from how we prepared all season. Lombardi and Landry went through the game film of the Colts with us one more time. The hope was to uncover some tendency that would give us an edge. Maybe we'd get lucky and catch a lineman setting his right foot a little differently on a pass play, alerting us to what the offense was going to run seconds before the snap of the ball.

Funnily enough, Baltimore had been in the league only six years, and that was only on account of the Dallas Texans folding. Then in 1954 the franchise hired an unknown 47-year-old assistant from Cleveland with zero head coaching experience in the pros, and told him to turn a bunch of young, discombobulated players into winners. The coach's name was Weeb Ewbank. A few years later, a construction worker from Pittsburgh, who'd been cut by the Steelers, borrowed some gas money from his buddies to drive to Baltimore for tryouts. That player's name was Johnny Unitas.

In 1957, a desperate Coach Ewbank decided to give the NFL cast-off a shot to lead the team. By season's end Unitas was named the league's MVP while the Colts took their place at the top of the NFL heap. Nicknamed "the Golden Arm," Unitas would spend the next decade or so terrorizing defenses around the league, rifling passes with cool precision to his corps of sure-handed receivers, including Hall of Fame receivers Lenny Moore and Raymond Berry.

We knew it was going to be a tough game going in. If our defense wanted a test, they'd sure get it trying to stop the duo of Unitas and Berry. As a backup corner, I had to be ready to step in. That meant paying close attention as Tom Landry showed us game film of the Colts. What made Unitas and Berry so hard to stop was the terrific speed and precision with which they executed pass plays. Unitas hadn't dropped back more than a few steps and the ball was already sailing out of his hand—and by then Berry had already made his cut to the sideline. *Bam! Bam!* Just like that. You send your defensive line on an all-out blitz. Unitas stands in the pocket like a man with ice water running through his veins. A second before they sack him... *Bam! Bam!* Too late. Unitas to Berry, 20-yard gain. Our best bet was to drop our middle linebacker back a little to his right to cheat against the sideline pass.

The fact that we had beaten them earlier in the season would only fuel their desire for revenge. When we met in November at Yankee Stadium, the Colts had a perfect record, and we were still struggling to find our identity. Both sides fought hard, but in the end we beat them on Pat Summerall's late–fourth-quarter field goal. The conventional wisdom is that if you've already beaten a team once, you have the upper hand against them should you face them again later in the season. But I can assure you that on the morning of the title game, no Giants player was strutting around, making guarantees of victory. For one, Unitas had sat out that first meeting with broken ribs and a punctured lung. What had happened seven weeks earlier was ancient history. And the fact that we had beaten the Colts twice in a row meant less than nothing to us. As for our won-lost records, you could throw those out the window. Shoot, they won their division. We won ours. Let's play.

I'm not sure how my teammates spent the night before the championship game. I know I stayed in my apartment and went to bed early. One unusual thing was that the entire Colts team had checked into the Concourse Plaza earlier that day. For all I know, Unitas could have been in the next room. But then, I didn't see anybody walking down the hall in black high-top shoes.

Game day started like any other: with 31 sit-ups in bed. I finished my stretching, went downstairs for breakfast, then made my way to a special players-only meeting. You'd think it would be to fire each other up, but it was to discuss whether rookies like me and Jack Kemp should get a full share. Of course, Jack and I didn't make a peep; we let the veterans sort it out. At one point, the conversation between Frank and Sam got pretty heated. Wouldn't that have been something? The biggest star on offense and our biggest star on defense getting in a fistfight seconds before we're about to play for the world title?

I struck out from the Concourse Plaza to Yankee Stadium on foot. After playing two Sundays in a row in frigid temperatures, to have a sunny day in the low 40s was a welcome relief. As Vince Lombardi led us in calisthenics for what turned out to be his last time, I had no idea that I was about to be playing in what's now commonly referred to as "the Greatest Game Ever Played." Or just how many people around the country were going to flip on their TV sets to watch that game a few hours later.

I'll never forget looking around the stadium before the game. I had never seen it that full or heard it that loud. Across the field stood Johnny Unitas. It was the first time that many of us on the Giants had seen him in person.

The Giants won the coin toss, and I went back to receive the kickoff in front of more than 70,000 cheering fans. The whistle blew, and Colts kicker Bert Rechichar sent the football sailing high into the air. It was a doozy of a kick. I took a couple of steps back in the end zone, caught the ball on the fly, and took a knee. And that's how, at 1:00 on December 28, 1958, in Yankee Stadium, the Greatest Game Ever Played got under way.

The performance that both teams delivered over the next four quarters set the standard for every title game to follow. I've never seen a knock-down, drag-out fight like that on a football field—then or since. The two teams kept going back and forth, neither one giving an inch. Late in the fourth quarter, Unitas led one of the all-time great drives, threading the needle to Raymond Berry with what felt like one improbable pass after another. You might ask, what happened to cheating over Sam Huff to take away the sideline pass? Unitas, predicting that the Giants would do just that, attacked the middle of the field with the calm demeanor that would make you think he was playing a preseason game. They used to say that when Clint Eastwood starred in a spaghetti Western he had two expressions: "one with the hat, one without." Well, that was two more than Unitas had when he went to work behind in the fourth quarter.

Unitas got the Colts into field-goal range, and then Steve Myhra kicked it through the uprights to tie the game. The next thing I know, I'm running out onto the field to receive the kickoff with seven seconds left in the game. I caught the ball in the end zone and ran it out to the 18-yard line. There wasn't enough time for our offense to mount a drive, so Conerly just fell on the ball and let time expire. The game was over—except it wasn't.

Our guys were roaming the sidelines, talking to each other but also trying to stay warm. The thermometer had really dipped. You heard players saying, "Well, it's a tie game. We've got to go back out there and break the tie." Not exactly a rallying call. But you have to understand, our guys had just been in one hell of a dogfight; we were a tattered, muddy unit, breathing out white plumes into the bitter cold.

Around the country, the buzz was building. The first ever title game to go to sudden-death overtime! People around the country were glued to their televisions.

By the time our captains, Kyle Rote and Bill Svoboda, met Johnny Unitas, filling in for their captain Gino Marchetti, who was sitting on a gurney on the sideline with a broken leg. The sky was dark. You could barely make out the spectators; you just heard their voices in the freezing cold. The lights had been turned on, giving the field the glow of a night game. It wouldn't have made any difference if we had known how many Americans were watching or not. After exchanging blows as we had for the past 60 minutes. There wasn't much that was said; there wasn't much that needed to be said. We had a job to finish.

The winning purse was also nothing to scoff at in those days. The players on the team to score first in the overtime period would receive around $4,700. That was more than half of my entire rookie salary. Of course, nowadays, a player's Super Bowl share is in the neighborhood of $80,000.

The Colts lost the coin toss; we would receive first. This was uncharted territory—for the players, for the league, for the TV announcers. Sudden death. First team to score wins.

At the same time the previous year, I was a college senior, home for Christmas, and Marilyn and I were probably pulling up to the Dairy Queen in El Paso. And here I stood, alone in the end zone of cavernous Yankee Stadium, the only lights in the place shining down on the players on the field. I glanced ahead at the back of my teammates' jerseys. They were lined up in our kickoff formation 20 yards up the field, rocking back and forth, waiting to block the onslaught of Colts players coming after me.

As for the people I knew up in the bleachers of the stadium, there was my wife, and that was it. She sat with all the other players' wives. The majorette was now a mother, and the cotton ginner's son was waiting to field the ball in the first NFL overtime game anybody had ever seen.

I couldn't tell you how many people back in El Paso were watching me as I stood alone in the end zone. I hadn't talked to my dad or my mom or my brother before the game. I would think they were watching it. I'm sure football fans from around that area were watching. But the others were probably celebrating Christmas with their family.

Rechichar kicked it off. I picked up the flight pattern of the football right away. It was going to be short. I took off like a rocket. As I sprinted up the field, never taking my eye off the flight of the ball, I squared my body up so that I would be directly under the ball when I caught it.

Nervousness never entered my mind as I took off after the ball falling from the sky. Normally, you want to pause a moment under the ball and then as soon as it's in your grasp, accelerate up the field. As always, I got to where I needed to be in plenty of time. I had never been late before—not to school, not to practice, not to training camp, not anywhere. And I was on time again. But rather than pause to catch the ball before taking off, I just kept running, catching the ball in full stride. By the time the ball hit my arms, I had a good head of steam going.

In a flash, I screeched on the brakes. The ball had slipped through my grasp. Instincts took over. I calmly reached down and felt around for the ball. I didn't even think about the pack of giant defenders bearing down on me. I kept feeling around. The whole time from when the ball hit the ground to when I picked it up was probably a second and a half. Frank would tell me years later that it felt like decades. A split-second before the defenders barreled into me, I retrieved the ball. A swarm of guys in white-and-blue jerseys piled on me.

I won't make any excuses. I didn't lose it in the lights or anything like that. I just muffed it—in front of 64,185 fans and 45 million viewers. Of course, it could have been much worse. Imagine if I had given the ball over to the Colts on our 20-yard line. Don't tell me there's no difference between a muff and a fumble. You bet there is.

On our opening possession, our offense couldn't get anything going and had to punt. Unitas took over at the Colts' 20-yard line. My recollection of the Colts' drive goes something like this. *Bam! Bam!* Unitas to Berry. *Bam! Bam!* Unitas to Berry. *Bam! Bam!* Unitas to Berry. Hand off to Ameche. Score. Game.

Do I remember seeing Frank or Kyle or Emlen right after the game? Not really. Nobody was talking to anybody. There was no, "We'll get them next year, Tex." There was just a locker room full of tired, beat-up guys quietly slipping off their pads and cutting the bloody tape from their legs. Hopefully, none of your teammates got hurt too badly. You showered, got dressed, and went your own way. Everybody went his own way.

Naturally we were disappointed that we lost the game. This was the world championship, the Super Bowl at that time. There's no chance to second-guess or to redo it. The game is over. The season is over. You're not thinking about next year. If anything, you're thinking about how you just lost your winner's share.

After the game, Conerly went back to work on his cotton farm in Mississippi, Gifford went back to California to make movies, and Kyle Rote went back to Texas. As for me, I returned to El Paso to be a plumber. With a four-month professional salary, I could pay back all the money I had borrowed from my folks, her grandfolks, and my brother to finish school. After that, believe me, there wasn't much left over.

Many people hadn't paid much attention to the NFL before that showdown in the dusk on New York City. But as word spread about this unbelievable game that had been played, even people who hadn't seen the game became curious. The national media ran with the story; so did the young suits on Madison Avenue. That championship made all the difference in the world.

Reflecting personally on that game half a century later, I feel honored to have been on the same field with so many great players on both sides of the field—an amazing 12 of us ended up in the Hall of Fame. It's become one of the most important contests in the history of sports.

It also makes me think about how life unfolds in different ways for different people. If I thought my big chance in life to do something great and memorable had come and gone in those one and a half seconds, I think the next 50 years of my life would have been a real drag. Instead, they turned out real fine.

I'm not saying that losing a big game like that wasn't disappointing. It was. Probably even more so to the older guys whose careers were winding down. I know Frank felt horrible that he had fumbled the ball twice, even though, as Lombardi came over and told him in the locker room after the game, we wouldn't have even gotten to the championship without him. But it wasn't the end of the world for Frank. He became one of the biggest sports announcers in the country. And so did our kicker, Pat Summerall. Lombardi went on to glory with the Packers. Landry took over an expansion team, the Dallas Cowboys, and turned them into "America's Team." See, losing that game wasn't the end of the world for any of us. That's just the kind of guys that we had that season. You keep doing your best. You keep grinding. Good things will happen.

No League

NOTHING STAYS THE SAME, and that includes football teams. After our loss to the Colts in the championship game, Vince Lombardi left to take over as head coach of the Green Bay Packers, a franchise that at the time boasted 11 straight seasons without a winning record. I heard that Lombardi's strict, hard-driving style rubbed a few players the wrong way in Green Bay. I can say that without exception, those of us whom he coached in New York thought the world of him. None of us would ever call Coach Lombardi a softie—or even "Vince"—but we never doubted his devotion to us, his players, or the great feeling he held for each and every single one of us. He had no favorites. He was coach, friend, and confidante to the youngest rookie and the oldest veteran. Quite simply, we revered him.

With a full season under my belt, I was primed and ready to make my impact felt when I got back on the field. In the fall of '59, I traveled up to Bear Mountain, New York, for the second part of Giants training camp. There I met Allie Sherman, the man replacing Lombardi as the Giants' offensive coordinator. Donning a stylish suit, tie, and fedora, Sherman paused to look at me. Of course, I had on my cowboy hat and boots.

"We don't wear sideburns in New York," he said to me.

"Well, I do," I replied.

Right then, I knew this wasn't Lombardi. Lombardi might explode on you, but at least he told you what he was thinking to your face. He didn't harbor any petty gripes. If something was eating at him, you'd hear about it—from one end of Manhattan to the other. Sherman was, well, different. He was reserved. He never yelled at me—not that I would ever give him a reason to. I came to meetings early, I never dropped a pass during workouts, and I was always the first one to finish wind sprints. But, gee whiz, every time I was around him, you'd think I was a skunk at a picnic. It was almost enough for a guy to take personally.

One morning at workouts, Allie Sherman was standing out on the field, watching the offense run through a series of dummy drills. He called for a sweep, a play that called for me to line up at left halfback and then swing around to my right, take the handoff from the quarterback, and accelerate around the corner and up the field. We ran the pattern, at the end of which, Sherman told us to run it again. No big deal. That happens a lot in pro ball. Maybe he felt the guard didn't pull wide enough. Who knows?

The players got back on the line of scrimmage and ran the play again. I got around the corner pretty quickly the first time, but I made sure to really motor around the second time. "Come on, Maynard," I hear Sherman call out. "Quit that long stridin' and get to runnin'."

I walked back to my spot in the formation and got ready to run the play again. The second the ball was snapped I sprang off the line like a bull released from its pen. I snatched the rock from the quarterback and sprinted around the edge. When I heard the whistle blow, I slowed up. *Well, if that doesn't satisfy him,* I thought, *I don't know what will.*

Sherman's voice rang out across the practice field. "I don't want to see those long strides, Maynard! This isn't a track meet!"

"Dang it, Coach," I said. "I can cover more ground in one stride then anybody you've got out here can cover in two."

Sherman exploded. "Get out of here!" he yelled. "Go stand down by the goal post! I don't want to see your face for the rest of the workout!" With all the players and coaches looking on silently, I started that long walk to the other end of the field, my helmet in hand. Sherman had really embarrassed me in front of my teammates.

I grew up respecting the authority figures in my life—my dad, my teacher, my coaches. As a matter of fact, I don't believe there was one time in my life I had ever talked back to a coach. But I was humiliated. At the same time, I was standing up for myself. You have to believe in what you're doing, unless of course, there's some evidence that what you're doing isn't right. To just say, "This isn't a track meet," well, that's true. But here was my question to him: what in the world difference does that make? I'd been taking long, easy strides for years, and nobody yet had been able to stay with me one-on-one. Did he want me to start writing left-handed, too? Maybe he'd like me to hold the pencil between my thighs and write that way. Hey, if it ain't broke, don't fix it. If something's working right, you keep on doin' it. If it's fouled up, then you make a change.

For the rest of practice, I stood alone at the other end of the field, watching as the offense went through the rest of their running drills and then, completed all their passing drills. Never in my life had I ever missed a practice—not in middle school, not in high school, not in college, not since I was 13 years old, when I played my first organized football. To miss that first one hurt unbelievably.

At the end of practice, I entered the locker room and walked over to my locker, past players milling around and changing out of their uniforms. As I passed Alex Webster, sitting in front of his locker, I said, "Gee whiz, what's the matter with this guy?"

"Don't pay attention to him," somebody called over. I turned around. Sam Huff was sitting at his locker. "You just keep running," he said.

I don't know why Sam Huff took to me when I was a rookie. Maybe he saw in me some of what he saw in himself—he wasn't the fastest linebacker in the league and I sure wasn't the biggest half-back, but we were going to work harder, study harder, and practice harder than the next 20 guys on the field. I hit the showers, not sure if the steam was coming off my body or out my ears.

I got the notion that Sherman had it out for me, so I was determined not to give him an excuse to get rid of me. Three weeks before the regular season kicked off, we had a big preseason exhibition game in Bangor, Maine. It shows you what small business the NFL was that the Maine Jaycees were able to get two professional franchises to come play at tiny Garland Street Field for $20,000 per team. We would be facing the Green Bay Packers under their rookie coach Vince Lombardi. It was fitting that one of his first games as head coach for the Packers would be against the Giants, where he had been an assistant for the past five years.

The Packers and the Giants were staying at the same hotels. When Lombardi ran into Huff and some of his old Giants players in the lobby, he got so choked up he could barely speak.

Not surprisingly, we had never played on a field that small or in such bad condition. The lights hung so low over the field that it was nearly impossible to pick up the ball in flight. On a very deep kick, you might not see the ball at all—you'd just hear it bounce to the ground behind the goal post. I did my best under those poorly illuminated conditions, managing to field the ball cleanly except for one time, when the ball slipped through my grasp. Now, the errant play didn't cost us the game; it didn't even cost us a touchdown.

Despite all Lombardi's offensive weapons, such as Paul Hornung, Jim Taylor, and Bart Starr, we shut them out, 14-0.

In the locker room after the game, Lombardi knew that it was not the time to berate his young team but to offer gentle encouragement. "Gentlemen," said Lombardi, "the defense you just faced might be the best in NFL history."

The next day we were back at Bear Mountain. Around 7:00 in the morning, I was in the cafeteria eating breakfast with the other players. Jim Lee Howell came up to the table. He told me to come into his office and to bring my playbook with me. The guys sitting around me quickly looked down so as to avoid making eye contact with me. They knew what I knew, what every player in the league knew. Anytime you're told that the head coach wants to see you and that you need to bring your playbook, you're either being traded or cut. Most of the time it's cut.

Howell and Sherman were waiting for me when I walked in. Howell told me I was being released. I was shocked. The only ammunition Sherman could use against me was my muff the year before against Cleveland and the one in that exhibition game against the Packers. In both cases, the error didn't lead to an opposition score, and what's more, we didn't just win both those games, we dominated them. Plus, I was having a good training camp. I hadn't dropped *any* passes. I had the system down perfect. I hadn't given them anything but my full effort. I hadn't done anything wrong off the field. I never came late to practice. I never missed a meeting.

"Why?" I asked them. Neither man gave me an answer.

"Why aren't you keeping me?" I repeated. "Nobody has beaten me out."

"We're going with Joe Morrison," said Sherman. Joe Morrison was a rookie from Cincinnati taken in the third round.

"That's the guy who's taking my place?" I said. "He's a nice guy and all, but I can run backwards faster than he can run forwards."

Later on, I learned that the coaches had taken some kind of vote on whether I should make the team or not. Tom Landry wanted to keep me. Allie Sherman didn't. To this day, I still don't know what his problem was with me other than that he didn't like that I wore Levi's and cowboy boots. What difference did that make? What a man wears or what his father does for a living has nothing to do with what he can do on the field.

Lombardi couldn't have cared less about my sideburns. He might make a comment from time to time about my cowboy attire but it always good-natured. Like the time he said to me, "Where'd you say you went to college?

"Texas Western, sir."

"Never heard of it."

"Where did you go?" I asked.

"Fordham University."

"Well, Coach," I said. "I've never heard of that place, so I guess we're even."

He could tease me about going to a tiny school in Texas because I knew that he didn't really care where I went; he was only interested in whether I was dedicated to excellence. As for your clothes or your hometown accent or your skin color, it didn't concern him one bit.

I listened to every single comment a coach ever made to me—from Mike Brumbelow to Sammy Baugh to Tom Landry to Vince Lombardi. I'd think on it long and hard. I'd ask myself, was there something about how I played the game that I needed to change? Maybe I had to tweak my stance or alter how I carried the ball or improve my footwork on a diving sideline pass. But what in the world did it matter how I ran if no defender on this planet could catch me? Besides, how do I know that Allie Sherman knew how to run? I never saw him sprint or even lead calisthenics like Lombardi. So he had played with the Philadelphia Eagles in the '40s. He rushed for a grand total of 44 yards. Excuse me, *negative* 44 yards. Before he took over as offensive coordinator, he had been a scout for the Giants—and in my opinion, he knew as much about football as those turkeys up in Washington know about honesty.

Shoot, any other coach would have been blessed to have a guy with my speed; they wouldn't care if I was running upside down on my hands. I felt like saying to Sherman, "Hey, don't mess up a good thing. Right or wrong, this is the way I've been running my whole life. It's my natural gait, so to speak. It's the way I've run since I was leaping over wooden sticks in a vacant cotton gin lot. Since I was playing six-man football at Three Way High School. Since I went down to Austin and won the Texas State title in the low and hi hurdles. It's how I got into college. It's how I got my degree. It's how I won the Blue-Gray game for my hero Sammy Baugh. It's how, as a ninth rounder from Texas Western, I was the only one out of 27 draft picks to make the Giants team in 1958. And it's how, as a rookie, I got the chance to play in the first sudden-death championship in NFL history."

When I left Jim Lee Howell's office, I thought about calling Marilyn, but instead I went back to the cafeteria. Most of the time I didn't eat much breakfast—maybe a piece of toast or a grapefruit. But I sat back down at the table and probably ate the biggest breakfast I'd ever had in my life. Hey, I didn't know where the next meal was coming from. There was no doubt I was going to leave the Giants camp with a full stomach.

I packed up my stuff, including all the special football gear I had brought with me from Texas Western. When Kyle and Frank heard that Coach Sherman had cut me they couldn't believe it. They told me, "Hey, keep your chin up. Some other team is sure to pick you up off waivers soon enough." We said our good-byes and that was it.

Marilyn was down in El Paso with Terry. Picking up the phone in the dorm to call her and tell her I'd been cut, that was a tough thing to do. Even thinking about it now gets to me. I don't think I've ever felt so devastated as I did in those couple of hours after being cut. In an instant, I was jobless and had no income. I wanted to crawl up under some rock. But I also thought about my wife and baby daughter in El Paso and how they were depending on me. I didn't know what I was going to do. But I knew I had to do something. So before leaving Bear Mountain, I called up Don Sutherlin, my friend from Giants training camp the year before.

I'd kept in touch with Sutherlin even after the Giants had released him. From time to time, I'd check in to see how things were going for him in Canada. He'd tell me he was enjoying life playing up north and how his team, the Hamilton Tiger-Cats, had made it to the Grey Cup, the CFL's equivalent to the Super Bowl.

On the phone, I asked him if there might be a spot for me on the Tiger-Cats. He told me he would go and talk to head coach Jim Trimble. Meanwhile, I went to my room and packed up my bags. I was fourth in the league in kickoff returns my rookie year with the Giants, averaging 28.3 yards a return, and yet here I was on my way out the door. Crazy.

I didn't get to say good-bye to Em Tunnell. If I had I would have thanked him for teaching me so much about football and life. He might have told me to keep my chin up. Actually, he probably would have wanted to take me to the Red Rooster nightclub to cheer me up. Maybe buy me a cashmere jacket to go with my cowboy hat. And I would have told him, "The old coat I have is still in good shape, why would I get another one?" And he'd probably just laugh and say, "You're not lying, Tex."

Later in Green Bay, Em would become teammates with Paul Hornung. This is what the man selected 108 spots in front of me in the 1958 draft had to say about him:

> Emlen Tunnell was the king of Harlem because he spent every quarter he ever earned there. He invested in businesses and was a soft touch for somebody who was down on his luck. If anybody from the streets needed fifty dollars, they knew where to go. I promise you that at that time, if Tunnell had been walking down one side of 125th Street and Sugar Ray Robinson down the other, Tunnell would have easily drawn the bigger crowd.... Emlen was seen as kind of a father figure to the black players. Emlen didn't see black players or white players, he just saw ballplayers.

I'm happy to say that I can attest to that fact.

In the end, neither Jim Lee Howell nor Allie Sherman would give me an answer as to why I'd been cut—in fact, they even tried to stiff me on my ticket home. The Giants had an agreement with players that if the team released them, they would pay for their return flight. Sure enough, just before I was about to leave, the Giants told me they'd heard something about me going to Canada, and they weren't going to pay for my plane ticket. I said, "I ain't going to Canada. You give me cash money now so I can get home."

I went down to the bus station and caught the next Greyhound to Manhattan and then onto LaGuardia Airport. The bus trip from Bear Mountain to LaGuardia took about two hours, but it felt whole lot longer than that. Just getting from Howell's office to the train station was one of the longest trips I'd ever taken—and I used to ride a mule six miles to school! I did a lot of thinking on that ride to the airport, and most of it wasn't too rosy. I didn't know what my next step in life would be. I needed help, but there wasn't anyone who could help me. There was no reason to call my parents; they couldn't help me. I was 24 years old and scared.

When I got to LaGuardia, I had no reservations. I had a big decision to make: either I was getting on a plane to El Paso, or I was getting on a plane to Toronto. I could go back to El Paso, and maybe in a few days another team would pick me up off waivers. Then again, maybe not.

I called Sutherlin again from the airport. He told me that he had spoke to Trimble. Turned out that Trimble knew about me from his time as a scout with the Giants a few years earlier. He told Sutherlin that if I came to Hamilton he'd give me a tryout. So, I bought a one-way ticket to Canada's Steel City, courtesy of the New York Giants.

Sutherlin picked me up at the airport and drove me to Hamilton. I sure was grateful to him for talking to Trimble on my behalf, just as I had been grateful to my buddy Corbell for talking to Coach Brumbelow at Texas Western. If anything, the stakes were higher this time around. Before it was just me I had to worry about; now I had two other people to consider: my wife and my daughter.

We arrived at the stadium and I went inside to speak to Trimble in his office. He told me to come to the next few workouts and he would see if he could use me. Shortly thereafter, my wife called me and told me to come on home—she had spoken to the athletic director of the El Paso school system, and he was going to give me a job teaching seventh grade P.E. class. At that moment, I didn't exactly tell her what I was thinking.

I spoke to my brother, Thurman, and he just told me to think it out in terms of what I could afford. That night in Hamilton, I bought a New York newspaper. I opened it up to the sports section and flipped through it until I came to a story about me. The headline read, "NFL reject." The next morning I arrived at the Hamilton Tiger-Cats practice field. I didn't say anything to anybody. I just went out there and started running pass patterns with their offense. I don't remember the weather that day in Hamilton, but I guarantee you, there was plenty of shine on the field.

Afterward, Trimble came up to me in the locker room and told me that if I wanted, I could be on the team. Sutherlin gave me a little smile when I taped my name on the locker near his. When I got back to the hotel, I called Marilyn on the phone and told her to pack some warm clothes, grab the baby, and fly up 2,000 miles north. For the next year, Hamilton, Ontario, was going to be our home.

When Marilyn and Terry arrived in Hamilton, the three of us moved into an apartment complex with several other American players—there were 12 of us. I guess it was no different for my Marilyn and Terry than it had been for my mom and me. They didn't know how long they would be living in Canada. They didn't know when they'd have to suddenly pick up and move. Just like with my dad, the road I traveled for work would be the same road my family traveled. I still didn't know what the future would hold for us, but I knew one thing: it wasn't going to involve teaching badminton to a bunch of middle-schoolers.

Around that time, there had been some rumblings, back in America, about Lamar Hunt starting his own professional football league. Growing up in Texas you knew about the Hunts—they were only the richest family in the state, maybe the entire country. Lamar's old man, H.L. Hunt, had started out in the cotton business just like my dad. But whereas my dad stuck with it, H.L. gave it up to try his luck in the oil trade instead. He bought a bunch of land in West Texas from an old wildcatter named "Pop" Joiner. By 1960 the wells he had built across those many acres of barren ground were pumping out $200,000 worth of oil a day.

Lamar loved football and had even played some receiver at SMU, backing up none other than Raymond Berry, the legendary

Colt wideout who would later team up with Unitas for the greatest drive in history. The 27-year-old decided he wanted to buy himself an NFL franchise. Improbably, the NFL spurned his repeated offers. Fed up with the politics, Lamar approached another young oilman from Texas named Bud Adams, knowing that the monopoly of NFL owners had also crushed his dream of owning an NFL franchise, and said to him, "If they won't let us into their league, well then, heck, we should just start our own." On the off chance they actually went through with it, I refused to sign an option with the Tiger-Cats.

Meanwhile, things were working out just fine in Canada. The Tiger-Cats were paying me a good salary. I was having a blast playing football again. Our team was in the midst of a great season. And, most important, I got to wear No. 13 on my jersey.

On our team, I served as the extra flanker on offense and the fifth cornerback on defense. The ultimate goal didn't change. It was still to score the most points and win the game. But I had to quickly deal with the different football rules north of the border. The field was a good 10 yards longer and nearly 12 yards wider. There were 12 men to a side instead of 11 and three downs instead of four. All of this translated to a wide-open passing attack. To me, it was a lot like playing six-man back in Three-Way. Wild shootouts ensued, which was as fun for me to be a part of as it was for fans to watch.

Another difference between the leagues was that in the NFL, a kick returner could call for a fair catch or take a knee in the end zone. What's exciting about that? Nothing. Well, the CFL had a no-fair-catch rule, so returners *had* to run it back. As a result, you saw more spectacular plays (as well as collisions) on punt and kickoff returns than you ever did in the NFL. To this day, nobody has done anything about changing the rule here in the States, but we need to do what the Canadians do: make 'em run it. That would be a lot more exciting than a dead ball.

A few games into the season, I got a telephone call from Vince Lombardi. It had taken them a week just to track me down. He told me that the Packers had picked up my waivers. I asked him, "Do I have to come? I'm happy here." He could have forced me to play for him under an agreement between the NFL and CFL. He said he wouldn't press the issue. Even though Lombardi would turn the Packers into one of the greatest dynasties in NFL history, I never regretted turning down his offer. What's more, I would always be thankful to him for letting me follow my road of choice.

My first season with the Hamilton Tiger-Cats ended with us going to the Grey Cup, the CFL's championship game. There we would face the rival Blue Bombers of Winnipeg. Days before the contest, and almost 10 years before Super Bowl III, Jim Trimble, known for stirring the pot with Winnipeg, gave what you might call the Canadian version of the Guarantee. "We'll waffle 'em," he said. "We'll leave them with lumps on their front and back." In one of the most exciting Grey Cups in history, we took an early lead on the Blue Bombers only to watch them fight back for a 35–28 win. The next year, the Winnipeg fans presented Trimble with an actual waffle. To make matters worse, Trimble and Hamilton would go on to lose the Grey Cup to the Blue Bombers three times over a four-year period. Twenty years later, my son Scot played for Winnipeg, and they won the Grey Cup. That's a little bit of personal history that I'm proud of.

With the season over, we flew back to Texas in December, and I went to work at a Chevron refinery.

On my lunch breaks at the refinery, I would thumb through the newspaper, keeping a close eye out for any breaking news about Lamar Hunt and his attempt to found his new league. I imagined how great it would be to play for either of the proposed Texas franchises: the Houston Oilers or the Dallas Texans. But then I'd play in any of the cities being discussed—Denver, Los Angeles, Oakland, Boston and Buffalo—just so long as it wasn't back to New York. Naturally, the AFL owners weren't about to stick a team in a city where they would have to compete with the New York Football Giants, the most famous and successful team in the NFL.

Deep down, I always believed that Lamar Hunt and the other AFL owners would get it done. First, men like Lamar, Bud Adams, and Barron Hilton didn't just have the money, they also had the brains and the ambition. Second, our title game against the Colts in 1958 had led to an explosion of interest in football across the country. If there was a demand for pro football in cities as far-flung as Denver and Buffalo, why not give it to them?

At the same time, I knew that I couldn't depend on the league getting off the ground. I could be working at the refinery for a long spell. But that was okay. It was a real good job.

In August 1959, I read in the newspapers that the AFL owners announced that the new league would start playing games in September 1960 and that ABC was going to televise all the games. Knowing that a television network was going to cover all the games, I felt in my heart that the league was going to be successful. The irony was not lost on me: the game I had lost as a Giants rookie had created enough national interest in pro ball to warrant the birth of a second league—and I could get a second chance.

The other irony was that I assumed Sammy Baugh, a Texas legend, would end up coaching in Dallas or Houston. But when it was announced where he was coaching, it ended up being the Titans—*of New York.*

When I heard that, I didn't have to think twice about my next move. Where Sammy Baugh was going is where I wanted to go—I didn't care if that was New York or the North Pole. First off, I knew Sammy Baugh would give me a fair shake. Second, he was one of my all-time heroes, and if he hadn't selected me to play for him in the 1957 Blue-Gray Game, the Giants probably would never have heard of me.

I called Sammy Baugh on the phone. "Congratulations. I see you got the job at the Titans," I said. "Hey, I wanna come play for you."

He was tickled to death. After all, he had watched me for three years in college, so he knew what kind of wheels I had. He also knew the kind of person I was. I wasn't a rabble-rouser. I didn't drink or smoke. I was just a dedicated football player. You might even say he got a No. 1 draft choice just by picking up the phone. He worked out a contract with me right then on the phone. I told him I wanted a no-cut, no-release, no-see-ya-later contract. I come to play, and I come stay.

Sammy said, "Are you kidding? You got nothing to worry about. You're a heck of a lot better than the guys we have coming to try out."

Just the same, I said, I'd like the part about the no-cut, no-release in writing.

The Titans receivers coach, "Bones" Taylor, flew down to El Paso to sign me to a contract. His wiry build earned him the nickname Bones, but it was his speed that made him Sammy Baugh's favorite target on those great Redskins teams of the late '40s and early '50s and the most dangerous and explosive receiver of his era. At the same time Sammy Baugh was rewriting the rules for what a quarterback could do, Bones was doing the same at receiver. Of course, when this broomstick from a small-town in Arkansas showed up at Redskins camp in 1947, they shook their heads and chuckled. I knew the feeling. Eight years after he made the team as an undrafted, virtually unknown walk-on, he held every receiving record in Redskins history.

If you were to equate the receivers to cars, then Bones was the original model: tall, rangy, and as fast as greased lightning. "His secret is that he can clip off six yards in two steps," wrote *Washington Post* sports reporter Jack Walsh following the 1952 season. "That means Bones has a stride of nine full feet. When you consider that a thoroughbred race horse has one of approximately 20 feet, you can see that Taylor is making the maximum use of those long legs of his." Added *Redskin Insider*'s Michael Richman: "He looked more like a basketball player than one of the NFL's finest receivers. But his physique was really a source of torment for defenders, for what he lacked in brawn he made up for in speed. He escaped those trying to catch him with long strides that made it seem he was galloping, plus beautiful fakes. He was deceptive, consuming chunks of yards even when he was coasting."

According to Richman, Bones had been tackled from behind only once in his career—just before crossing the goal line on a 57-yard run, he was corralled by Steeler Ed Kissell. "Kissell might not have made the tackle if Bones hadn't worried about fumbling and wasted a step to tuck the ball closer to his chest," Walsh wrote.

But now, sitting in front of me in El Paso, Texas, Bones had more dings on the frame and more miles on the engine. I told him that my dream was to be a defensive safety. Bones said, "Maynard, you're more valuable as a receiver." I said to him, "How about I play both ways?" But Bones said that he felt if I played defense it would take away from me becoming the great pass receiver he believed I could be. He could help me become the best of the best, he said, but I needed to dedicate myself to the position, heart and soul. I signed the contract and it was official. January 1, 1960, I became the first Titan of New York.

Thurman called me up from Abilene and asked if I had gotten the no-cut, no-release part in writing. I told him, "You bet I did. I also made sure they guaranteed that I got to wear No. 13."

No Team

AS FAR AS RAW DEALS GO, I felt that I had gotten a doozy from the Giants. But all the bitterness I carried with me from Allie Sherman's anti–Don Maynard campaign was outweighed by the thrill I had about going to play for Sammy Baugh in the AFL. It might not have been the NFL but it was a pro league—and I had the best coach in the world—a certifiable pass-attack junkie! Plus, I got a pretty good raise from what the Giants had paid me in my rookie season. With my no-cut, no-release, no-way-I'm-going-anywhere contract in hand, I breathed a big sigh of relief and started looking forward, not backward.

There was no sudden change in my daily routine; I continued working at the refinery. After all, I wasn't going to see a paycheck from the Titans until I flew up north for training camp in July. With no word of my signing in the press, nobody at the refinery had an inkling that I was going off to play in the AFL come summer. My wife and brother knew and the Titans knew. I didn't tell another soul. It was nobody else's business what went on in my life.

I didn't see much of a difference between the AFL and Chevron. Both were corporations. One happened to be in the oil business, the other in the football business. The AFL had developed a business plan and secured financing. Now they needed employees. Well, I threw my hand in the air and said, "I want to work for y'all." Well, naturally, I added, "Y'all need to send me the plane ticket to fly out there."

While in El Paso waiting to report to Titans training camp in July, I landed my first endorsement deal. The Sinclair Oil Company paid me $500 to promote a special offer they had cooked up: come in for a fill-up and get a free Don Maynard kicking tee. For the commercial, they had me pretend like I was kicking off in a game. They filmed the approach, the kick, and follow-through, and then used the footage for local TV and print ads. Around the same time, James Garner was appearing in Warner Brothers' big action movie, *Up Periscope*. His costar was Frank Gifford; mine was a plastic orange tee. Don't even try to get me to say which was the better performance. (I can kid my dear friend. He would soon go on to become a truly first-rate sports announcer.)

By that time, my parents had moved to Odessa, Texas, a real oil town. They've always played real good football down in Odessa. That's the place *Friday Night Lights* is based on. It was about 300 miles away from El Paso—and a lot farther than that from New York City—but I'd always try to make it down for the holidays.

Meanwhile, Thurman, who became known as Ken, had taken a job at El Paso Natural Gas. He was the head clerk out at the compressor station in Guadelupe, 100 miles due east of El Paso, where they pumped natural gas all the way from Houston to Canada. As the head clerk, he took care of all the office work. By then, he was married with four boys. He worked there for the next 13 years before becoming an FBI agent. In fact, all four of his boys followed in his footsteps. Later, he and his wife had a daughter; she became one of the top FBI ladies in the country.

He and the family would drive down to El Paso for groceries every two weeks. When they came to town, they stayed with me for the night. I always looked forward to seeing my brother.

My sister moved to Amarillo, Texas, where she worked as an insurance representative. One year, her company flew her to Atlanta and gave her a national award—the highest that anybody in her field could receive. She was a very sharp individual and did very well. I guess we all shared the belief that it doesn't matter what route you take in life—it could be sports, business, or law—you might as well give it your all. In the end, she did the best she could, my brother did the best he could, and I did the best I could.

As for my best buddy, Corbell, he'd been coaching the high school football team while I was off playing in the bright lights of New York and then the bitter-cold night of Ontario. It was good being home and getting a chance to hang out with him. We'd sit around his den or mine, talking back and forth for hours about football. I would take out a pad of paper and a pencil and draw up plays that I had seen Vince Lombardi employ. Then Corbell would ask, "What if you did this or that?" When we got to bouncing ideas off each other, inspired offensive schemes just kind of came to life.

In mid-July 1960, I flew from El Paso to LaGuardia Airport. I was moving on, like I had so many times before. Leaving my friends and my family behind wasn't any easier at 25 than it had been at 13.

Once I arrived in New York, I took the Greyhound bus up to the University of New Hampshire. The size of the student population there was about 4,000—which wasn't much less than the entire population of Durham, the sleepy New England town in which the school was nestled.

I knew that the team had sent out a press notice that it was conducting open tryouts for the Titans of New York, but I didn't expect every Tom, Dick, and Harry who'd ever laced up his high-tops to show up at the small wooded campus in New Hampshire hoping to make the squad. I approached Sammy Baugh, who was showing a bunch of newbies the correct way to drop back and throw the ball.

At Baugh's first practice with the Washington Redskins, coach Ray Flaherty challenged him to prove why he was worth all the hype. "You see that receiver out there?" the coach said. "I want you to try and hit him in the eye." Baugh deadpanned, "Which eye?" At 46, old "Slingin' Sammy" raised that ball up to his ear, planted his cowboy boots, and fired a bullet into some young greenhorn's chest. I'd be willing to bet that it was the best pass that kid had ever been thrown, then or since.

As I came over to Coach Baugh, I asked him, "Just how many ballplayers do you plan to try out?" He spit a wad of tobacco juice on the field and replied, "As many damn players as it takes," he answered.

The constant influx of new players being thrown right into the pressure cooker made for a nutty scene. Coaches had to run extra workout sessions just to get a look at everybody. An equipment shortage did require them to share helmets and pads. But in this do-or-die atmosphere, guys weren't exactly swapping friendship bracelets.

Over the next three weeks, I watched the carousel of players go round and round, most of them the longest of long shots to make the team. I figured the Titans' first training camp wouldn't be run quite as smoothly as the Giants had run theirs, but I was unprepared for the three-ring circus I walked into. Those practices looked less like a professional workout and more like a herd of cattle that had gotten loose from their pen. One guy would be wandering in the wrong direction, another would be searching around for his helmet, while a third would be bent over by the goal post, trying to catch his breath after only five minutes in.

Among the unemployed veterans who showed up looking for a job were Sid Youngelman, a likable mad-dog sporting a few missing teeth and a loud Brooklyn accent; Bob Mischak, a former teammate of mine with the Giants who had found work at a telephone company in New Jersey; and Thurlow Cooper, a bruising tight end from the University of Maine who had been drafted and cut by the Cleveland Browns, then signed and cut by the Giants, finally hooking up with a team in Canada, just as I had.

Then there was Buddy Cockrell, who had played for Baugh at Hardin-Simmons and who had won two Texas State amateur rodeo titles. Cockrell wasn't the only player from Hardin-Simmons that Baugh had brought with him to the Titans. When Baugh got hired as head coach, one of the first guys he reached out to was his old starting quarterback, Ken Ford. After the 1958 season, "Model T" had returned to Abilene and got a job coaching the high school football team. I'm sure he thought his playing days were over, and he probably would have been right—that is, if Sammy Baugh hadn't rung him up. But then, why wouldn't he have? Who could better execute Baugh's offense than his star quarterback at Hardin-Simmons? Ford was practically an extension of Baugh. With my co-MVP in the Blue-Gray game starting at quarterback for the Titans, and with Sammy Baugh calling the plays, there'd be more bombs coming my way than the London Blitz of World War II.

I felt as if my buddy Ken and I were the only locks to make the starting team. But then, not everybody shared my opinion. "I can still picture him getting off the bus," recalled linebacker Bob Marques in William J. Ryczek's *Crash of the Titans*. "A cowboy hat, dungarees, cowboy boots, and one of those belt buckles. I thought, *Who the hell is this guy?* He was so skinny, I thought somebody was going to break him in half." Of course, I take exception to that—they were Levi's, not dungarees.

In addition to the assortment of NFL castoffs who showed up at tryouts to make a last-gasp stand, there was a mess of working-class Joes, some as young as 18, who disembarked in Durham, New Hampshire on a wing and a prayer. You had men showing up from all walks of life: truck drivers, war veterans, minor leaguers, college dropouts, out-of-work carpenters, and beer-gutted bouncers. By week's end, most of these would-be players had left on the same bus they had rode in on, and a whole new crop of boys would pull up with their duffel bags. "It was dog eat dog," recalled safety Roger Donnahoo, one of the lucky few to survive. "There were fights. There was kicking. There was punching."

If a newcomer came in looking to punch me, I welcomed him to try, so long as it was on the field. Naturally, he'd have to catch me first. A lot of defenders passed through camp that summer, but if you want to know how many were successful doing that, just ask Thurlow Cooper: "Maynard could run as fast as he wanted to. I never, ever saw him get caught from behind."

Tryouts like the one taking place in Durham—open to anybody with the desire and a bus ticket—were taking place all over the country: in Boston, Buffalo, Los Angeles, Oakland, Denver, Houston, and Dallas. This was America at its best. A fair and open competition based on talent, not lineage; on craft, not cronyism; on heart and grit, not dirty tricks.

In the end, Sammy Baugh estimated that nearly 400 players came through that first camp. Out of that group, only 45 were still standing at the end of the month. Those of us who remained boarded a plane in Boston and flew to Los Angeles to play our first game in franchise history. Every man on that 10-hour flight, at one time or another, had wondered if he had played his last meaningful football game, including me. We all shared the same thought: *How lucky am I?* None of us were looking for fame or fortune; we just wanted to have a paycheck for playing football. We wanted to have somebody want us.

The AFL accomplished so many things—the biggest merger in sports, a groundbreaking national TV contract, an exciting brand of football that modernized the game—that it's easy to forget the impact on ordinary people, people who had been told they weren't good enough, not smart enough, not elite enough. There was a lot of that rubbish going on in our country. But in 1960 a few people were starting to stand up, not just for themselves, but for others who were being denied the God-given right to, well, life, liberty, and the pursuit of happiness! Just as Lamar Hunt stood up to NFL owners who thought they could keep people like him out of their club, another Texan by the name of Lyndon B. Johnson, then Senate majority leader, got the Civil Rights Act of 1960 passed despite his colleague staging a 43-hour filibuster, the longest in history.

By the start of the exhibition season, players were still coming and going, some via trade, while others seemingly walked in off the street. That said, I felt that we had pretty well solidified our offense. With Model-T at quarterback and Sunshine at wide receiver, we were ready to make some noise. Then, out of nowhere, Titans owner Harry Wismer announced he was bringing in a new quarterback. It threw our whole team for a loop.

Wismer had been a well-known sports commentator in the 1940s. He became a minority owner of the Redskins but was driven out by founding owner George Preston Marshall, largely because of his support for signing black players. A fast-talking hustler to his core, he took a wild stab, proposing to air football on prime time, broadcasting a taped replay of Notre Dame's game on Sunday night. This was 17 years before *Monday Night Football* came along and changed the sports landscape. Although that scheme was a bust, as were many others the constant salesman cooked up, he deserves credit for at least one thing: his plan for the networks to share broadcasting rights equally among all the AFL teams did more for the sport of football than you can imagine. Shoot, not only did it help the AFL to survive after people had declared it dead, but not long after, a young Pete Rozelle announced he had signed the same kind of deal with CBS, setting the groundwork for the NFL to grow into the most popular and lucrative sport in America. Problem was, although Wismer matched Lamar Hunt in nerve, he didn't come close in money.

Al Dorow was the quarterback that Wismer had signed. He was a 31-year-old veteran who had played three years with the Redskins and one with the Eagles. After Philly cut him, he ended up kicking around in the Canadian Football League for a couple of years. The reason Wismer, a Michigan native, was so high on Dorow is that the quarterback had been an All-American at Michigan State, which just happened to be Wismer's alma mater. Needless to say, making Dorow the quarterback pleased his friends in East Lansing. To be fair, he was a real fine quarterback. I just didn't see what was wrong with Ken Ford, is all.

Wismer showed up with Al Dorow and basically told Sammy Baugh, "This is your quarterback." It was hard to swallow, but you have to understand that at the end of the day, the guy with the final word is the one who writes the checks—and that wasn't Sammy Baugh. If that's who Wismer wanted to play, that's who was going to play. There was nothing Coach could do. As for all those months Ken and I had spent working together, day after day, until every single pass pattern was crisp and perfectly timed, until our chemistry was so good that we felt like we could read each other's minds? Well, that *whoosh* you hear is the sound of it all getting sucked down the drain.

For our first exhibition game of the season, we showed up to play the Chargers in the massive Los Angeles Coliseum. The Chargers were loaded with a lot more talent than we were—they had a better financial situation—and their coach, Sid Gillman, was one of the great offensive minds of all time. Gillman had the perfect quarterback to run his high-powered offense. It was my friend and fellow backup rookie at the Giants, Jack Kemp. That afternoon our defense was no match for the accurate, mobile Kemp. The first game in Titans history would go down as a loss.

Next, we flew down to Sacramento to play the Raiders on their home field, a sprawling missile facility operated by the Aerojet General Corporation, which coincidentally made Titan missiles. Unfortunately, we suffered a second defeat. My only consolation was that I had my first breakout day as a Titans receiver, catching nine passes for 135 yards. After our exhibition game against the Raiders, we flew down to Abilene, Texas, for the city's first-ever meeting between two pro teams. In a dry, blazing heat, we took the field to battle the Houston Texans at the Abilene Public Schools Stadium. Some of my teammates from areas farther north inquired how I could have grown up playing football smack in the middle of dry, dusty cattle country. I told them it wasn't like the cattle could get onto the field (at least not most of the time).

As it turned out, we could have used a couple of cows lined up in front of the goal line to stop the Texans from scoring. Nothing else seemed to work and we got spanked for a third straight time, 38–14. After the game, Ken Ford told me the bad news that both of us had expected: he'd been cut. The only reason they had kept him around for the game in Abilene was that he was a local sports hero and that the game's sponsor, the Shrine Club of Suez Temple, figured his name would be good for box-office sales. I'm sure it broke Sammy Baugh's heart to see his quarterback left out in the cold like that. I know that Coach argued strongly on Ken's behalf, but Wismer wasn't hearing any of it. "Man, I'm really sorry to see you go," I told Model-T as he gathered his stuff from the dressing room. It was weird. I was on the train, and my buddy wasn't. He never played football again.

Although I felt bad that Ken didn't get more of a chance to keep his job, I had to accept the fact he was gone—and quickly. I wasn't mad at Al Dorow. He was just another guy trying to make a livelihood. But I did wonder how in the world Dorow and I were going to make up for five lost weeks of training camp. Thankfully, Dorow was quick to pick up Sammy Baugh's offensive schemes, and the more time he spent practicing with the rest of the squad, the better we got. Plus, he added his amazing ability to scramble, either to buy more time to throw or to take off for a first down. Sammy Baugh also was able to snag Bill Mathis, a halfback from Clemson, who had played in the same Blue-Gray game as Ken and me, and who Baugh had coached.

Another key last-minute pickup was Art Powell, a tight end from San Jose State, whom the Eagles had released after he refused to play an exhibition game in the segregated South. Sammy Baugh didn't care about any of that nonsense. He intended to give Art Powell a fair shake. For one, Sammy was the kind of guy who would buy the whole bar a round, who judged a player only by what he could do in that space between the two sidelines. What did any of that other stuff matter? It might have mattered to some blue-blood owner up in the nation's capital, but it didn't matter to Vince Lombardi, and it sure as heck didn't matter to Sammy Baugh. We were all riding in the same stuffy train cabins, were all staying in the same dingy motels, and were eating at the same roadside diners. I can assure you, if Sammy Baugh is buying a round of beer, he's buying *everybody* on the team a beer—no exceptions. I can also assure you that if we have to run 50 laps, the whole team is running 50 laps. When Powell got there, I was the host of his welcoming committee. After all, my only thought was this: *Shoot, maybe now teams will finally stop double-teaming me on every play.*

After traveling everywhere from Durham to Los Angeles to Abilene, we arrived in Buffalo, still looking for our first-ever win as a team. In that game, our new-look offense, with Mathis at running back and Dorow throwing to the receiving tandem of Powell and me, broke out in a big way, putting up 52 points against the Bills on the way to the first victory in Titans history. It felt really good to get a win under our belt with the regular season just around the corner.

After all the miles we had covered as a team, we were ready to head back to New York for the regular season. When I found out that the Titans would be playing their games at the Polo Grounds—which the Giants had shared with the New York Baseball Giants before they moved to Yankee Stadium in 1956—I told some of my fledgling team-mates, "Hey, I know a hotel that's only one stop away. It's a 15-cent subway ride and you're there." Soon after, many of my new team-mates and I checked into the Concourse Plaza, the very same hotel where I had lived as a Giants rookie. Gee whiz, what were the odds?

As strange as that was, even stranger was that the Titans, a bunch of guys who the NFL had deemed has-beens, never-weres and never-gonna-bes, wound up living together with the Giants and Yankees, a group of world champions and high-profile celebrities, including Mickey Mantle, Frank Gifford and Sam Huff. But what-ever beef there might have been between the established and rebel leagues, the players on both sides got along just fine. In fact, many of us would go out do dinner together or have drinks together or play cards together.

The Giants had such a winning football team in 1958 that, of my 35 former teammates, I'd say about 30 were still on the roster—and most of them still lived at the Concourse Plaza. The Yankees were also in their prime, and most of the guys I knew from before—including Mantle—were still there. I appreciated those guys helping me find my way when I came to New York to play in the pros; I didn't have to think twice about giving a few pointers to my new teammates, many of whom had never even been to New York City before.

My wife and I had already lived in the city a full year so we knew where the grocery store was, where the barbershop was, the nursery, the post office. We could recommend where to go downtown for dinner or the best route to take on the subway. Marilyn was happy to see a lot of the Giants' wives, with whom she had been friendly. Conerly's wife helped out a lot. She had been around for many years. You always go to people who have experience or who know the area. Marilyn and I were glad to be able to step into that role with the young Titans couples.

Although I was coming back a Titan, my past Giants teammates greeted me kindly. Naturally, I enjoyed seeing all my old friends— Kyle, Frank, Em, Sam, Andy, and Alex. Many of them had told me that they felt I had gotten a raw deal and that they were glad to see me back in New York. The guys had no problems with me playing for the Titans. Their attitude was, *Good luck to you and your league. I hope it works out for both of you.* And they meant it.

For all the well-wishes we got from the guys on the Giants teammates, the press never gave us a chance. They counted the days to our demise. Over the next couple of years, Harry Wismer and the media carried on a heated grudge match. To be fair, Wismer was a born rabble-rouser prone to drunken outbursts and outlandish publicity stunts. Still, that said, a day did not go by where the press didn't have something downright mean to say about the Titans. Reporters were always comparing the Giants and the Titans; they were first-class winners, and we were the cash-strapped losers. I expected the press to throw mud to see what stuck. But it was my coach and my friends standing there covered; I didn't much care for that. To reporters, the Titans were a joke, Wismer was just a drunk,

Sammy was just a faded star, and I was still just the world's greatest fumbler. Well, we'd see about that.

As a player, when you walked into Yankee Stadium, you knew you'd arrived. Everything was first class. The dressing rooms were spotless, the showers clean, the media room state of the art. When I first walked out onto the Polo Grounds, I was stunned by how dirty and run-down it was. It was as if the owners of a house had just up and left. There was clutter and trash strewn everywhere. Looking at the field, I surmised that the last time the grass had been mowed was some time before the Civil War. Going from Yankee Stadium to there was like going from the Taj Mahal to the Kings Inn Motel in Paris, Texas—and if you've ever been there, then you know, it's not good.

Just a week before our home opener, the maintenance crew was still doing everything they could to dress up the stadium and make it at least presentable. They had to double-check just to make sure the water was working and the lights would actually come on. While they had guys painting line markers on the field, others were filling in a gully that ran from one 40-yard line to the other. When you walked into it, it was like stepping off a stairstep. We christened it "Wismer's Gully."

The regular season couldn't come quickly enough. I was so excited to play for Sammy Baugh, that I swear, even if the Giants had asked me to come back I would have told them no thanks. I wanted to repay Baugh for giving me the chance to show my detractors that I could play and that I could be a good receiver. And there's one way I knew how I could do that: help the man win ballgames.

The season started with little fanfare and few spectators, but hey, at least Wismer's Gully had been raked over. Of the small crowd who showed up, most of them were Giants fans who couldn't get a season ticket and decided to go across the river to check us out. I had been playing under the bright lights of Yankee Stadium, and now I was playing in a mostly empty, run-down stadium. But what choice did I have? What choice did any of us have? We were a bunch of the players who had been either released or cut by the NFL. Some were playing in the AFL because it was close to home and because they still had that fire in them to compete, even if it meant for little money and even less fame. Then there were others, like me, who believed that the AFL would eventually take off and that we could make a name for ourselves in the league. And until then, the feeling was, *Hey, as long as I'm getting to play football and still get a paycheck, I'm happy.*

Despite its condition at that time, the Polo Grounds was still one of the greatest places for spectators to watch a football game. Its horseshoe shape made for perfect vantage points no matter what the seat. There were spots in Yankee Stadium, like in right field, where you couldn't get a good view of the action on the field. In Yankee Stadium, the visitors' bench was about 40 yards from the sidelines; in the Polo Grounds, both benches were right next to the field.

Those people who saw us play at the Polo Grounds in those first couple of years wound up seeing some runnin', gunnin', and high-flyin' football, the likes of which you couldn't find anywhere else. Every time our offense took the field, we put on a show for the fans. Al Dorow threw for a league-high 26 touchdowns, and either Powell or I caught 20 of them. But as fun as our aerial circus was to watch, it didn't always translate into wins. Our defense struggled, and we ended our debut season with a respectable 7–7 record. Personally, I had a great year. I caught a lot of deep passes, and I also turned a lot of 10-yard receptions into 30-yard gains. There weren't too many catches when I didn't get a first down. When the season was over, I had amassed 1,265 receiving yards, second in the league behind Houston's Bill Groman, and pulled in 72 receptions, second behind only Lionel Taylor of the Denver Broncos.

During the exhibition portion of our second season, we played a game against the Boston Patriots at Philadelphia Stadium. The Acme Food Corporation was giving away one ticket for every $10 worth of groceries you bought. I thought, *Gee whiz, that sounds kind of silly.* Well, when I walked out there I was dumbstruck over the enormity of the crowd. One of the guys who knew I was an ex-NFL player said, "You've never played before that many people in a game."

I told him, "I've never played before that many people in a whole football season in college!"

Later, it came out in the paper that 73,916 people had come to see the ballgame. I thought, *Man alive, that's a lot of groceries.* We ended up beating Boston that day, and I ended up receiving a Most Valuable Player trophy. I played in front of almost as many people on that day as I would eight years later at Super Bowl III in Miami. I've always said that my claim to fame is that I was MVP of the Grocery Bowl.

We started off the next season playing well, winning three of our first four games. But as the season wore on, gaping holes in our defense and a rash of injuries on offense doomed any hope of winning a championship. Again we finished 7-7. Unfortunately, while we were having the time of our lives, Harry Wismer was losing his shirt.

Poor ticket sales were to blame, but all the negative publicity the press heaped on him sure didn't help. Meanwhile, Wismer and Sammy Baugh were at each other like cats and dogs. Wismer wanted Baugh gone, and Baugh wanted to be gone. The only problem was that Wismer wanted Baugh to quit, so he wouldn't have to pay him for the last year of his contract. Wismer, refusing to fire Baugh, went ahead and just hired a second head coach—Clyde "Bulldog" Turner, who had played several years for the Chicago Bears. Wismer figured that when Baugh heard the news that he had been demoted he would quit in the name of pride rather than report to the upcoming Titans training camp at some small state campus in the Pocono Mountains. Well, Wismer figured wrong.

Baugh found out where camp was being held (not like any of his players would tattle, ha ha) and showed up ready to start work at his demoted job—*as kicking consultant*. "I will be mighty happy teaching boys to kick for $20,000 a year," he said.

When we saw him leaning against the fence at the farthest edge of the field in his Levi's and cowboy boots, we, his players, couldn't help but share a bemused smile. Technically, we might not have been his players anymore but in that moment it felt like we were. A lot of us greeted him the way you would a returning sea captain: with great affection and respect.

Coach and I both shared what some New Yorkers might call "a cowboy image"—not the most popular look in Manhattan in 1960. I never thought about shopping for new clothes on Fifth Avenue, and I'm sure Coach Baugh didn't either. Sammy had worn cowboy boots and Levi's way back when he was a Redskins player. I had dressed the way I had since middle school, before I even knew who Sammy Baugh was. That's the way it ought to be. A man should have the right to choose the clothes he wears and the car he drives. I'm a Ford man. Well, maybe the next guy is a General Motors guy. I like pickup trucks. Okay, maybe somebody else prefers a station wagon. I never bothered anybody. I never tried to be different or a rebel. I did my thing in New York, just as I'm sure Sammy Baugh did his thing in Washington, D.C.

With two coaches and one team, it would have been easy for things to go haywire at training camp up in East Stroudsburg, but Slingin' Sammy had too much class to cause problems for Bulldog Turner. Besides, his problem wasn't with his replacement. So Baugh made sure to stay off to the periphery. Meanwhile, stout, red-nosed Harry Wismer marched around camp, stewing like a game hen in a Crock-Pot.

I don't know if the school officials had been expecting us, but the fact that they didn't water the field once that summer sure seemed odd. Most likely, Wismer had failed to pay them. As camp wore on, the field dried up until it got as hard as concrete. After a couple of weeks running on that hard surface, some of my teammates complained that their legs felt like dead weights. But it didn't bother me any. It was similar to field conditions in West Texas.

After some time, it became apparent to Wismer that Baugh wasn't going to bend. Reluctantly, he returned to New York and announced to the press that he would pay Baugh his full 1962 salary. By then, Wismer was so broke he had to set up a payment schedule with Baugh. The last time Wismer would meet with Baugh would be to hand him the signed agreement. After Baugh had that piece of paper, he left training camp. All of us knew where he was going—or at least we had a pretty darn good idea.

In all the years that Sammy Baugh played in the NFL, he had always gone back to the Double Mountain Ranch once the season ended. Located about 80 miles from Abilene, Texas, the 7,600-acre parcel of land was purchased by Baugh in 1941 at $200 an acre. He returned there again after the Titans released him. Then the University of Tulsa coach asked him to come and work with his young quarterback, Jerry Rhome. Baugh helped develop him into an All-American. Baugh spent only a year in Tulsa before the Houston Oilers made him their new head coach. After one losing season in Houston, Baugh headed back to his ranch where he and his wife and former high school sweetheart, Edmonia, spent the next 25 years raising their five children. Despite Wismer's promise, Baugh never did get paid in full.

As far as I'm concerned, Baugh isn't just one of the greatest quarterbacks to ever play the game, he's also one of the greatest coaches. It's like my Titans teammate Larry Grantham once said of him: he could draw up better plays in the dirt than most coaches could on a blackboard. Both on and off the field, he was one of the fairest people in the world, and I consider it a great thrill and honor to be able to say that I played for him, from Alabama to New York City.

In all the years since the Titans let him go, I have kept in touch with him. I would call him from time to time. He shared a birthday with Charley Pride. Actually, their birthdays were close together—on the 17th and 18th. I never could remember which was which, so I'd always call both of them up on St. Patrick's Day with my birthday wishes.

Edmonia died in 1990. They had been married for 52 years. Sammy died 18 years later, a week before Christmas in 2008. "There are a lot of old football heroes," he told a Dallas reporter a decade later. "Who needs to be a goddamn football hero? Listen to me a minute. I've been happier the last damn 10 years than I ever have been in my life." And that was the truth. Football was his job, the ranch was his dream, and those rough, barren prairies of West Texas were his home.

No Joe

SAMMY BAUGH WASN'T THE ONLY ONE from my past to show up to training camp in East Stroudsburg, Pennsylvania, in the summer of 1962.

Prior to leaving El Paso, I jumped in my turquoise 1955 Ford coupe and drove over to my buddy Corbell's house. Through some mechanical tinkering on my part, I had retrofitted the seven-year-old car to run on a hybrid of propane and gasoline. I set the 40-gallon propane tank in the trunk. Let's say you step on the accelerator but the car won't get any faster; that's the time when you flick it over to gasoline. Heck, you get the same mileage with propane as you get with regular gas but for a whole lot less money. Let's say gasoline was 30 cents a gallon in El Paso. Propane was probably a nickel a gallon. When you save that much on fuel, you realize it's a pretty good deal.

The main reason I added a propane fuel system on my '55 Ford was that propane burns 100 percent clean, which means that your engine will run four to five times longer than if you use regular fuel—plus it doesn't pollute the environment like gasoline. A lot of people are not aware of the things that are out there, then and now. It only took the brains in Detroit another 40-odd years to figure that one out.

Driving east to New York City that summer, I kept to the inter-
state, where there were always places to stop and get propane. Lots
of farmers in West Texas used propane for their tractors, so finding
it locally was no problem. But after you get out of farm country, getting propane is a bit trickier.

I was sitting in Corbell's kitchen when I told him and his wife
the great news: I had gotten him a tryout with the Titans. From the
look on their faces, I got the feeling that they didn't exactly share my
enthusiasm. After a weighty pause, his wife said to Corbell, "What
about the job you took as head coach of the El Paso high school
football team? It starts in a few weeks."

Not a problem, I interjected. Corbell and I will go up there
and he'll try out. If he makes it, fine. If he doesn't, then he comes
home and starts his new coaching job, and the folks over at the high
school are none the wiser. It's a win-win.

After a bit more discussion and reassuring on my part, I finally
talked Corbell into coming up to East Stroudsburg with me for tryouts. That was, on one condition: the doctors assured him that the
concussion he had suffered in high school wouldn't make it dangerous for him to play football again. We had a local doctor examine
him and everything checked out perfectly. He had the green light.
That's when Corbell decided, *Let's go get it.*

Playing in the pros was something a country boy from West
Texas might occasionally daydream about while riding his tractor
back and forth across a cotton field, but it wasn't something he
considered a real possibility. For someone like Corbell, a chance like
this only came around once in a blue moon. What's more, he knew
it and he was grateful to have it. Still, his decision to leave El Paso
and go up to Titans camp to try out for the team was probably more
my doing than it was his. I had seen his talent, and I felt certain that
if the Titans could see his versatility, they would find a spot for him

on the team. After all, he could fill in at three different positions—quarterback, punter, and field-goal kicker. I was sure that even if he didn't make the team on the strength of his arm, he would on the power of his leg.

Going into our third season, Harry Wismer moved the Titans training camp to the campus of East Stroudsburg State Teachers College. We also had a new coach in Bulldog Turner, and Larry Grantham was the only defensive player left over from that first training camp in New Hampshire.

Although Corbell arrived to camp a long shot, he had managed to stick around by the time the exhibition season got under way. As fate would have it, he almost outlasted me. I was recovering from a hamstring injury, suffered on the hard, brittle turf at the teachers college. I was doing everything in my power to get back on the field. Apparently, Harry Wismer felt I wasn't doing enough, and he told the press he was trading me to the Boston Patriots. His outbursts had grown more frequent with his escalating financial issues, but it was still a surprise to hear I was off the team. Despite his announcement, I was still a New York Titan when we hit the halfway point of the season. When a reporter asked for my opinion on Wismer's popoff before the season, I answered, "I tried not to let what he said bother me. You know how people get ulcers? They let things like that bother them. Not me. You know all that trouble with Cuba? I didn't let that worry me one bit. There was nothing I could do about it."

By the last exhibition game, Corbell was still on the roster. At that time, he came up to me and said, "Listen, in a couple of days I'm supposed to be starting my head-coaching position down in Texas." He then asked me what I thought he should do.

I knew that this was probably Corbell's one and only chance to play pro ball. What's more, being on the same team would be a thrill for both of us. The problem was, if he didn't report to his coaching job the next Monday, he'd be fired before he even started. His family, in preparation for the new job in a new town, had already moved to a house near the school. I told Corbell not to worry. I would talk to Bulldog and the other front-office guys about getting him a guaranteed contract, like the one I had.

I went to them and said, "Well, you got to give my buddy a no-cut contract or he's gotta go home and start coaching." I don't know exactly why I pushed so hard. Maybe a part of me felt like I owed Corbell for the time long ago when he went to Mike Brumbelow and asked him to give me shot to play at Texas Western. He had helped me when I was in a tough bind, and now I was in a position to return the favor.

After the Titans' front office told me they wouldn't give Corbell a guaranteed contract, I thought long and hard about what I would say to him. I had no doubt Corbell was going to make it in the pros. But if he did, then for how long? With the Titans, I'd already seen more quarterbacks pass through than I could remember. And some of those guys had left not because of a lack of talent but because of politics between the coach and the owner and the front office. Heck, maybe Bulldog would treat my friend fairly, and if he was going to release him, at least make sure to wait until after the season ended. But he could just as easily let Corbell go after the second game of the season. Then what?

I walked around camp a while. When I ran into Corbell, I told him that the Titans had refused to give him a no-cut contract. But I also told him that I believed he was going to make the team, without a doubt. "In that case," he asked me, "what should I do?" It was with a heavy heart that I told him he should go back to Texas.

I had thought about what my brother had always told me: you have to be honest with yourself about what you can afford to lose. I knew that I could afford to lose my buddy. But my buddy couldn't afford to lose that job back home. I knew he would be happy coaching those high school kids and that the job would allow him to feed his family for years to come. Don't get me wrong, it would have been great for him to make the team, and I really think he would have. But family comes first. The next day, Corbell got on a plane and went back down to Texas to start his high school coaching job. That would be the extent of his one-month pro career.

In his first year as head coach, Corbell led his team to the quarterfinals of the state tournament. What's more, he ended up taking them to the state playoffs in all three years he coached there. One year, I was coming through those parts and went to see how he was doing. I asked him about his offense, knowing it would be high-flying in the mold of his mentor and mine, Sammy Baugh. He said, "Oh, we don't hardly throw the ball. Maybe two or three times a game." I said, "Gee, why not?"

"Well, because I've got three running backs and all of them average nine yards per carry," he told me. That just blew my mind. But it's like I always say, a great coach isn't always the one who has the most, but the one who makes the most of what he has.

Today, Corbell is retired and enjoying golf. And a sand trap is one place you don't have to worry about linebackers charging at your head.

As concerned as I was for the financial well-being of my friend, I suppose I should have been just as worried about my own. In the press, rumors were flying that the eight AFL teams were hemorrhaging money and that after only one year, the league was in danger of collapse. Many predicted that the New York Titans would be the first team to go belly up. Wismer had made a nice chunk of change in broadcasting rights, but it was a fraction of the dough that a couple of Texan oil tycoons named Lamar Hunt and Bud Adams had made. Now, the local papers were reporting that Wismer was running out of funds. But then, how could I worry about that? I was having too good of a time.

In those early days, we were the most pass-happy bunch of fellas you would ever see. If our league had a motto, it would have been: *throw first, ask questions later.* One might wonder how our new league became a wide-open aerial circus. It's like I said: good coaches are going to evaluate their players, then figure out where the most talent lies. If it's the offense, they're going to build their team around the offense. If it's the defense, they're going to build their team around their defense. In the case of the eight original AFL teams, the most talented players were gathered on the offensive side of the ball. The thinking was, *Hey, if we score enough points we can make up for our swiss-cheese defense.* Was it exciting to watch quarterbacks fill the skies with pigskin spirals? You bet. Of course, if you wanted to win in our league, it was also required.

The coaches and players can't take all the credit for those weekend shootouts; those rich, renegade owners had something to do with it, too. See, they knew that when it came to signing the game's most talented ballplayers, there was no way they could compete with the NFL owners—at least not right away. *That's okay,* they thought, *instead we'll put on a show of unearthly firepower that NFL fans have never seen.* Heck, I was all in favor of it.

With all the available money used to stack offenses with fast, veteran playmakers, the defensive cupboard was left bare. In the Titans' first two years, linebacker Larry Grantham was the only one to stay. The other 10 starters on defense were traded, demoted, or cut.

Larry Grantham was an interesting guy. Everybody told him he wasn't good enough to play in the NFL. He was too small. He was too slow. And so it was that Grantham was one of the hundreds of hopefuls to show up in Durham, New Hampshire, for that first

Titans tryout in 1960. Apparently, I was the first guy he saw when he stepped off the bus that July afternoon. "He had those long sideburns and he was sitting on one of those old New England stone walls wearing cowboy boots, Levi's, a big Western hat and a belt with a huge brass buckle. The belt had number 13 on each side where it rode the hip and the word 'Shine' across the back of it. The whole thing was unreal," Grantham said. "I mean, where was the rodeo?" Maybe he should have asked Buddy Cockrell.

We might have had small crowds and so-so records, but in many ways those early days with the Titans were just as special as the ones I enjoyed as a Jet. With Art Powell and I spread out on the two ends, quarterback Al Dorow had a field day. A few seconds after he snapped the ball, he'd find that one of us—if not both of us—had broken free from our defender and gotten as open as an all-night diner. Forget about shutting us down. Against our pass attack, the defense was lucky if they could just survive the first quarter.

Al Dorow and the other great veteran gunslingers—guys like Houston's George Blanda, Buffalo's Jack Kemp, and San Diego's John Hadl—had all the time in the world to throw the ball. Although they hardly needed it—not when they had explosive receivers like Charlie Hennigan in Houston and Lionel Taylor in Denver and me running roughshod over the league's hapless cornerbacks. I wouldn't have wanted to be some rookie free agent told he had to stop any of us crafty speedsters. No, sir. Those young corners didn't have the first clue how to defend against the pass, let alone stop the aerial attacks devised by offensive masterminds like Sid Gillman and Sammy Baugh.

Instead of writing about our explosive offense, or about how players like Art Powell, Bill Mathis, Larry Grantham, and I—who had all been discarded by the NFL—were emerging as exciting stars, or about our fun, loose, and colorful clubhouse, the press spent the first two years of our existence focusing on empty seats and the fact that we weren't the Giants. They took delight in contrasting the small, ragtag group of fans trickling into the Polo Grounds with the droves of well-heeled spectators cramming into Yankee Stadium.

Once we got word that the parking lot outside the Polo Grounds was overflowing with cars. We thought, *Hey, it looks like there's finally going to be a big turnout.* We soon realized that most of the vehicles belonged to Giants fans looking to save a buck on parking. All they had to do was leave their car in our lot and take the subway across the river to the 161st Street stop, where they would come out right at Yankee Stadium. It's not as if we didn't have *any* folks sitting up in the stands, although an unusually large number of them had brought radios with them. Then it dawned on me: they were listening to the Giants game going on at same time about a mile away.

Some might say it was inevitable that any football team that dared to put down stakes in New York would be compared to the Giants, especially with Wismer stoking the flames, saying in the press that the Giants were afraid to play us because we would beat them. Ha. This was a team that had Y.A. Tittle at quarterback, a team that still had Frank Gifford and a host of other stars. They would have kicked our butts all over the field. We laughed off Wismer's boastful claims as hot air (explaining to a reporter why he chose the name Titans he responded, "What's bigger than a giant? A Titan."). A few other people needed to get a sense of humor.

I couldn't understand why so many people wanted to see the Titans fail. What's so bad about giving guys like me a second chance? It's not like we had anywhere else to go. I had already come through the NFL and the CFL. The next stop for me was likely teaching P.E. to eighth graders in El Paso. For those who wanted to see us go down in flames, the 1962 season would be all they could ask for and more. But even when we lost a game, our team was entertaining as heck to watch and—you know what—when the Titans collapsed, we did so spectacularly.

Actually, our third and final season started on an optimistic note for the players. Harry Wismer had married the widow of rumored New Jersey racketeer Longy Zwillman. Word was that as a result of this blessed union, he had come into a whole lot of money. *Maybe money would no longer be an issue,* we thought. But no sooner were things looking up, than, for some strange reason Wismer, just prior to our season opener, traded our tough-as-nails star quarterback Al Dorow to the Buffalo Bills. Once again, it looked like I was without a quarterback.

I remained friends with Dorow for a long time after that. After playing one more season with the Bills, his arm finally gave out. Rather than send him to the doctor, the Bills decided just to cut him. He returned to Michigan State, where he was still a beloved figure, and became the Spartans' offensive coordinator. Later, he worked at an RV distributorship in Champion, Michigan. Over the next 19 years he worked his way up to become its national sales manager. In 1992 he finally retired to Sierra Vista, Arizona, where he remained a proud member of Arizona's NFL alumni chapter.

I would go out there and see him a couple of times a year. In terms of his ability, he was a really fine quarterback—solid arm, smart as a whip, and one outstanding scrambler. My loyalty to Ken Ford made it difficult to fully embrace Dorow when he arrived to the Titans, but over time Al earned my respect through his tenacity to hang in there in the heat of battle. I watched him take one vicious pounding after another only to get back up and call the next play —and for a salary below his pension check! Outside of football, he was just a good friend. I am sad to say that a friend of mine called me not long ago from Sierra Vista, to tell me that Al had died. Knowing him, he'll get into heaven on a fake pass and scramble.

Days before our season opener, Wismer signed Lee Grosscup to replace Dorow. Grosscup had come over from the Giants where, as a rookie like I was, he had been penalized for the crime of not fitting in. Why was he branded such a rebel? His hair was longish for those days, and he had a habit of writing his thoughts in a journal. To coach Allie Sherman, his inability to conform to the way an NFL player should act and look—crewcut hair, blue blazer, and *no sideburns*—made him suspect. Although I didn't give one hoot what Sherman thought of me, it really tore up young Grosscup. Heck, I didn't care if Grosscup was the next Truman Capote so long as he could deliver the football with accuracy. In any event, Sherman made sure he got the same sentence that I did: permanent exile to an "inferior" league.

Grosscup's signing wasn't the only big event to occur just before our first game of the season. A week before, the team staged a minor coup against our loud, cigar-chomping owner, led by the newest member of our team, Curley Johnson. Everybody liked Curley. He was a free-spirited, motormouthed Texan who took no guff from anybody. It was a run-in with coach Hank Stram, his coach in Dallas, that led to his release from the team just before the season. Wismer quickly snatched him up to be our punter and backup fullback. But when Curley went to the bank to cash his $1,500 signing bonus, the check bounced. As it turned out, he wouldn't be alone.

Let's clear up some of the false rumors that still persist to this day. First, the only time the issue of bounced checks came up was in our third season, at the tail end of Wismer's ownership. Let's get another thing straight. No Titans player ever failed to get a paycheck. Now, cashing that check right off? Well, that was another story.

At that time, the only bank branch in the city willing to honor our checks was the Irving Trust office at 39th Street and Madison, where Wismer had his last remaining account. On payday, which was usually every Tuesday, Wismer hadn't put enough money in the account to cover all the Titans coaches and players. Meaning if you weren't one of the first guys to get to the bank after practice on Tuesday, you might be plum out of luck. You might have to wait around three or four days for the check to clear.

You should have seen our clubhouse on Tuesdays. The second the whistle blew to end practice, you'd have 35 guys rushing in from the field to grab their paychecks. With our checks in hand, we'd race each other downtown. There wasn't enough time to take a shower. Heck, we still had our cleats on as we hightailed it down the length of Manhattan.

Naturally, I left all my teammates in the dust. I'd be saying, "Thank you, ma'am," to the teller as I put my money in the front pocket of my Levi's. As I walked away from the bank window, the other guys were still running, out of breath, down to the 50s. Later that day, Larry Grantham would walk into the Concourse Plaza, wearing a defeated expression. I'd look up and give him a smile, and say, "How goes it, Larry?"

"It's no fair, Maynard. How the heck am I supposed to catch up with you?"

Then we found out that the coaches were in the same boat. "On this particular day, none of us had seen any real money for several weeks," recalled teammate Alex Kroll. "But we practiced as usual. Suddenly defensive end Ed Cooke noticed that the coaching staff had disappeared. 'My God!' he shouted. 'Paychecks!' With an animal roar we stampeded from our formations, scrambled up the rickety steps into the locker room, and there, sure enough, stood George Sauer Sr., holding a stack of pay envelopes. Madness. Every man for himself. Skinny backs to the rear. Big linemen first. As each man received his check, he made his break for the 155th Street subway entrance, depending upon his indebtedness and his personal-hygiene habits. Some showered and dressed in street clothes. Some merely dressed. Some just threw raincoats over their sweat suits and changed shoes. Then came the great race to 39th Street. The coaching staff probably had gotten a two-or-three-subway-stop head start on us, but nearly everyone received real money that day."

I didn't like that some of the guys had to wait days in limbo to get their money—especially a hardworking pal like Larry—just because he couldn't get to the bank as fast as me. But I had gotten used to the bizarre routine, I guess. I reckon Curley Johnson didn't feel the same way, because he went up to the front office and yelled at them to give him his darn money. Instead, the Titans released him.

As I mentioned, we were a real close-knit group. It was common for players to go out for a beer together on a Saturday night. Such was the case on the night after Curley was shown the door. How could we just sit by and let Curley get the shaft? It wasn't right. Larry Grantham felt strongly we should do something. He explained his plan.

The next day, Curley showed up to the scrimmage looking disheveled and badly hungover, knowing that Bulldog Turner had been told to keep him off the field and that Curley was days, if not hours, away from being without a job. But moments before the whistle blew to start the game, our fullback Bill Mathis came up lame. Funny, considering he was just fine seconds earlier. Bulldog had no choice but to play Curley. That's when the strangest thing happened—whenever Curley ran up the middle, nobody on our defense could seem to get him down. I watched him make Larry Grantham miss tackles that I had never seen him miss before. Ever. For three quarters, he took over the game in what would be the best rushing day of his life. After a performance like that, Bulldog had no choice but to keep him.

The Curley Johnson episode was behind us, but it wasn't the last time we players took matters into our own hands. With our home opener in Buffalo just days away, we held a players-only meeting. We decided that we wouldn't practice until Wismer gave us paychecks that didn't elicit laughter from every bank teller in the city.

Wismer exploded. "Fine, you don't want to practice? Then neither will your coaches." Needing to prepare for the Bills, we had no choice but to meet up and practice on our own. Everybody showed up in sweatpants. As soon as the players got on the field—most of them young and inexperienced—they didn't have a clue what to do. That's when the veterans took the reins, so to speak. Guys like Larry Grantham, Bob Mischak, and I wound up running the most lively, organized practice of the season. I called upon all those plays that I had worked out with Corbell over the years and worked them into the game plan. (Later, after we went out and beat Buffalo 17-6, some of the guys joked that maybe we could do without coaches for good.)

Somebody called up Lamar Hunt and told him what was going on. The next thing you know, we had all been paid in full and Turner was back in charge. Lamar had taken care of it, no questions asked. We had made it to Buffalo in the nick of time. We checked into the Sheraton Hotel in downtown Buffalo, but there was still no sign of our quarterback. I thought that it might be a nice idea to meet him, you know, considering in a few hours we were going to have to go out and play together for the first time ever. Finally, Grosscup arrived at the hotel, just hours before game time. "Bulldog Turner was having lunch with a couple of other coaches in the dining room," recalled sportswriter Larry Felser. "Grosscup came in. Bulldog told him to sit down, gave him the game plan—what there was of it—on the linen tablecloth for the next two hours." By the time I introduced myself to Grosscup, it was in the dressing room, while I was changing into my uniform. We went out there and just winged it. Somehow or other we wound up crushing them, triggering the Buffalo fans to send a barrage of beer cans raining down on us. By some estimates, 3,500 beer cans had been thrown on the field, an even more impressive number when you consider that the stadium didn't sell beer in cans.

The press continued to gossip that our paychecks had bounced because Wismer had run out of dough. In fact, the reason that any checks bounced was that Wismer had closed down his account at the Irving Trust in the Bronx and opened that new one in the downtown branch. Unfortunately, not all the players were made aware of this fact. So, when they tried to deposit their paycheck in the defunct account on 160th Street it went, *boing, boing, boing.* But if you went down to the one in Manhattan—and you remembered to put on your track shoes—you had no problems.

Still, anybody who wrote that my Titans teammates and I feared we'd be out of a job for next season didn't know what they were talking about. As soon as all this business about unpaid salaries and bounced checks started up, the league set up a meeting between Milt Woodard, the assistant commissioner of the AFL, and the players. Woodward basically told us not to worry, that the league would guarantee our salaries. And with Lamar Hunt, you could take that to the bank. There's a story about how someone once told his father, the famous oil tycoon H.L. Hunt, "Your boy will lose a million dollars on his football team this year." "Well," he responded, "I reckon at that rate he'll be broke in another 150 years." So all that gossip in the press didn't concern me one bit.

I only had one question for Woodard: "What about the $1.50 charge our banks hit us with on these bad checks?" He told me to expense it to our new owner. I was working as a master plumber in the off-season in El Paso when I read in the papers that the league had found that man. His name was Sonny Werblin. I was thrilled.

As one of the most powerful agents in Hollywood, Sonny "In the Money" Werblin had made a lot of folks rich. Among his famous clients were Johnny Carson, Frank Sinatra, and Elizabeth Taylor. For more than 25 years he had worked at MCA, working his way up from an $85-a-month gofer to the president of what was then the top talent agency in the country. Having already made a fortune in show business, he hooked up with the AFL as its agent. After all, he was the guy who had negotiated that great TV contract with ABC. I figure that's why he threw a birthday party for AFL commissioner Joe Foss. Harry Wismer had too much to drink and uttered a nasty slur in the direction of Sonny, resulting in fists a-flying. The two men had to be separated but the jawing continued. Werblin got so mad he finally shouted to Harry, "Someday, I'm going to *own* your team."

When the league took over the team, Mr. Foss met Werblin for lunch and offered to sell the Titans for $1.35 million. Werblin handed him a $100,000 down payment, right then and there. As a player, let's just say I knew bounced checks weren't going to be an issue anymore.

If Sonny Werblin hoped to turn our bankrupt franchise into a moneymaker, he had his work cut out for him. But I felt that if anybody could transform the Titans into a first-class operation, it was him. The first thing he did was change our name to the New York Jets. Then he changed the team colors from blue and gold to green and white. He chose those particular colors because he'd been born on St. Patrick's Day. He was Jewish, but hey, you take your luck where you can get it. Kind of like me and the number 13.

Next, Werblin needed a new head coach, and not just anyone would do. He needed somebody who could build a championship culture despite the fact that we'd won diddlysquat in the past. So, who better than the man who took the Baltimore Colts from a lowly expansion team to world champions in five short years, Weeb Ewbank?

Who would have guessed that I would wind up playing for the very same coach who, on that December day in 1958 in Yankee Stadium, led his Colts to victory over my Giants team in what was probably the most famous title game in history. Back then I was just a shy rookie trying not to stand out in a bad way. I can still see Coach Ewbank and his golden-armed, crew-cut quarterback standing on the opposite side of the field as dusk fell over the stadium. Weeb might have been my adversary then, but he was my leader now. I might not have had the same feeling for him that I did Sammy Baugh—not even close—but that didn't matter. We had been thrown into the same mess, and if we were going to ever reach that light at the end of the tunnel, if we were going to take a team that nobody respected, that everybody thought was inferior to the city's other football team, and turn it into a winner, we'd have to do it together. It would be no easy job, but it sure would be fun trying.

For our fourth season, training camp had been moved up to a military academy in Peekskill, New York. Weeb showed up at that first Jets camp looking to make changes—and he carried a machete, not a scalpel. In the weeks that passed, I watched as my former Titans teammates got picked off one by one. Some of these guys had been with me since day one. They had driven all the way up to Durham, New Hampshire, to compete for a job against hundreds of other players, enduring those chaotic tryouts, to earn a spot on the very first roster in Titans history.

When my bright-colored car rumbled loudly into view, all the Titans players and coaches spun their heads around. After getting a load of my propane beauty, Bill Mathis dubbed it the El Paso

Flamethrower. That just goes to show you the knowledge of the people up there—it was a flame *burner*, not a flamethrower.

Propane is not so easy to come by in the suburbs of New York City. Lucky for me, there was a plant up in Peekskill where I would go once a month for a refill. I forget the name of the plant, but it's still up there. They asked, "Where are you coming from?" I told them, the New York Titans. "What's that?" "Well, it's your new football team." Over time, I got to know the people there really well.

The veterans would sit around the training room, an old coal bin, playing cards, drinking coffee, and smoking cigarettes. You could spot the rookies when they came into camp—they were the ones who weren't carrying window screens under their arms. They hadn't learned yet that there was no air conditioning at Peekskill. Of course, a lot of them would be sent packing before it ever mattered.

As for me, I never worried that Weeb wouldn't keep me around as a starter. Heck, if you could find somebody to come in and do a better job at receiver than I could, then go ahead. I won't say a word; I'll just walk out that door. I came into Peekskill the Titans' best receiver and I was gonna make sure I left the Jets best receiver.

Among the original Titans sent packing was Bob Mischak, who had played for the Giants with me before working as a telephone company supervisor. Weeb traded him to Oakland. He also sent calf-roper Buddy Cockrell to Denver. He got rid of Thurlow Cooper, the tough receiver from Maine. To everybody's surprise, he even dropped Lee Grosscup. Once again, I was starting the season without a quarterback.

Here's a list of the quarterbacks I'd played with since joining the Titans in 1960: Ken Ford, Al Dorow, Dick Jamieson, Johnny Green, Lee Grosscup, Butch Songin, Hayseed Stephens, and Bob Scrabis. Now, as the 1963 season was about to start, Ewbank had named

Dick Wood as the starter. He was one of several players Weeb brought over with him from the Colts. In Baltimore, he had been a third-string backup to Johnny Unitas, but I guess Weeb figured that at least the guy knew how to run his offense.

Just before the final game of the exhibition season, Weeb brought in one more of his Colts players, flanker Bake Turner. At practice that week, Weeb had Bake playing over on my side of the field. I don't even remember who Weeb was going to play over on the left side—I think one of his former Colts players—but I said to him, "Weeb, you're crazy. You don't need Bake over on my side. He ain't gonna beat me out. He's too good to be my number two. Stick Bake Turner on the left side. Now you have a balanced attack."

We had our last exhibition game at Rutgers Stadium. Trailing in the game, Weeb finally decided to try putting Bake and me on opposite ends of the line. In the remaining time, Bake ran a punt back for a touchdown, a kickoff for a touchdown, and caught a pass reception for 78 yards for a touchdown. At practice the following week, I went out for a passing drill, only I didn't see Bake at first. Then, I looked over on the other side of the field and there was Bake lined up wide to the left. I glanced over at Weeb standing in the middle the field, arms crossed, looking serious, and chuckled to myself.

Our first game of the season was against the Boston Patriots. They knew about my talent, but they were less sure about Bake. So once the game got under way, I got double- and triple-teamed, leaving Bake wide open. Naturally, Dick Wood went to the guy who had less guys covering him. I caught four passes for 32 yards that day. Bake caught 10 passes for 103 yards. And I felt great. I was happy the offense had performed well and happy for Bake, because he was a tremendous receiver who deserved the chance to play. Bake and I would end up rooming together for the next seven years.

Despite our success on offense, it was the same old story on defense. After that first loss, Weeb got rid of two more Titans. A week into our season, I was one of only 15 original Titans still on the team. Our next opponent was the Oilers, a team we had never beaten in our history (as in a perfect 0–6 losing record). Our 24–17 win over Houston would be the highlight of a season that had endured its fair share of battered wrecks and bounced checks.

The Jets' first season was in the books, and we had finished in last place. There were a few bright spots. My pals Bill Mathis and Larry Grantham, who had been there with me from early on, played in the AFL All-Star Game. Bake had a tremendous year, gaining 1,009 yards on 71 receptions to lead the team. In fact, I caught half as many passes as Bake and 18 fewer than as I had the year before. Big deal. I had a fine year with 38 catches for 780 yards and nine touchdown receptions. The fact that Bake had such a terrific year that he wound up winning the MVP of the Jets thrilled me to no end. That's the game of football. You just do your job.

When all was said and done, Weeb kept only four Titans—Bill Mathis, Larry Grantham, backup Curley Johnson, and me. I had been the first Titan of New York, and now along with Larry, Curley, and Bill (Moe was cut in '61), I had become the last.

With Bill Mathis returning at halfback, and Bake Turner and me making up the best receiver corps in the league, I felt good about the Jets' immediate future. But if we were ever going to be the best, we needed a place of our own to call home. That would happen as we moved into a brand-new stadium in Queens. But deep down, I knew that we needed more than that. We were still missing what we'd always been missing: our star quarterback. Then, on January 2, 1965, Werblin announced to the world that he had found him. And all it would take to bring him to our team was a rookie contract roughly 58 times larger than mine.

No Liftoff

DURING MY FIRST FIVE YEARS IN THE PROS, I spent my off-seasons as a master plumber. Then, the next seven off-seasons, I taught math, Texas history, and shop class in the various high schools in the El Paso district.

I liked teaching kids how to work with tools and machinery. Those kids came into my class with no idea of what went into building and rebuilding machines, but I guarantee you that by the time they left my class they did. I showed them that there was a science behind it, that you needed to be a strong math student, and that a little common sense didn't hurt, either. And, of course, I taught them, *don't ever be absent and don't ever be tardy*. And if any of them said, "Mr. Maynard, weren't you ever late or tardy to class?" I would tell them the truth: no.

When I wasn't instructing kids how to take apart an engine to figure out how it worked, I was working on becoming one of the top receivers in the pros.

Everybody on the team worked during the off-season, not just me. Bill Mathis took a job as a broker at Bear Sterns, Larry Grantham worked in a bank, Bake Turner built and remodeled houses, and fullback Matt Snell had a little construction business. A bunch of guys taught school up in Long Island. With an annual salary of $17,000, I was one of the highest-paid players on the Jets, and I never once considered quitting my off-season teaching job. Everybody worked. You had no choice. That is, until Joe arrived.

With the '64 season over, I went back to El Paso to resume my teaching job. One day that January, I went into town on my lunch break and picked up the paper. I read that Sonny Werblin had signed Joe Namath, the All-American quarterback from Alabama. Then, I saw for how much: $400,000! I thought, *Gee, that is a lot of zeroes.*

Right away, there was an outpouring of negative comments directed at Mr. Werblin for giving an unproven rookie that kind of dough. "He must be bonkers," the naysayers said, wringing their hands in anger. I didn't think he was bonkers, though. For one thing, I was one of the 25 million people who had watched Joe's performance in the Orange Bowl on New Year's Day.

In that game, Namath's Alabama Crimson Tide went up against the national powerhouse Texas Longhorns. There were precious few TVs in the state of Texas that weren't tuned into the telecast. Nobody had expected Namath to play after suffering a brutal late-season knee injury. But with the Longhorns beating the tar out of the Tide in the first half, Bama's legendary coach, Bear Bryant, figured he had no choice. He sent Joe onto the field.

As he made his way to the huddle, I could see he was sporting a limp, a fact that I'm sure didn't go unnoticed over on the Texas side-line. You knew the Longhorns' defense was going to pin back their ears and try to smoke him. Sure enough, they brought a steady, furious pass rush at him. But time after time, just when you thought, *Oh boy, he's done for,* a split-second before the defense pounded him into the ground, the ball would come rifling out of his hand. No matter how fast they got to him, Joe was that much faster, delivering a perfect bull's-eye to one of his receivers.

Desperate to find a way to stop Joe, Texas dropped all their guys back into the secondary. Now, he would have no choice but to run the ball. But they were wrong. Namath continued to throw one improbable pass after another. Earlier, Bama had been left for dead, but there was Namath refusing to let them go down. It felt as if it was Joe against the entire Longhorns team and their legion of fans. It was enough to make even a boy from El Paso start cheering for the kid. *Could he really pull this off?*

The game came down to a showdown at the Texas goal line. Joe handed it off to his fullback three straight times, but the Longhorns stuffed him on each attempt. On fourth down, Namath took matters into his own hands. Bad knees and all, he took it himself to the hole. He was stopped. About three inches short.

Although Alabama wound up losing the game, those who had attended the game and the millions who had watched on TV shared a feeling that they had witnessed something special. The final score wasn't what mattered. After all, when was the last time you saw a press pool, as cynical a bunch of folks as there was, greet a player—especially a *losing* player—after the game with the applause of appreciation?

So many folks cheered Joe because he had gone out there with a bum knee, stood toe-to-toe with one outstanding team, and refused to go down until time had expired. At the end, he was a battered and spent player, but even in defeat everybody marveled at the heart and determination he had shown in nearly bringing back his team. And maybe, at least on that day in 1965, his unwillingness to back down counted for more than the slick advertising of ad men or the fancy packaging of candidates or the back-door wheeling and dealing of Washington insiders or the win-at-all-costs ethos of Wall Street players. I tipped my hat to anybody who could pull that off.

To football fans across the nation and to the press at large, Namath was the $400,000 wunderkind. But he wasn't going to find any of that adoration when he showed up at the Peekskill Military

Academy, particularly from the veterans. It didn't matter who you were or what you had done in college. When you came through those training-camp doors, you were a rookie, plain and simple. Joe was no exception. The guys on the squad weren't going to accept him just because of his star reputation. For him to be considered one of us, he was going to have to earn our respect through something other than just raw talent. He had his work cut out for him.

When he arrived in camp that summer, Joe was green—and I'm not just talking about the color of his jersey. It certainly wasn't my first rodeo. My first training camp in the pros was in 1958, I was the first guy to sign with the Titans in 1960, and I was the franchise's longest-surviving player. Of the 35 players on that original Titans roster, Larry Grantham, Mike Hudock, and I were the only ones remaining. I knew the ins and outs, both in terms of what took place on the field as well as what went on off of it. I knew how to navigate between the practice field, the locker room, the front office, and the media area. Well, okay, maybe not so much the last one.

In those first few days of training camp, a lot of the talk going on among the veterans-only card tables was about our new, young quarterback—and it wasn't all positive. Some of the old-timers were sore that piles of money and publicity had been heaped upon Joe without him ever taking a single hit on the field. I didn't see it that way. As far as I was concerned, his contract was good for all of us. I thought, *If Joe is making that much money, heck, I can make more, too.* Still, I understood the way some of the guys were feeling—it wasn't that long ago we'd had our footraces to the bank.

The other issue, which had nothing to do with money, was that the fraternity among men in football was not dissimilar to that of the military. Rookies were supposed to pay their dues. That's how it's always been and how it ought to be. You come in and you keep your opinions to yourself. As for starting, you don't even think about it. You're thinking, *Maybe I'll get lucky and see some playing time.* And you're definitely not the highest-paid player on the team. In fact, you're probably paid the least. Certainly, that was my situation with the Giants, as it was for most of our veterans. Which is why some of the veterans resented that Namath was viewed as special. But there was a good reason for that—he was special. After all, the 22-year-old kid was being touted as the franchise quarterback, and as such, was expected to lead the team to success right away—not to mention do it under the bright lights of New York City.

There was another reason that Joe's record-breaking contract and publicity didn't bother me. I had played with more than 25 professional quarterbacks before he came along. So, yeah, you bet I was glad to have talent of his caliber on board.

The first days of camp are the toughest for a rookie. You're far from home, in many cases for the first time. You're living with a bunch of guys who already know each other well, so you're an outsider coming into a tight brotherhood of players. But Joe was having twice as hard of a time fitting in, with some of the veterans still stewing over his megacontract.

On Rookie Night, newbies had to stand in front of the team and give a rousing rendition of their alma mater's fight song. The razzing was all in good fun. But before Joe had barely started singing "Yea, Alabama" the guys drowned him out with a chorus of "There's No Business Like Show Business," a not so subtle jab at his already-burgeoning "Broadway" Joe image. I looked over to see Joe's reaction. He didn't look bothered one bit.

His cool demeanor carried over to the practice field, which was a good thing, because some of the veterans were intent on sending the rookie a message. To avoid getting the quarterback hurt, defenders are ordered not to hit him during practice drills. In fact, he wore a red jersey to signify his special status. But when Joe snapped the ball, some of the veterans appeared to have forgotten the rule and hit him anyway. Most of the time, the defender would just bump him or give him an extra shove backward. It was a way of letting Joe know that they could have laid him out if they had wanted to. A few times, Joe would actually get pushed back into Weeb, who was watching from behind the offense. But Weeb knew if he tried to fight Joe's battles for him, the young quarterback would lose even more credibility. Joe had no choice but to take it.

"Hey, can't you see?" he said once. "This red jersey means, 'Do not touch.'"

Gerry Philbin was the defense's leader in the anti-Joe campaign. A couple of times, he really grabbed him hard or pushed him down. We had one veteran linebacker by the name of "Big Chief Wahoo" McDaniel, a Native American wrestler, who also went out of his way to hit Namath. Once he even knocked Joe right on his ass. Joe popped up off the turf. It was one of the rare times I saw Joe have words with a teammate.

I felt that Joe should be given a fair shake. I greeted him the same way I greeted the other 25 quarterbacks who had come before him. He came in and we shook hands. He didn't strike me as nervous. He was sure a lot more outgoing than I had been when I was a rookie. He knew he belonged.

I had been curious to see how the rook would handle himself on the practice field. Sure, he had gained experience playing under the legendary Bear Bryant at Alabama. But playing in college is a far cry from playing in the pros. The offense Joe would be running would be more complicated, the defenses he would face would be faster and more aggressive, the techniques he needed to defeat those defenses would have to be more advanced, and the traps he would need to watch out for would be numerous.

Over the years, people have asked me when I knew that Joe and I could do something special together. I'd say, *after one day of practice*. It started with a 10-yard pass route. As I turned my shoulders, the ball hit me square in the chest. I'd never seen a quarterback deliver the ball that fast. The next time, I ran 15 yards down the field. As I turned back, the ball tagged me right in the breadbasket. So I ran a 20-yard slant route. I sprinted down the field, cut across, and then just as my eyes turned back upfield, the ball hit my hands. I thought, *Holy smokes, this kid's accuracy is unreal.*

The only concern I had was the strength of his arm. It wasn't that he didn't have enough zip on his ball. Just the opposite—he had too much of it. I went out for a deep fly pattern, sprinting the whole way, and he overthrew me by a good 10 yards. "You don't have to show me your arm," Weeb shouted at him. "If you couldn't throw, you wouldn't be here."

As I jogged slowly back to the huddle, I passed some young sportswriter on the sideline. The look on his face said it all. "Man, I've never seen anybody overthrow you, Maynard."

Me neither, I thought to myself. *Me neither.*

Practice ended. Joe walked off the field by himself as usual. I came up behind him. He peered over his shoulder. I don't know if he thought I was another veteran coming to jump him—Big Wahoo had already done that, jumped on his back and knocked him down while we were running laps one day. He stopped and just looked at me. I said to him, "I'll help make you a better quarterback, and you're gonna make me a great receiver."

The next day, at practice, we got right down to work on our warm-up drills. I said to him, "Here's what I want you to do. The minute you get the ball, I want you to throw it. One step, raise the ball, throw it. One step, raise the ball, throw it."

"What are you going to be doing?"

"I'll be going out for a five-yard pass route. I'll be cooking as I reach the fourth yard. That's when I'm going to round off to the left, real smooth-like. When I reach that fifth yard, you'll have already thrown the ball. If our timing is right, the ball should hit me in stride. Shoot, I won't even have to look back for the ball. It will be on my right shoulder. I'll turn up field and that's it. I'll be gone."

"Shit, man, what if I throw it to you too quickly?"

"I'll tell you what: I challenge you to do that."

The snap went to Namath. He took one step back, raised the ball, turned, and released. As I came streaking into view, he put the ball on my right shoulder—a little bit out in front of me, where I could catch it and turn upfield without ever having to slow down. I jogged back over to him. "That's called a quick out," I said, tossing him the ball. "Here, we call it a cherry route." For the next 30 minutes, we ran that same five-yard route over and over again until we had it perfect.

What Joe had yet to experience was the incredible speed of pro defenses. When the linemen or linebackers, and maybe even a defensive back, came on a blitz, the quarterback was lucky to blink twice before kissing his ass good-bye. But if you could master the quick out, you could turn their blitz against them. Punish them for their aggressive play. With that said, there's a reason so few quarterbacks in history have ever mastered the timing route—it takes unbelievable vision, calm, footwork, and accuracy. And even if you somehow get all of that down, it won't matter if you don't have one other thing—and that's trust.

Every play in football is like a stage performance. The receivers and tackles are the actors. The quarterback is also an actor, but he's also the director and the playbook is the script. The better the script, the less need there is for the actors to improvise. You can't worry about anybody else remembering their lines; you just have to remember your own. If you take care of your end, and everyone else takes care of his own end—basically, if everybody just does his job to the best of his ability—the results will be outstanding.

Sounds easy enough—except it rarely happens that everybody works in such perfect harmony. You have receivers cheating routes, making their break to the left or right early so they get open before the other receivers. It happens. And what it does is screw up the timing of everybody else, just like an actor reciting his lines early or walking on stage before his cue.

Consider our leading man, the quarterback. He has the toughest job of all, because, as I said, he's both actor and director. This dual role can be tricky because he alone must decide where to go with the ball—and all of this within a couple of seconds because a gang of mouth-foaming, 250-pound behemoths are bearing down on him. At the same time he acts individually, he must be a part of a larger whole. This means trusting the larger scheme to unfold and trusting his guys up front of him to keep the charging stampede at bay, and trusting his receivers to be at exactly the right place at exactly the right time, because if they aren't, then it's going to be him who throws the interceptions and hears the boos of 60,000 fans.

Trust is the hardest thing to teach quarterbacks. They either get it or they don't—and most don't. They're used to orchestrating the performance of their team. They like being in control of the action—and their great talent has given them a false confidence that they can do just that, that they can dictate the outcome of events in a game.

You can't really blame them for thinking they can do it themselves because, well, they *have* done it themselves in the past. But when you get to the pros, you discover it's a whole different ball of wax than high school or even college. Shucks, Joe had an almost supernatural cannon for an arm. He could throw a tight spiral 60 yards with perfect trajectory. I'd seen him almost single-handedly beat the Longhorns in the Orange Bowl. And now he'd been given a record-breaking $400,000 contract and made the cover of *Sports Illustrated*. Go tell somebody like that not to try making the exceptional happen on his own.

The whole trust thing is even harder is if you're short on talented receivers or if you have selfish or inexperienced receivers. Luckily, we had just the opposite on the Jets. Joe was joining an offense with the most talented corps of receivers in the league.

It started with the two veterans, Bake Turner and me, and then with our two rookies, George Sauer and Pete Lammons. Coincidentally, Pete and George had been on the University of Texas team that beat Joe and the Crimson Tide in that classic Orange Bowl. As a matter of fact, Lammons, who played both linebacker and tight end for the Longhorns, played an outstanding game, intercepting two passes, recovering a fumble, and catching the pass that set up the Longhorns' last touchdown. So Lammons and Sauer came to the Jets already good friends.

They fell in easily with Bake and me. And wouldn't you know, all of a sudden, we had four receivers who were all from Texas.

During those six weeks of camp, we stayed out on the field for hours, sometimes long after practice, working on those passing drills. I could see that Namath hadn't come to the NFL just to collect a big paycheck. I didn't see a prima donna but rather a young man who was determined to relearn his footwork and timing, who was ready to get his hands dirty, and who was hungry for knowledge. A guy like that didn't need to improve—he was already an outstanding player—but he was determined to raise his game just the same. Even if that meant nothing short of rethinking everything he thought he knew about playing football. It was clear to me from day one that he was willing to do that.

Then, we practiced the same route at different depths. I'd run a 10-yard route, a 15-yard route, then a 20-yard route. On the quick out—the five-yard route—Namath takes a one-step drop and throws it. On the 10-yard route, he takes a three-step drop and throws it. On a 15-yard route, he takes a five-step drop and throws it. We had it down to a science.

When Weeb saw what Joe was doing in practice, he started getting on his case. "You're throwing it too fast," Weeb would tell him. He would whip out his stopwatch and started timing him. "Too fast. Too fast." But I knew different. It was like when Allie Sherman told me to shorten my strides ("Too long. Too long."). But I knew the very thing Sherman wanted to whip out of me was my greatest gift. And so did Sam Huff, which is why, after Sherman had made me sit out practice, he told me, "You just keep on running."

We spent 20 minutes a day doing nothing but running those pass routes for six straight weeks. *It's all up to Joe. He's got to throw the ball early.* And that is why I challenged him on those quick outs.

Sometimes we'd draw it up on the blackboard beforehand, but it wasn't until we got out there and ran it against our own defensive players that we got the opposition we'd be working against. But it's just like anything that you do over and over: you get better at it.

When I saw Namath hang his head after a rough practice in which Weeb had been criticizing him, I'd come over to him and say, "Hey, rookie, you just keep throwing."

We took a bus to the Allentown School District Stadium in Allentown, Pennsylvania, for our second exhibition game.

As Mark Kriegel wrote in *Namath: A Biography*, "The driving rain and muddy field were not the ideal conditions for a young quarterback trying to show what he could do. But after calling eight consecutive running plays, Namath threw the bomb. That time, he didn't overthrow Maynard. Instead, he hit him on the dead run,

60 yards for a touchdown. Most remarkable, though, was the ball's perfect trajectory, a path that defied the fierce elements. Almost 40 years later, Dave Anderson says, 'I can still see that ball, like an arrow, cutting through the rain like it didn't exist. That was the moment you knew: this guy was different.'"

The season was starting in a few days. We had one last team meeting, just for players. Before breaking off, Mike Hudock, an original Titan, asked if anybody else had anything he cared to say. All of a sudden, Joe stood up in front of the team. The room fell silent. All 35 pairs of eyes—veterans, rookies, free agents, special-team players—were on the young quarterback. He said, "Some of you are concerned about how much I'm making." He paused for a second. "I'm getting as much from the Jets as I can, same as you. We're all doing the same thing. We're all playing a game we love. Now, if anybody's still got a problem with me, speak up now. If you want to go outside and take care of it, let's go."

Maybe it was too much to ask of anybody, let alone a rookie, to lead our team out of the weeds. What's more, he was a rookie who showed up to his first training camp with a huge target painted on his back. I didn't know if he could become the leader we needed him to be, but for him to walk into what you might call a hostile environment and deliver the speech he delivered, facing his anonymous critics head on? Well, gee whiz, the kid was off to one heck of a start.

• • •

That September we returned to New York, but by then we had a new home in Queens: Shea Stadium.

I didn't think any ballplayer could come to New York City and stick out like a sore thumb more than I'd managed to do as a rookie with the Giants in 1958. But gosh, Namath was sure gonna give it his best shot. First off, the kid comes out to our first practice in Shea

Stadium wearing the brightest white shoes you've ever seen. I mean, you could see those shoes from space! For a guy everybody was gunning for, he sure had made himself easy to find.

It turned out that before he arrived to camp he had told our equipment manager, Bill Hampton, that he wanted his shoes to be laced right over left and wrapped with tape until they were completely white. Maybe to some people that sounds crazy, but it didn't to a guy who refused to play in the pros unless he got to wear No. 13 on his jersey. As a matter of fact, I had been making special requests since day one. I needed my cleats to be white—unheard of at the time, but it was the color I had always worn. I also had them equipped with exactly 24 spikes on the bottom—even in the instep—which gave me better traction than anybody else. Bill had the Puma Shoe Company make them for me, and when I came into the locker room at Shea, sure enough, there they were, bright white and beautiful! And just as I had asked, they had put a piece of sponge underneath the tongue of my shoe, then made two small slits so I could thread the lace through it. That prevented the tongue from ever slipping down during the game.

Realizing that half of his time was going to be spent taping Joe's shoes, Hampton put in one more special order that year. This time it went to the Magnus Shoe Company: one more pair of white shoes.

It was assumed that if you played ball, you tried to emulate the legendary Johnny Unitas with his crew cut and black high-tops. But Joe didn't seem interested in emulating anybody. A lot of folks assumed that Namath's disregard for football tradition was just another calculated ploy to get more attention. So were his brash comments, his flashy shirts, and his constant presence on the party circuit. I could see why people might think that, but having spent all those weeks with him up in Peekskill watching him go over game film long after the other players had headed to the local bar, I realized that he wasn't putting on some big show. Nope, it was just the way he was.

Although I felt comfortable shooting bull around the propane tank with the guys, Namath was in his element painting the town red with a stunning blonde on his arm. I showed up to camp in the El Paso Flame Burner; he showed up in a big Lincoln Continental. I wore country-and-western belt buckles around the city; he wore dark sunglasses. I liked to drink whole milk; he preferred Johnnie Walker Red. Every morning, I woke up early in my house in the suburbs of Long Island and did my 31 sit-ups in bed. Joe woke up—who knows when?—in his penthouse in the city with a pretty new gal in his bed. I'm guessing he skipped the sit-ups.

Those white shoes he wore were ridiculous looking, but I had to give it to him—he was letting everybody know that he wasn't changing for anybody, and if you don't like it, well, you can stuff it in your pipe. His white shoes were no more an act of rebellion than my cowboy boots were. I was being myself, and Joe was being Joe.

Just the same, I saw the young rookie get the same grief that I did for marching to his own drum. If the Giants thought my hair was long, they should have seen Joe's shaggy mane. The New York press guys, who followed him everywhere, were always unfairly comparing him to the Giants' longtime star quarterback Y.A. Tittle, who fit their notion of the way a quarterback should act and look to a T. He wore black high-tops, not gleaming white shoes. I'm guessing that Joe didn't see a good reason to cut his hair, other than to conform to the standards of how a football player should look, and that was no good reason at all. It was the same deal with me. When the Giants told me to shave my sideburns, I refused. How's looking like everybody else going to make me a better player? I could be wearing a barrel around my waist, and I would still outrun anybody. Joe could be wearing Wahoo's feathered headdress, and he would still throw a better ball than anybody.

Dealing with special equipment requests was nothing new for Bill Hampton—I'd been making them since the day I arrived there. Besides the cleats, I told him to ask the people at Champion Knitwear to create a jersey for me out of a special, lighter material with tiny holes in it like screen wire, so the air could breathe through it. I didn't know how they would accomplish it. I just told Bill what I wanted Champion to do. After all, they were the textile people, so naturally they would figure out how to make it happen. They delivered me exactly what I had asked for, and that's how I became the first player in America to wear a mesh jersey. After that, Champion started making mesh jerseys for other players in the NFL, and eventually it became a big seller for them.

In those days, shoulder pads went down as far as your armpits. Well, to protect my sternum, I had them drop the shoulder pads to the bottom of my rib cage. The manufacturers hadn't made them that way before, but they did for me. I wanted to wear as little protection as I could get away with—I estimate than I carried five pounds less than any other guy in the league.

• • •

As fate would have it, our first game of the season was at Houston's Rice Stadium. I hadn't been back for years, not since I had transferred to Texas Western after my freshman year. There I stood, on the same field where I had stood up to my coach, challenging the wisdom of doing wind sprints before practice. I looked up at the light posts towering above me, those same light posts my uncle and I had climbed up and painted during the summers of my youth.

On that opening day in September, the thermometer was nipping at 100 degrees. In other words, it was typical football weather in Texas. I couldn't believe how many fans had turned out—around

52,000. But if they came there to get a glimpse of Namath, and I suspect most of them did, they were out of luck. Namath didn't play one down that day. Instead, Mike Taliaferro led our offense. It was no disrespect to Namath that he didn't start. Mike had a very strong arm and was a fine quarterback. Namath understood, and he wasn't bitter at all.

The following week, after losing our season opener in Houston, we returned home for our first-ever regular season game at Shea. With the exception of Namath, nothing created more interest in the Jets than the move to our new stadium. A record 53,658 fans showed up that evening for our game against the Kansas City Chiefs. Even if half of them were Giants fans who hadn't been able to get tickets for their own team's game, it still meant that over 25,000 people had showed up for us. Heck, it was a bigger crowd than we'd ever had in the Polo Grounds.

We trailed in the second quarter, and Mike had only picked up 24 yards through the air. Weeb replaced him with Namath, to the delight of the crowd who had been chanting "We Want Joe!" from the start. Joe didn't do much, and we slipped further behind. The Chiefs led 14–3 in the fourth quarter. If we were going to do something, now was the time.

The quick out was called. Joe and I had been running that play over and over again during those six weeks of training camp and month of exhibition games. I had told him how and where I wanted the ball thrown. I told him, "I don't want you to wait. One step back, pivot, throw." But then, telling somebody is one thing, having him do it is another.

The ball was snapped. I broke down the field. *One one thousand, two one thousand, three one thousand...* I cut left. As I streaked across the field, the ball hit me in full stride. The moment the ball was in my grasp, I took off. Meanwhile, the defender, who thought I was already running full speed, was left in the dust after my sudden burst of speed toward the end zone. The crowd went wild as I crossed the goal line, completing the 37-yard scoring reception. Joe had thrown his first touchdown as a New York Jets quarterback. We wound up losing the game 14-10, but something more important had occurred in the mere seconds it took for us to score a touchdown: the formula for great future success had been laid. From then on, Joe and I knew it without discussing it, that when each of us executes his part to perfection.

Weeb named Joe the starter for the following week's game. It couldn't have been a tougher test, facing the defending AFL champion Buffalo Bills, led by Jack Kemp, my fellow castoff from the '58 Giants. The Giants had done as poor a job of judging his talent as they had mine. In Buffalo, Kemp became one of the premier quarterbacks in the game. It would take a Herculean effort for Namath to outgun the veteran sharpshooter. What's more, Namath was going against the No. 1 defense in the league.

After falling behind 13-0 in the second quarter, Namath led an impressive comeback against a very tough defense, throwing 40 times until he had closed the gap to 26-21 in the fourth quarter. In the end, Kemp was just too much, scoring a late touchdown to cement the Bills' victory. Namath had shown off his potential, but it didn't change the fact he had thrown two interceptions, that he still didn't have complete faith in the short timing routes, or that our team was still winless going into our fourth game of the season.

You had to be blind not to see that Namath was the total package. He had terrific arm strength. His release was lightning quick. He could read defenses like a seasoned veteran. And he was deadly accurate. And yet, the question that remained, at least in my mind, was whether he could embrace what we were trying to do. In other words, could he learn to let go and put faith in all the great weapons he had on his side of the field? I knew that if Joe could do this, he might just take our team to football's promised land after all. And if he couldn't? Well, then he'd have to settle for just being rich beyond his wildest dreams, adored by millions, and having any girl in New York City he wanted.

Going into the eighth week of the season, we'd managed to win just one game. That was really disappointing, considering all the talent we had on our roster. Up to that point, Mike and Joe were still sharing the quarterback duties. The problem with both of our young, inexperienced quarterbacks was the same: they were used to winning games in college purely on the strength of their arms. But that wasn't going to fly in the pros. The coverage was too good, too tight, too smart. The ability to throw a football through a concrete wall was impressive, but it wouldn't win you games. It was all about timing and precision. And that's what I had tried to teach Namath day after day during that summer at Peekskill Military Academy.

Our next game was a rematch against the Kansas City Chiefs, one of the AFL's elite teams. The game started with Mike under center and Namath relegated to the bench. In the first half Mike heaved one long-distance missile after another. It was the same old story—trying to win the game with one heroic throw from his powerful arm.

He didn't have to worry about his receivers. We didn't miss assignments, drop passes, or fumble balls. Even when the team came out on the short end of the score, our unit had performed at a very high level—I guarantee you that. In fact, I would put the four of us up against any other receiving corps that's ever played the game.

Mike needed to trust us the way we trusted each other. We didn't have to cheat on any pass routes just because one of the other guys had his play called in the huddle. We never even considered it. Personal stats weren't something that any of us cared about. It never entered our minds. Bake, Sauer, Lammons, and I were all too close for that. We were having too much fun playing together. We couldn't care less who caught the most passes.

At the half, Mike's numbers had not been good. He had thrown two interceptions, and he hadn't gotten the ball to me once. We were lucky to be down only 10-6. It was the perfect time for Weeb to bring in Namath—and that's just what he did.

As the third quarter got under way, Namath started moving us down the field, not with dazzling long bombs, but rather by using the short, accurate passes that we had worked on in practice. It was as if you could see him slowly letting go of the reins that had been so tightly in his grasp.

As our offense drove down the field, Joe was no longer orchestrating the events of the game but letting the events in the game inspire his choices. He was giving it over, and this had allowed him to remain cool and calm in the center of the tornado of pass rushers, to see the plays develop in front of him in a way that most quarterbacks never could, and to deliver a perfect dart in that tiny window of space where only his receiver can catch it.

With the ball on the Chiefs 31-yard line, we huddled up for the next play. At that point, a field goal would have left us one point behind. Namath called the play in the huddle. It was the quick out. He would need to throw a perfectly timed ball. There was no room for error. It would be all about trusting the pattern. Bake and Sauer lined up wide to one side; I lined up wide to the other. Namath hiked the ball from the center. He took a one-step drop and raised his arm.

Meanwhile, I had run out for the pass. The defender was draped all over me. *Round at four yards. One yard. Two yards. Three yards. Round!* I sprinted around the corner, gaining half a step on the defender. I knew the ball would be there. I didn't even think about it. As I raised my arms up to catch the pass, I felt the ball stick against my chest. And then I was off to the races.

The defender gave chase. We were both running full speed. I could hear his footsteps closing in on me. Just as he was about to catch me, I kicked in the afterburners. I start pulling away from him at the 20-yard line, and by the 10 he was fading from my rearview. I crossed the goal line with nobody near me. The whole play had taken less than 10 seconds. Joe Willie to Sunshine. Jets lead 13-10. The defense, sensing victory was ours, stepped up and held the Chiefs scoreless for the rest of the game.

On the plane back to New York, we were all celebrating the win—the coaches, the players, the rookies, the veterans, the black guys, the white guys, the Southern players, the Northern players, Broadway Joe, Chief Wahoo, Bake, T-Bird Mathis, and me, Shine.

Sure, everybody had been impressed with Joe's outing—not many rookies could come off the bench after halftime, his team trailing, and pull out a win in the loud, hostile environment of Kansas City's Municipal Stadium. But that's not why our spirits had been lifted, especially when it came to Joe. I could see him smiling, not because he had earned his first win, but for the same reason everybody else was smiling. It wasn't just that we'd come from behind to win, it was that it had taken all 35 guys—on offense and defense—to do it. We all felt so good because, rather than try to do it on his own, Joe had trusted his veteran receivers to make plays. And his veterans, in turn, had trusted him. We all ran our routes correctly, knowing that Joe would make the right decision as to who to throw to and when. No one individual had saved the day; our victory had been a total team effort.

Weeb didn't need to make the announcement. Everybody knew that Joe was going to be our starter from that day on. The $400,000 Kid had finally become a New York Jet.

And the New York Jets had liftoff.

No Knees

THE SUMMER HEAT IN TEXAS CAN BE UNBEARABLE. It's worse still if you're stuck inside your car or truck. Then it feels like cruising around inside an oven turned up to "Broil." Today, you can simply turn on the air conditioner, but back in 1965, most American cars that rolled off the factory assembly line weren't equipped with climate control, as it was considered a luxury for the very rich—men like Lamar Hunt and Sonny Werblin, for example. The rest of us had to roll down the window or use the fan-yourself-with-your-hand method. Well, that didn't seem like the most effective cooling system to me. So, I went ahead and designed my own air-conditioning unit, built it from scratch, and installed it in my propane-powered '55 coupe. It worked great. I might not own a Cadillac like Sonny Werblin, but I guarantee you that I stayed just as cool in my Ford.

I had a cousin who was a Texas highway patrolman, and I got to thinking about him, working his eight-hour shift in the sweltering Texas heat. His job was hard enough without having to bake all day inside his patrol car like a Butterball turkey. Deciding to take matters into my own hands, I drove to the highway patrol department offices in Midland, Texas, to try to sell them on the idea of letting me install my custom-made air-conditioning unit in their patrol cars.

I walked right into their office and told my cousin's bosses that if they let me install air-conditioning units in their vehicles it would keep their patrolmen cool during their long shifts and they could do their jobs better and more comfortably. Plus, I could do the work myself and it would be a whole lot cheaper than Ford or General Motors. They were skeptical at first, but I wasn't leaving their office until they said yes. When they saw how determined I was, they told me I could go ahead and do it.

Over the next couple of off-seasons, I continued to teach at the high school in El Paso and worked nights in my garage, refitting cars with my AC units or propane conversion systems. On the weekend I would drive around Texas and New Mexico, selling my homemade air conditioners, probably traveling many of the same routes that my father had traveled years earlier with his cotton gin. Sometimes two or three people would come out together, and I would show them how I could put an air-conditioning unit under their dash or add a propane system to their pickup truck. Each year I'd try to go to the head office where I would present a demonstration to the highway patrol or state police. They got so popular that a couple of units were sold nationwide. I had a pretty good little business going each summer before I went down to football.

I personally campaigned for the state of Texas to put factory air-conditioning units in their highway patrol cars. It wasn't right to ask those men to sit in their cars all day, parked on the scalding black-top, as they tried to slow down reckless speeders. (Of course, I never broke the speed limit, unless you count the occasional kick-return or deep pass pattern.) All my hectoring was for naught. I never could get them to agree to do it.

By the spring of 1966, the AFL could no longer be seen as some laughingstock venture that was destined to fold. Namath's decision to spurn the established league and sign for more money with the upstart one was not some strange event but rather a symbol of the AFL owners' willingness to engage in all-out warfare with the NFL, not just picking off a few high draft picks, but achieving supremacy over them.

Sonny Werblin's signing of Namath had been a game changer. It felt like suddenly everybody in New York panned their heads from the Bronx to Queens and said, "Hey, wait a minute. There's a stadium there, too." Finally, we were getting the kind of crowds that poor old Harry Wismer wouldn't be around long enough to see. I guess I still felt for him, even after he'd announced that I'd been traded to Boston that one time, because I knew how awful it was to get beat up in the New York press, for whom ridiculing the Titans of the AFL was daily sport—that is, when they weren't singing the praises of the Giants.

Joe did more than bring some much-needed excitement to Shea Stadium. His star power was a boon for the other AFL franchises. As we visited other teams—in cities like Houston, Boston, Oakland, and Buffalo—we began to see more and more people in the stands.

The league's upswing came as a shock to many folks but not to me. Even the NFL owners finally had to admit that the AFL had become a force to be reckoned with. Compelled by their own self-preservation, they started talking merger. Not surprisingly, Lamar Hunt was not ready to make nice. And why should he have been? After all, it was the NFL owners who had shunned his request for an expansion team in Dallas. They wanted a fight. Well, now they had one.

As for Sonny Werblin, I never sensed he had any interest in conceding anything to those same people who thought he didn't belong in the football world. When Giants owner Wellington Mara said, "Football is not a hobby for us," you got the feeling he was referring to our showbiz honcho.

But Mara had no choice but to face facts: New Yorkers were growing more interested in the Jets every day. We went from playing before 7,000 spectators in the Polo Grounds, many of whom were Giants fans, to 64,000 fans in Shea Stadium, most of whom were loyal to the Green and White.

What's more, the once-mighty Giants had sunk so low under Allie Sherman that in 1966 they posted a 1–12–1 record. In his infinite wisdom, Sherman traded Sam Huff—one of the greatest middle linebackers of all time and the heart and soul of the team—to Washington in 1964. If you thought I was upset at Sherman, boy, you should have seen Huff. "As long as I live," Huff said, "I will never forgive Allie Sherman for trading me." He swore he would get back at him. Sure enough, he got his chance when the teams met in D.C. the following year. The Redskins didn't just beat the Giants; they put up the most points ever scored by a single team in NFL history. The Redskins had already put up 69 points on the Giants when, toward the end of the game, they were able to tack on a few more. While Washington coach Otto Graham had been momentarily distracted, Huff sent in the field-goal team!

With the crowds swelling, our reputation around the country growing, and our team improving, Werblin could hold out for as long as felt like it. That June, right before I was getting ready to head up to Peekskill, the news broke: the two leagues had agreed to a merger after the 1969 season.

Not everybody was happy about this announcement—including me, for one. I'd taken enough ridicule from the NFL for 10 years. Keep 'em separate. Also, I knew a big reason the merger was to get a handle on player salaries, which had skyrocketed as the fight over top draft talents heated up between the two leagues. The players didn't seem likely to benefit from any partnership. I felt we should just have two separate leagues and then play a championship game between the two leagues at the end of the season.

Al Davis, owner of the Oakland Raiders, didn't want the leagues to merge either, and he was good and vocal about it. Known as a man who did things his own way, I had nothing but admiration for him, both as an owner and a businessman. He even impressed me during his brief time as a coach. He also treated his players real well. His feeling was that we had the NFL on the run, so why concede to them? In the end, the other AFL owners overruled him.

I reported to training camp in July. On the first day, I saw Joe strolling easy-breezy through the military academy with his Irish Setter, Fancy Pharaoh, at his side. Every player knew the rules: no wives or girlfriends were allowed in camp. Pets were also prohibited. Now, my feeling was, if Joe wanted a dog, that was his business, not mine. But Fancy Pharaoh's presence in camp that summer left some of the other veterans bent out of shape. It proved that Namath was free to flout the team rules just because he was, well, Namath. During a team meeting, it came to a head.

"Why can Namath have a dog but nobody else can?" asked a defensive veteran.

"That's different," Weeb quickly declared. "That's our mascot."

If Weeb said Joe's four-legged redhead companion was the mascot of the New York Jets, then she was. Maybe it was fitting. Joe and she had the same happy-go-lucky nature and, of course, she had my speed. As for complaints about Joe breaking the no-canine rule, that should have been the least of anybody's concerns. The way Joe saw it, you could file your complaints under "I don't give a rat's tinkle what you think."

While Joe brought Fancy Pharaoh with him to training camp, I brought a couple of cases of HomeCare cleaning fluid with me. It was a chemical cleaner that was nonflammable and nontoxic. You could take a quart of the cleaner concentrate and dilute it down with water and get yourself 10 quarts. I sold it as a cleaner. I was helping the local Lions Club raise funds. If everybody in the room bought one—let's say there were 60 players—that's $60 right there. And if a couple of people bought one for their neighbor, it would be even more. Or everybody could take 12 quarts and then go around to their neighbors and sell it to raise money.

I demonstrated how it could remove lipstick from a wall by spraying some on a lipstick-stained board. I did a few different demos. When I was finished, somebody said, "I can't believe that a product that effective isn't harmful." And I said, "It's nontoxic. Here, I'll drink some for ya." Then I poured some in a little breakfast glass—it wasn't much but enough to get my point across—and I drank it. That was around noon. I went out for practice that afternoon. Well, the way the chemical product worked is that it took the oil out of lipstick or grease. Wouldn't you know, it reacted in my system. It took all the moisture out of my mouth. Gee whiz, you talk about cotton mouth! My mouth got so dry that I couldn't keep any moisture in it. So every time I finished a play I would walk over to the ice bucket and get a piece of ice about the size of half a golf ball and I'd put it in my mouth to get the moisture back. I had a hard day of workout just trying to keep from getting dehydrated. Everything was bone dry—my mouth, my tongue, my lungs. But the important thing was that the Lions bought all the cleaner I had brought them. Later, I got all kinds of compliments that it really did work. "Yeah, but we ain't drinking any of it like you," they said. *That's all right, 'cause I ain't ever drinking it again, either.*

I guess you could say I went the distance to prove my point, like the time a couple of my teammates questioned my claim that I could run exact pass patterns as well as anybody who ever played the game. They, like most other people, assumed I was just a speed receiver, as opposed to the Colts' Raymond Berry, who was known as a great possession receiver. So I told them to stick around after practice and I would prove that what I said was the truth. Well, a couple of the guys hung around on the field, waiting to see what I was going to do. I took out a blindfold and tied it around my head. I said to them, "Okay, I can run a five-yard route. I can run a 10-yard route. I can run a 20-yard route. They can be square ins or square out. And I won't miss it."

As I ran the pattern, blindfolded, I counted in my head, *one one thousand, two one thousand, three one thousand*...then I made my break to the sideline. I reached my hands out a few inches in full stride. I felt the ball hit my palms. I secured the ball and got my feet in before going out of bounds. As I took off the blindfold, I gave everybody a smile.

I had always done things a bit differently and that didn't change with the Jets. What did change, however, was that now, in Joe, I had a quarterback who shared my feeling that the only way to move forward was without fear. He was just as willing as I was to defy the established playbook. Not in some silly, self-congratulatory act of rebellion, but rather to add a never-before-seen dimension to the game.

Joe had a natural aptitude when it came to football. Every year they tested the rookies on their knowledge of the playbook. Joe scored 104 correct out of 106 questions. What's more, he spent as much time watching game film as anybody I've ever seen. In fact, I can assure you that he spent just as much time with that projector as he did the ladies. His desire to raise his game was evident to me. I saw the attentive look he wore during team meetings; I saw the hours he spent poring over game film and the pounds of ice the young man went through trying to bring down the swelling of his battered knees. That was important, to witness this with my own eyes, because it would have been easy to assume from his hard-drinking, playboy lifestyle that he wasn't interested in reaching his true potential. It was just the opposite. Namath wasn't interested in being great; he wanted to be the *greatest*. As far as I was concerned, that sounded a whole lot like someone else I knew.

Even in 1966 I could see how NFL teams operated in the same uniform way. The sweep, which Lombardi had developed in New York with Gifford and Webster and later perfected with Hornung and Taylor, was the pattern that many offenses still depended on in order to score. It was as if there were an accepted style of play to go along with the accepted style of dress. Now, I had no problem following the "proper" technique, but not on account of it being the conventional wisdom. If there was a better way of doing things—whether it was designing a car or running a pass play—it made no sense *not* to go in a new direction. It didn't matter if that road had never been traveled before, if it held dangers unknown and the potential of disaster. So what? It's better than being content with "good enough."

And I felt that when it came to the passing game, there was a better way of doing things. My problem was that I wasn't shy about telling folks my ideas on the subject. It was the same characteristic that earned me a one-way ticket to El Paso by way of Canada. But, as I had learned from the situation with Bake Turner, Weeb was more receptive to input from his players—to a point, at least.

My relationship with Weeb depended on which hat he was wearing at the time. When it came to him as a coach, I liked him about 95 percent of the time. The only times I ever had a problem with him as a coach was when he called some boneheaded play that usually ended up with Joe throwing an interception. On a couple of occasions, I griped to him about how he was screwing up our quarterback with the plays he told him to run. He was great all week, but a few times he should have stayed home on game day.

Our daughter, Terry, is always full of laughter. And, as you can see, our son, Scot, took to football early on! PHOTO COURTESY OF THE AUTHOR

My eyes are already downfield as I make a move on a Patriots defender.

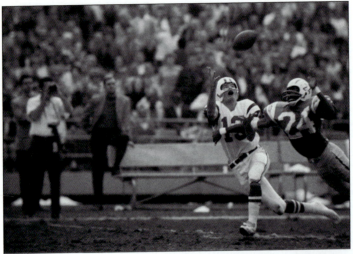

Top: Joe and I had our rhythm down so well that I could always count on the ball being exactly where I expected it.

Center: Two friends celebrate victory in the AFL Championship Game. Next stop: Super Bowl!

Bottom: Jim Turner remains a good friend to this day. Here, he and I are awarded trophies by the Catholic Youth Association.

THIRD WORLD CHAMPIONSHIP GAME/JANUARY 12, 1969, ORANGE BOWL, MIAMI, F

I was surprised to find out that the programs for the Super Bowl featured lucky No. 13. PHOTO COURTESY OF AP IMAGES.

The scene at the Orange Bowl in Miami for Super Bowl III. PHOTO COURTESY OF AP IMAGES.

Joe and I take it all in.

"You put it up and I'll go get it."

Matt Snell gets in for the score.

I love to golf—and I wouldn't be caught on the links without my cowboy boot spikes. PHOTO COURTESY OF THE AUTHOR.

Longtime equipment manager Bill Hampton is an unsung hero in the Jets organization. PHOTO COURTESY OF THE AUTHOR.

Taking in the sights at Super Bowl XXXIII (from left), V.A. George, TWU teammate Jackie Meeks, legendary coach Tom Landry, me, TWU teammate Ken George, and my son, Scot. PHOTO COURTESY OF THE AUTHOR.

At the Pro Football Hall of Fame with Scot; my HOF placard (left). PHOTO COURTESY OF THE AUTHOR.

Nothing is more important than family. At a Jets-Cardinals game with (from left) my son, Scot; grandchildren Tanner and Tyler; son-in-law Rusty; and daughter, Terry. PHOTO COURTESY OF THE AUTHOR.

I'd also gripe to Weeb that he wasn't treating his players the way they ought to be treated. Sometimes he treated us like boys instead of men. For example, he'd have us all write down on a piece of paper what we wanted for dinner on the road. As a general manager, I always said he was cheap. He'd steal from his wife. But, away from football, as a man—well, I loved him.

The other good thing about Weeb was that he surrounded himself with some really fine young coaching minds, men like Walt Michaels, Buddy Ryan, Chuck Knox, and Clive Rush. More important, he didn't interfere with their duties as assistant coaches, which was to direct their position group.

Clive played only a year of pro ball, for the Green Bay Packers in 1953, but he went on to apprentice under the legendary Woody Hayes at Ohio State and Bud Wilkinson at Oklahoma. What I respected about Clive was that although he brought impressive credentials with him to the Jets, he was receptive to ideas or suggestions from players. And that's really all I ever wanted from a coach, for somebody to consider my ideas regarding the passing game, no matter how strange or different they might sound, and not just discount me because I might talk or dress a little differently.

Up at Peekskill, I told Clive that I had an idea, a kind of unorthodox way of running the pass play. He said he'd like to hear it. Well, that's when I told him my theory about how if I rounded my turns I could gain half a step on the corner every time, and then if Namath got rid of the ball in under three seconds, delivering it to me with pinpoint accuracy, I would have a clear path to the end zone. Now, if I had brought this idea up to Allie Sherman, he probably would have told me I was crazy, and by the way, shave my sideburns. As a matter of fact, I would not have been surprised if Clive laughed me out the door. Oh, *it's just a matter of getting rid of the ball under three seconds and throwing a perfect strike 20 yards down the field.* Except that we were talking about Namath, and Clive didn't laugh.

Over the next six weeks, I trained Namath on how to run my special fade pattern. I told him, "If I break it to the outside of the defender, then all you have to do is throw it to my right shoulder. If I run it to the inside, then you throw it to my left shoulder." That was the key—throwing it to the correct shoulder. I wasn't going to turn back until the last possible second—that way I would never have to break my stride. If, in that last moment, I turned and the ball was coming down on the wrong shoulder, I wouldn't have time to adjust my body to make the catch. A throw to the wrong shoulder on that particular play equaled sure disaster.

Meanwhile, the rest of the offensive guys and I spent night and day, practice after practice, devoted to getting down Clive's offensive plan until we could run it in our sleep. The offensive line had one job: keep Joe upright long enough to find the open receiver and rifle a tight spiral to him. Our job as receivers was just as straightforward: get open for Joe. Now, we had so many talented skill players that the defense couldn't cover all of us at once. If they decided to double-team me downfield, that might leave Lammons open in the middle of the field or Bake Turner open on the short side. Okay, but what about if they drop everybody back into coverage? Well, then Joe can toss it lightly to our rookie halfback as he swings out to the flat. It was scary how, over and over again during passing drills, Joe would drop back, survey the field, and throw it to the open guy—and the whole sequence probably took no more than three seconds. *Three seconds.* Quarterbacks weren't supposed to be able to connect with their receivers that fast. But Joe Willie and his Lone Star Receivers weren't too interested in what people said you couldn't do. We were having too much fun seeing what we *could* do.

Each time Joe and I connected in practice, the defender covering me got beat. And the more we worked on it during camp, the more times we connected. By the time we reached the exhibition season, it didn't matter if Namath threw it to me 10 yards downfield or 20 yards or 30 yards or 40 yards—we were in synch on every pass.

I couldn't wait for the season to start so we could unveil our new high-powered offense. But then, in an exhibition game against the Houston Oilers, Joe injured his knee while stopping 315-pound tackle Ernie Ladd on a fumble return. As a result, he was listed as questionable for our season opener against Miami. Oh, and did I mention that NBC was broadcasting the game at a special time, Friday night, so the whole nation could tune in and watch us?

It wasn't until the third quarter of that game in Miami that Namath finally limped onto the field on his balky knees. He hadn't thrown a pass for weeks, and it showed. He threw an interception that was returned for a touchdown.

The following week was our home opener at Shea Stadium. We were hosting Houston, the same opponent that had injured Joe's knee just a few weeks earlier. Houston's defense was scary good. So good, in fact, that the previous week, they had held the Denver Broncos without a first down in the entire game.

The attendance for our game was 54,681—the high mark for an AFL home opener. You couldn't help but feel the energy of the loud, cheering fans.

But Houston scored the first points of the game on a George Blanda field goal. As soon as Namath took the field with us, his Lone Star Receivers, there was a feeling that this was it—go time. In the huddle, Joe called a 61 route. As we approached the line of scrimmage, we didn't know where Joe was going to throw the ball, but Joe knew exactly what George Sauer was gonna do on the left side—he's going to curl 20 yards downfield. Joe also knew what I was gonna do on the right side—I was going 30 yards downfield on a fly pattern. Pete Lammons was cutting across the middle on a 10-yard slant, and our rookie halfback Boozer was swinging out into the flat.

The ball was snapped. As Namath shuffled back in the pocket, all of us receivers broke. Even though we were all running separate routes at different lengths, we did it in perfect unison. Namath raised the ball up to his ear, pivoted, and threw it to a wide-open George Sauer. George caught the ball and turned upfield for a 67-yard touchdown. Then in the second quarter, he found Matt Snell for a 25-yard touchdown pass. On the next drive, he hit Pete Lammons on a 13-yard pass for a touchdown. By the time we went into halftime, we were up 21-6.

We were all feeling good, but nobody was happier than I was. It didn't matter to me that I hadn't personally caught a touchdown pass. Why should Joe Namath throw the ball to me when I have two or three guys hanging on me and when he can throw it to George Sauer or Matt Snell or Pete Lammons? All three of those guys are going to beat any defender in the league one-on-one. A great quarterback can't play favorites; he needs to read the defense and take advantage of the mismatch. Namath understood that a lot better than guys with twice his experience.

Coming out in the third quarter, as I broke off the line of scrimmage, the defender came up and grabbed me. I knew I would be late getting to the spot where Namath expected me to be. I shook the defender and broke toward the sideline. But instead of cutting at a sharp angle, I rounded my turn, which allowed me to continue my pace unbroken.

I streaked downfield, never once looking back for the ball. I had faith that when I turned my head back for the ball it would be there. Sure enough, at that moment, I caught sight of the white laces of the ball spiraling down over my right shoulder. With one step on the defender chasing me, I reached out and grabbed it in full stride. At least, that's what I had led the defender to think. Like a track runner who kicks in the afterburners as he turns for the home stretch, I put my pedal to the metal. As soon as I got behind the defender, I was gone. Namath to Maynard. Fifty-five yards. Touchdown.

So what about the defender grabbing me at the line of scrimmage who threw off my timing? Well, I had never stopped counting in my head—*one one thousand, two one thousand, three one thousand...* so all I had to do was make my break at the 15-yard line instead of the 20 to make up for the lost time. Joe would never know that I made this adjustment. From the angle that he's looking from, I might be five yards shorter in length, but I'm only an inch different in height.

All I was doing was applying the same science I had watched my dad use to build our wind-powered water tank, the same physics that went into laying pipes through a house, the same geometry I used to design a better rooftop air-conditioning unit, the same math that I taught my shop students to use when building a storage chest.

Houston's defense had never seen our kind of offensive weaponry before, and neither had our next several opponents. After five games, we were undefeated with one tie. Joe, who quickly proved how sharp he was at reading the field, landed on the cover of *Sports Illustrated* under the headline, "Jet-Propelled Joe Namath." Knowing that we had such great balance in our passing game gave our offense tremendous confidence going into the second part of our season.

In mid-October, we flew down to Houston for a rematch against the Oilers. Every so often, Weeb should have stayed home on game day, and that contest was definitely one of them. Let's just say that some of his play calls left something to be desired. He got Namath intercepted twice, sending in his plays. I finally went over to him and said calmly, "Joseph, don't listen to him for nothing. All he can do is tell you where the restrooms are located. You call your plays or you ask me and I'll fill you in."

Unfortunately, we wound up losing that game 24-0 and then the next one to the Raiders 24-21. But that was nothing compared to what came next. In front of a full house at Shea, Namath would suffer the worst game of his short career against the Buffalo Bills. He took a beating from the Bills defense, but he kept throwing. And although he threw for more than 300 yards, he also ended up with an ugly five interceptions. After the barrage of hits he suffered, it was amazing he could walk off the field on his own.

Joe's knees were in such bad shape that he needed painkilling shots on game day just to make it out onto the field. After all the promise we had shown in September against Houston, we wound up winning only two more games the rest of the season, finishing in third place in the Eastern Division with a 6-6-2 record. But that wasn't the worst of it. Before Joe went his way for the rest of the year and I went mine, he told me the bad news. He was going in for surgery on his knees.

With the exception of a few high-profile guys like Namath and Houston's Heisman-winning rushing star Billy Cannon, players still needed to work a second job in the off-season to cover living expenses. I suppose a few guys hustled enough in endorsement deals and public appearances that they could afford to do little to nothing during those six months away from the game. Well, if they felt they didn't need to work in the off-season and could still live the lifestyle they wanted and maintain it well into the future—when arthritis, joint replacement surgery, or any of the other gifts of those brutal Sunday battles came to pass—I wished them all the best. As for me, I went back to El Paso every winter to work as a plumber or teach shop class until camp started up again in July.

No Guarantee

I SHOWED UP TO PEEKSKILL IN JULY 1967. I was eating my break-fast when all the old guys appeared, one after another—Bake, T-Bird, Larry Grantham, George Sauer, Curley Johnson. Soon thereafter, I saw Namath. It was the first time since the end of season, when he hobbled his way out of Shea and into the operating room. He looked good. Rested. The Florida sun had always been good tonic for him, as it had been once again in this off-season. His hair was long and shaggy and his sideburns were bushy. Weeb wanted him to get a haircut and to shave his sideburns. He even set up an appointment for him with the local Peekskill barber, who ran a tiny little shop in town. Joe told him he couldn't do it. Weeb asked him, why not? Joe said that his mill-worker dad had told him never to go against the union and, well, the local barber's one-man shop didn't have a union. Gee whiz, I wish I had been smart enough to think of that one when Jim Lee Howell and Allie Sherman tried to force me under the razors. But that was Joe for you. He was one smooth customer.

Weeb could get as steamed up as he liked. At the end of the day, there was nothing he could do. Joe was Sonny's boy. Heck, Joe and Sonny had more all-night meetings in the finest cocktail bars in Manhattan than you could count, always at the best table in the joint. What Joe did in his free time was no business of mine.

Personally, I liked to wake up early, do my 31 push-ups, stretch, eat some breakfast, and get to team meetings early. It didn't bother me any that many considered me odd for not drinking. I made a promise to Granddad Sharpe, and I was going to keep it. Besides, when I saw some of the other guys dragging their sorry selves into morning meetings after a long night, I was darn glad to be a teetotaler.

Weeb didn't get on me for the same reason that Brumbelow or Lombardi didn't get on me—I never gave them a reason to get on me. I did everything that was asked of me. Except, of course, change the number on my jersey—that was always gonna stay No. 13.

As a matter of fact, I was still the only guy in the league who wore No. 13. I don't recall how the pregame ritual started, but only tight end Thurlow Cooper was allowed to pull my No. 13 jersey down over my shoulder pads. Recalled Cooper, "He would not let anyone touch that No. 13 jersey except me. A couple of times I sent Roger Ellis over, and Maynard went berserk."

I also refused to wear a chinstrap, even though it was mandatory. If they want the helmet they could have it, but my head's not going to be in it. Instead, I had the equipment manager build me a special helmet that was molded to my head. It involved stuffing extra padding around the cheek area. It worked just fine, and I didn't have to wear that stupid chinstrap.

He might have been "Broadway Joe" to the rest of the world, but inside the locker room he was just "Joe" or "Namath." Occasionally, I would call him "Joseph" when I wanted to make sure I had his full attention in a meeting or workout. I might say, "Now, Joseph, this is how we needed to run this slant pattern." It was like when I was a kid. When my mom or dad called me Donald, I guarantee you that they wanted 100 percent of my focus, and you can bet I gave them it. But Joe was a good listener. He always showed me respect, and believe me, that respect went both ways.

The feeling around camp was that we had the firepower to make a serious run at the Eastern Division championship. Joe had two years of playing experience under his belt, the chemistry between him and the rest of the offense had only gotten better, and after all those years in the weeds, our defense had developed into one of the best in the league. Not only was Larry Grantham still flying around making tackles, but now we also had Gerry Philbin, an outstanding defensive end from Pawtucket, Rhode Island. He had a great knack for getting to the quarterback, as Joe had unfortunately learned during workouts. But the good news was that when it came to the actual game, it was the opposing quarterback he put a hurt on.

Over the next six weeks, we trained rigorously to get ready for the regular-season clashes ahead of us. That meant going out on the field and practicing twice a day, no matter how bad the weather. Maybe it was because we were training on a military base or that we were forced to live together in cramped quarters and our days were filled with drills and more drills or that we worked out for hours in the heat and the rain—but nobody ever forgot that he was there to do a job.

Even in the harsh conditions of training camp, we had our fair share of laughs. We'd run drills for hours in the pouring rain until the field looked more like a lake. Weeb would say, "Well, we're staying out here unless we get some lightning." And I'd say, "But, Weeb, what about all of us who are afraid of thunder?" Looking at Weeb, I was pretty sure he'd never done a single jumping jack in his life. But I'll tell you what, when that first streak of lightning finally burst across the sky, Weeb outran everybody to the dressing room. Shoot, even I couldn't catch up to him.

The day before our first exhibition game we got hit with another storm, just one of many that our team would endure that season. Our star quarterback was nowhere to be found. No Joe. No Fancy

Pharaoh. They said he'd gone AWOL, that he was too busy enter-taining himself with booze and broads to bother showing up for our first game. But that was just plain wrong. Truth was, Joe had gone home to Beaver Falls, Pennsylvania, to care for his brother, who had come down with the infamous Doylestown flu, which had made his legs go numb. Their mother was a right mess with worry, and Joe, who loved his mother deeply, wanted to be there to comfort her and the rest of his family.

The press was not worried with such little burden as "facts." They didn't care that he'd come to Weeb beforehand and asked him for permission to tend to a personal problem only to be told no. I suppose Joe could have told Weeb the nature of his requested absence. I also suppose that it was none of Weeb's business. If Joe said he had a personal problem, it was serious. That's all Weeb needed to know. It sure wasn't worth my time to judge the kid. I was busy stretching and working on my pass routes and trying to get ready for months straight of physical abuse.

When Namath returned, guys wanted answers. A players-only meeting was called. Joe stood in front of the team and said he was sorry that he had let everybody down. He wouldn't use his sick brother as an excuse, even if it was as good an excuse as any. But even with him back, we were not at full strength going into our season opener in Buffalo on September 10. Sam DeLuca, our veteran left guard and offensive captain, had wrecked his knee in the preseason. The first quarter of that game ended in a scoreless tie. As the second quarter began, Namath hit me on a 19-yard pass for a touchdown, giving us a 7-0 lead. Shortly thereafter, Namath dropped back in the pocket, raised up his arm, and released the ball like an arrow across the sky.

Meanwhile, I was sprinting down the field, covered by the cor-nerback. I made my move, like a race car taking a smooth curve around the track, and rounded up to the left, maintaining my high speed. No way the corner could keep up with me. The moment I get a step on him, I turn my head back, and at that very second the ball descended into my arms. See ya later. I'm gone. Fifty-six yards. Touchdown. Before you could blink, we were up 14-0. By the time the fourth quarter started, a Jim Turner field goal had extended our lead to 17.

Just when everything looked like it was going our way, the wheels came off. First, Cornell Gordon's season ended after he got hammered in the knee on an interception return. Then, the big blow. With two minutes to go in the game, Matt Snell, our Mr. Do Everything, absolutely decimated—you guessed it—his knee. Even with my two touchdowns and my 106 yards on five receptions, we blew our 17-point lead to kick off the year with a loss.

At first, it looked like we might just survive losing Snell. Boozer, a sixth-round rookie, stepped in at halfback and proved to be a dangerous weapon, using his elusive speed to pick up big chunks of yards while providing us with the balanced attack that was crucial to keeping our high-powered offense humming.

Leaving our season-opening collapse behind us, we flew out west to face our next opponent, the Denver Broncos. We were down 17 points on the road when our offense exploded, ultimately snagging a 38-24 win. I made four catches for a total of 141 yards—good for an average about 35 yards per catch. Lammons also had 141 yards receiving while Sauer chipped in with 84 yards and a touchdown. In total, Namath had thrown for a career-high 399 yards and set a new team mark.

The next week we played our home opener against the Miami Dolphins. Our offense put on its most entertaining show yet, as Joe threw for an incredible 415 yards and three touchdowns. I led the team with 121 receiving yards on four catches. Our offense was rolling.

AFL teams had a reputation for lots of passing, but a receiver averaging 100 yards a game was a rare feat, to be sure. To average 30 yards on every catch was rarer still. But I was just doing the same thing that I'd been doing since I was at Texas Western: getting open, catching the ball, and then running like the dickens to the end zone.

As rare as it was for a receiver like me to average so many yards per catch, it was equally special for a quarterback to break the 400-yard ceiling. But Namath did it by doing the things we had worked on so hard—the quick and exact timing of the ball's release, hitting the right target, and hitting him in the right space. Our offense might have looked flamboyant to the public, but each play was constructed like a finely tuned watch, the many parts working in perfect unison.

Our offensive unit performed so incredibly well together that between Namath and us receivers there was only one time in nine years that we weren't on the same page as we ran our pass pattern because as individuals we were dedicated to our work and also because we were committed to the goal of winning as a team over personal glory. We were a close-knit group. There were no egos and no jealousy of one another. We were all rooting for each other to play well.

Grantham, Bake, T-Bird, Curley, Sauer, and I were just a bunch of regular, easygoing guys from Texas. We enjoyed fishing and hunting and playing cards, but most of all we loved to play football. And once you got past the fur coats and the llama rugs and the penthouse suite, Namath was no different than we were. He grew up in a working-class steel town in Pennsylvania. He might not have embodied that spirit on the outside the way Johnny Unitas did with his close-cropped haircut and stoic personality, but make no mistake, Joe was a tough, hardworking, and dedicated ballplayer. He didn't carry airs about him. He was a real guy—likeable, funny, and cool-headed. Because he was just a down-to-earth fella, like the rest of us, he was able to take the constant ribbing that happens among teammates and even poke fun at himself.

We all teased each other in that way that brothers who would do anything for each other might get on one another. Everybody had a nickname. We called our free safety Bill Baird "Rabbit" because he was just about the quickest Jet on the team, other than me and maybe Bake Turner. Rabbit was also the smartest defender I've seen since Emlen Tunnell. Weeb called Gerry Philbin "Puppy Dog" because of his roving ability. Larry Grantham could guard inside and outside the blocker, so Weeb nicknamed him "Chigger," because chiggers zip around in the air so quickly.

As for how Bill Mathis got his nickname, well, I'll take credit for that one. Mathis was so hung up on owning a Thunderbird that whenever we were on the road and we had some killin' time, he and I would stop into the local Ford dealership to check out the car of his dreams. I'd say to him, "Why in the world do you want to waste your money on a Thunderbird when you can get a Fairlane, which is just as good for a whole lot cheaper?" But Mathis wasn't hearing it. A Thunderbird was what he wanted, and you couldn't change his mind. So I started calling him T-Bird. Over time, the rest of the guys started calling him that, too, or sometimes "Bird" or "Birdie" for short.

Everybody knew that I was careful with every dollar I spent. As a result, they would kid me about my thrifty habits, but at the same time, they were never disrespectful. What can I say? I wasn't like our government—I didn't waste money. I was a good saver. Did it get down to writing down every nickel and dime I spent in a little notebook, as some have suggested? I don't think it went quite that far, but I was very good about getting a receipt for everything. I learned exactly what items I could deduct, and at the end of the year you bet I wrote them off—plane tickets, gas bills, motel bills. Shoot, I'd get a receipt for the 25-cent toll whenever I crossed over the Triborough Bridge.

To me I was just a good bookkeeper, but boy, did my teammates like to tease me about my spending oddities, if you want to call them that. It was the same thing with me not drinking or smoking—I took some guff for it, but it was always good-natured kind of teasing. I'd be in a bar drinking a Coke. But I'm not there to drink, I'm there to be with my teammates and enjoy their company. We would take a pool of cars to the bar or restaurant after practice—three or four offensive guys in one car, three or four offensive guys in another car, and a couple more in the last car. Most of the time, we're sitting around, talking football—how our offense or defense is going to stop our upcoming opponent. Sure, a few guys might be drinking heavily but our minds were all on the same thing: winning the big game on Sunday. It was like a business meeting, except that our business didn't take place in a boardroom, it took place on a football field.

Being from Texas wasn't the only reason that T-Bird, Curley Johnson, and Larry Grantham got to be such close friends. We all lived out in Long Island together and shared rides to the stadium together, our families hung out on the weekends together, our kids went to the same school and played after school together, and our wives all became good friends, as well. When you play together on the same team for 10 years and you're all neighbors, you get to know each other pretty well.

A few of the single guys chose to live in Manhattan, where they could be closer to the action. But their attitude was the same as the rest of ours. We came to New York to play ball. It's what happens when you're all stuck together for six brutal weeks of training camp and four weeks of preseason, followed by four or five months of the regular season, making the same cross-country trips, staying at the same hotels, eating the same food, working out in the same torrential rain, and removing bloody tape in the same trainer's room. We couldn't help but become friends. And forging all those friendships is just an added bonus to the job. Sure, we also came up to make money at it, but it was mostly for the fun of it, for the love of the game. We all loved to compete and to win.

What a guy did off the field was no one's concern but his own. The married guys might drive back to their homes in Long Island after practice, while the single guys might take a date out for cocktails or dancing in the city. Okay, well, they didn't have to worry about going home to a family or kids, or fret over grades or homework. We didn't need to live the same life, we just had to play football the same way.

Besides, it's not as if the married guys and the single guys never hung out together. We saw each other plenty off the field and at the team functions throughout the season, from speaking engagements to banquets and charity events.

I remember the front office once gave us all these big, wide green and white ties that said "Jets" across them, which they asked us to wear at public events. I told them, "I don't want that tie. It looks ridiculous. What do you need a necktie for anyway?" Well, at a team function later that season, I showed up wearing a similar tie, only much narrower.

Joe said to me, "Where in the world did you get that tie?"

"Well," I said. "You remember those ties they gave us? I put the tail piece in the front."

"What did you do with the big piece?"

"I was checking the oil in my truck and I needed something to wipe the dipstick, so I used the front of the tie. It had oil all over it so I threw it away. I figured I don't really need that wide of a tie anyway."

Joe should have been the last guy to laugh. Here was a guy who you'd see walking through the hotel lobby at sunrise wearing a Hanes T-shirt under his team blazer, a pair of Bermuda shorts, and dark shades, with a wad of tobacco in the side of his mouth.

During the season and after home games, we married guys from Long Island would take our wives into the city. We'd head downtown to Namath's restaurant, Toots Shor's, or one of the other nightlife spots popular with the players. Of course, I was the designated driver during the football season, taking home the married players after they'd had a few too many. That was one time I bet they didn't mind that I don't imbibe.

We were a few games into the season and the whole team was clicking, on and off the field. Not only was Joe having a magical season, putting up crazy numbers, but I was also having the best season of my career. Most important, the Jets stood alone at the top of the Eastern Division. Without question, Joe's celebrity had a lot to do with the crowds suddenly filing into Shea Stadium. In 1965 he had won AFL Rookie of the Year, as well as the heart of just about every female in the five boroughs, eligible and otherwise. In 1966 he led the league in passing.

But if you ask me how we won over so many skeptical fans, I think it was the soaring heights to which we took our passing game. There was a feeling that maybe the impossible could be achieved, and it was a feeling that went beyond tie-dye–clad hippies. You could see that spirit everywhere in 1967, from Shea Stadium to Cape Canaveral, where the Apollo Program was progressing full speed ahead. The Soviets had already completed the first soft landing of the moon, the United States had launched the first successful weather satellite, and a South African doctor performed the first heart transplant. Texas Instruments had unveiled the first handheld calculator and the Boeing 737 had made its first flight. Even Evil

Kneivel had successfully launched his motorcycle across a row of 16 cars. And, well, Joe Willie and his Lone Star Receivers were breaking into the stratosphere with their own kind of magic: the "Jet propelled" kind.

We played one more classic against our old nemesis, the Houston Oilers. In the second quarter, Joe hit me for a 30-yard touchdown score, putting us up 14-0. But in the second half, Joe threw me a pass that was intercepted by Miller Farr, a cornerback who returned it 51 yards for a touchdown.

On the next possession, he threw it my way again and, wouldn't you know it, Miller Farr stepped in front of me and picked off another pass. Namath threw a third interception, this one returned 43 yards for a touchdown. The only good news? At least Miller Farr didn't get that one.

The boo birds of Shea called for Weeb to bench Joe after his third pick. But Weeb wasn't going to give up on Joe, and neither were the rest of us. Our offense kept battling. Unfortunately, Joe also kept throwing interceptions. He wound up throwing a total of six in that game, an unbelievable number for anybody. If they expected Joe or any of the rest of us to throw in the towel—even after his fifth interception—they had the wrong group of guys. Trailing by only eight points and with time running out, Joe drove us down the field, despite getting hit after every throw. He moved us all the way to Houston's 3-yard line. Boozer took the handoff for the score. Only we were two points short.

Except that the game wasn't over. See, the AFL did a lot of things differently than the NFL. For example, it was the first to put the players' names on the back of their jerseys. As a matter of fact, we were the only team in the league to print a player's nickname on the back of his jersey, a distinction that belonged to a linebacker named Wahoo McDaniel. The public address announcer at Shea would say, "And the tackle made by Wahoo!" Later, the announcer would say, "And the tackle made by—guess who?" And everybody in the stands would shout back, "Wahoo!" On occasion, I think sometimes he got credit for a tackle he hadn't made just so the crowd could yell, "Wahoo!" And there was another AFL rule that the NFL didn't have, one more pertinent to this game: the two-point conversion.

We were down by two points, and we had no choice but to go for it. We lined up in our formation. Standing across from me was Miller Farr, who had eaten us alive that day. He stared at me with intense eyes, bouncing up and down. I just stood there, still as could be. I heard the ball snap. *One one thousand...*Farr came up to block me. I faked one way, then went the other. *Two one thousand...*Farr took the bait. That's all I needed. I blew past him as he spun around to give chase. *Three one thousand...*I streaked across the end zone.

Meanwhile, Joe had shuffled his feet, turned, and released the ball just as the defense slammed him down for the umpteenth time that day. The ball floated up toward me. As I reached up to grab it, I felt one of the other Houston defenders grab me. I never took my eye off the ball even as the defender did everything in his power to pull me down. The moment I had the ball in my grasp, I crashed down to the turf. I got up, the football still secure in my hands. We might not have won that game, but they didn't beat us. They couldn't. We wouldn't let them. Final score: 28–28.

But then, to everybody's surprise, our season went up in flames just as quickly as Apollo 1's command module had done on the launch pad during a preflight test, killing three astronauts. The rest of the 1967 season was as frustrating as any season I'd ever played. If you can believe it, 15 players on our team had knee operations. It was probably the biggest injury bug to ever hit a ballclub in a single season. Yet despite all our injuries, we still came within a half-game of winning the Eastern Division. That was small consolation as we said good-bye to each other and went our separate ways into the off-season.

Finishing the '67 season as one of the AFL's top receivers with a league-best 1,434 receiving yards felt great, but it wasn't going to help me pay for the office that I wanted to add onto my house. And as great an honor as it was to receive the Jets' MVP award, Joe Blow at the auto shop wouldn't take that as payment for the shell I needed for the back of my pickup truck. My financial situation had improved greatly since my first job, delivering newspapers on my bike, but it didn't mean that I had forgotten what my brother, Thurman, had taught me way back when: *You need to think about if you really need something before you go ahead and buy it.* Well, I could have spent that first paycheck from my paper route on anything my heart desired—candy, toys, or a mixture of both—but I bought myself a flashlight because I figured when I rode my bicycle home in the dark, I might just want to see where I'm going. I don't see why the New York Jets writing my paychecks should make any difference. I would have happily traded in the honor for that one to give us the Eastern Division title.

Winning MVP didn't mean I played any better. It was just the way the cards fell. My stats that year had more to do with the way each game unfolded than anything else. Our team ran the ball when we had to run it. Namath threw the ball when he needed to throw it. It didn't matter if it was Sauer or Lammons or Bake or me. But when he threw it to me, I just made sure to catch it.

Quite frankly, I didn't give a toss about recognition. Don't get me wrong, I appreciated my teammates voting me their MVP. I felt I had been as good as any receiver in the league for a while and it was nice to be recognized—especially to be recognized by the only people whose opinion mattered worth a darn to me. With that said,

I knew the main reason I put up extra great stats that year was that we finally had a balanced offense. In other words, our opponents couldn't afford to double- or triple-team me without paying dearly for it. As far as I was concerned, I had gone out there and played to the best of my ability. Individual stats meant nothing; what mattered was how the Jets did in the won-lost department. And we weren't there yet.

Usually, the only way to get them to forget something was to go out there the next week and play well. Well, for me, it took a little longer to lose my bad reputation in New York. It took a good seven years. I learned that most of the time, the best thing to do was not even read the papers. Weeb used to say to the rookies, "Don't believe all you read in the newspapers or hear on the television."

My whole life I had been trying to do things better, to do them as perfectly as possible. It was this impulse, this passion, this calling that Joe and I shared. Together we designed and ran pass plays that embraced common sense as much as they did intuition, a balance of precise science and improvisation. Outdated rules were hindrances to be shit-canned, on and off the field. A bold step forward could come only when you no longer feared trying things a little differently, regardless of what other people might say.

I guarantee you that neither Joe nor I lost any sleep over that. It was clear to us that lot of so-called smart people didn't know what they were talking about. And that was okay. They could lecture us all they wanted on fashion or religion or politics or the length of our sideburns, for that matter. But there was one thing that nobody was going to tell us: how to operate a passing game. Come to think of it, same goes for propane conversion systems and air-conditioning units, too.

Back in El Paso, when I was tightening a pipe in the refinery's boiler room (*one game*) or when I was installing an air-conditioner under the dashboard of a camping cruiser (*one game*) or when I was mowing the backyard on my John Deere (*one game*) I had one thing on my mind, and that was how close we had come to winning the Eastern Division. One game. That was all.

Okay, I probably wasn't thinking about how those 15 knee operations cheated us out of a playoff berth while I was fishing for trout in the Pecos River. But then a man in waders really shouldn't have anything on his mind. He should just cast his line in the rippling water and let his worries float gently downstream.

No Heidi Ho

BY 1968 SONNY WERBLIN HAD TAKEN a struggling Titans franchise, characterized by low attendance and a ticket operation that was run out of Harry Wismer's living room, and turned it into a first-class franchise. In addition to that, he'd forced the huge and profitable New York Giants to share, at least partially, the biggest stage in the world. He also negotiated the TV contract with NBC that all but singlehandedly rescued the AFL. What we earned as football players was a pittance compared to what today's players make. Still, the sight of 35 big men in cleats making a mad dash through the streets of Manhattan to cash their game checks was a thing of the past. And as a result of Werblin's $400,000 contract to Joe, we all ended up getting a raise. So that was a good deal.

That off-season, all of the players received a letter notifying us that Sonny Werblin had been bought out of his ownership stake in the Jets. The new group in charge assured us that nothing would change with regard to our situation. We were going to continue to have a first-class operation. That was a relief to hear.

Later on, some people said that Werblin had been ousted, but I was in the dark as far as that goes. So far as I knew, that was a business deal between businessmen. They were the bosses and we were the hired help, so to speak. So I figured we were going to just keep doing what we were supposed to do once it came time to report to training camp.

The other big news in that off-season was that training camp was being moved from Peekskill, where it had been for years, to a new location: Hofstra University in Hempstead, Long Island. There were no complaints from me. The facilities at the military academy were rough—cramped, humid quarters, bad cafeteria food, and a mediocre field. On the contrary, everything at Hofstra was first-rate—good food, big dressing rooms, and a real nice practice field. Shoot, the dorms were even air-conditioned! You have no idea how nice it was not to have to bring a window screen to training camp.

I had to hand it to Weeb for insisting that his guys train under better conditions, ones more suitable for professional ballplayers than military cadets. The move to Hofstra absolutely gave our team a big lift. A lot of the players didn't live too far away. Now it was possible for guys to spend their free Saturdays at home with their family. With everybody feeling happy and comfortable, we could put all our focus where it belonged—on taking the Eastern Division crown from the Houston Oilers.

With only eight AFL teams, I'd say that each team had a rivalry with everybody else. That's just the way it was. But we had a little bit extra rivalry with the Oakland Raiders—at least after Joe arrived in 1965. The fact that he lacked a lot of mobility wasn't exactly a secret to the other teams around the league. It was nothing new, therefore, for defenses to make reaching Namath and making him pay their primary objective. However, a couple of the Raiders defenders went a little too far in their zeal to hit Namath, delivering some late blows. Of course, the press liked to blow these couple of incidents out of proportion, until everybody believed that the two teams had this "simmering animosity" between each other.

The towering 6'8", 275-pound Ben Davidson had a reputation as the biggest, baddest bully on the Raiders' defense. In fact, he couldn't have been a nicer, more regular guy. He started his pro career with the Giants until Allie Sherman condemned him to the scrap heap, just as surely as he had me. Ben wound up as a reserve player on the Redskins, but they dumped him shortly thereafter when he came to camp a mere 40 pounds overweight. After Washington waived him, the Jets expressed interest in signing him. Davidson couldn't wait to come back to New York, because now he shared a goal with Sam Huff and me—to prove Allie Sherman wrong. As it happened, the Raiders informed him that they had purchased his contract and that if he refused to come and play for them they would ban him from playing for anybody else.

Although Ben didn't get to show Sherman up in New York, he did get a second shot in Oakland, where he transformed himself into one heck of a defensive lineman. With his handlebar moustache and some of the wild tales he told (such as cruising around Mexico on a motorcycle) added together with one or two late hits on Namath, gave the press the perfect symbol of the "bad guy Raiders." Ben didn't break the law. He didn't bother anybody. So what if he rode a motorcycle? I knew a lot of guys who drove motorcycles, only they didn't get much publicity for it. Heck, even I rode a motorcycle. A Yamaha 250. But then I guess I'm not playing defense or knocking the socks off quarterbacks. But as far as I'm concerned, Ben wasn't a bad guy at all. Quite the contrary, he was a great player. If all people want to remember are a few late hits, they can do that. What I remember about Ben is how much tougher he made beating the Raiders.

And he wasn't the only member of the Silver and Black who we had to contend with. Dan Birdwell was another outstanding Oakland defender. I've known him since high school. He had grown up 30 miles away from me, in Big Spring, Texas. We were friendly, having competed at the same track meets. I ran the hurdles, he did the shotput and discus. But even though he was a friend and I was always impressed by his athletic talent, on game day, he and everybody else on the Raiders was the enemy.

Sometimes we would stay in Oakland through the week before we went down for our next game in San Diego. It was not unusual for Jets players like me and Larry Grantham to get together with our "enemies," like Ben Davidson and Dan Birdwell and work out at some gym or grab dinner or play a round of golf.

What people have to understand is that each AFL team played every other team in the league twice a year. As a result, all of the players got to know each other well and many became good friends. Nobody competed harder against each other than we did, but at the same time, that rivalry began and ended on the field. Maybe because we were all in the same boat. For nearly 10 years, the press looked on us as second-class citizens to the NFL. It made us feel as if we were united. And we were all out there to play and have fun and enjoy the games. So, for example, every time I came to Denver, I'd catch up with my pal Goose Gonsoulin, who I'd known since before the league existed. But on the field of play, he was there to win, and you can be sure I was too. During the game, the only friends you have are the ones wearing the same color jerseys.

Through the first three games of the 1967 season, the Raiders defense had dominated their opponents. In their season opener, they thrashed the Broncos 51–0, holding their offense to just three first downs in the entire game. Next, they pounded the Patriots at home 35–7. Surely, their next opponent, the league's reigning champion Kansas City Chiefs, led by strong-armed star quarterback Len Dawson, would put a dent in their armor. Nope. Instead, the Raiders defense held Dawson to just 150 yards passing while delivering five sacks and forcing three turnovers for their third-straight win. And we were up next.

Our first meeting of the 1968 season took place on a cold and gusty Saturday in October, in front of a Shea Stadium crowd of more than 63,000. As expected, the Raiders were blitz happy. Joe responded to the furious rush by calling "25 Lag," a play that was disguised to look like a pass that was actually a run. In order to fake the defense, Namath had to hold onto the ball until the Raiders defensive line advanced deep into the backfield. At the same time, his blockers would release and let the foaming-mouthed defenders get through to Namath. Only when Ben Davidson and his posse were a step away from pounding Namath would the quarterback hand it off to Emerson Boozer on a draw. Suddenly, their defenders had to spin back on a dime and try to capture Boozer. By the time they reacted, it was too late. Boozer had already busted up the middle and was streaking into the open field.

The key to pulling off the play hinged on Namath's ability to sell the play to the defense, which meant waiting as long as he possibly could before giving up the ball. As a result, he got leveled every time he ran that play—and he ran that play a lot that day.

Raiders defender Tom Keating remembered all the licks they got on Joe: "In those days, the goal post was on the goal line. "I hit Joe Namath and knocked him right into the goal post just as he was dumping the ball. Just mashed the shit out of him. I thought I'd killed the guy. He stood up. He was okay. And Dave Herman was yelling at me. I didn't do anything! They didn't take him out. The next play, he threw like a 60-yard pass to Bake Turner. Now, what does that tell you?"

With the Raiders' blitzing defense, there wasn't much time for us, his Lone Star Receivers, to get open for him. But then excuses weren't going to be much help to Joe as he got hammered by multiple guys. He got one pass off to tight end Pete Lammons but Pete was dropped for a one-yard gain. He found Sauer one time but he managed to pick up only three yards. And that was pretty much it. It was my job as a receiver to try to bail out Joe when he absolutely had nowhere else to go. I wound up accounting for just about the entire sum of our passing attack that day. It wasn't much—86 yards on four catches—but it was just enough help for Joe to pull out an improbable 27-14 victory.

Stung by our victory, the Raiders defense, nicknamed the "11 Angry Men," would go on a quarterback rampage around the league, emerging from their reign of terror with eight straight wins. But that whole time, they had been gearing up for revenge against us—awaiting our arrival to Oakland-Alameda County Coliseum in Week 13. I guess the fact that we had denied them a perfect regular season hadn't exactly endeared us to them.

Going into our second-to-last game of the season, I had lost track of how many of my teammates had been knocked out by knee injuries. I know it was in the double digits. Emerson Boozer, the kid who had done a fine job filling the big shoes of Matt Snell, took a blind shot to the knee in Kansas City and was carted off the field, done for the season. That was a big loss. But there wasn't much use crying about it.

The more guys dropped like flies, the harder I worked as a receiver. As it would turn out, I was putting together my best season ever, breaking away from defender after defender and streaking for touchdown after touchdown. There was no catching me that year, not the way I was going. Although I was glad to be playing so well, what really made me happy was that we were going into Oakland tied for first place with Houston and vying for the Eastern Division championship.

Unfortunately, Joe was starting the Oakland game with a broken bone in his ankle, which he had suffered in that wild comeback against Houston earlier in the season when we connected on that two-point conversion. He'd also managed to mangle his thumb on his throwing hand. Not that anybody knew any more about his bum ankle or swollen thumb than they did about how his knees ballooned like a pair of cantaloupes in the training room after each game.

Joe's knees were so bad that his dad had asked him to quit football so he wouldn't batter them further. *That wasn't possible,* Joe surmised. *They couldn't get any more screwed up than they already were.*

That's not to say Joe was thrilled about being a fixed target for the Raiders. "We used to have a saying: 'the one-eyed monster never lies.' Talking about the projector," said Namath. "If you looked at the film, Big Ben [Davidson] did things that were uncalled for. The Raiders were always a little extracurricular." Although this was true, Joe never once whined about it to the officials or even us, his teammates.

"Namath was a hell of a guy," recalled Tony Veteri, AFL head official. "He never moaned when he got hit. He never moaned about anything." Not that it would have done him any good.

On December 17, we took the field in Oakland before 53,000 fans and a national television audience. Oakland was a tough place to play. Their fans had a reputation for being loud and, more to the point, crazy. They would throw bottles at the visitors' sideline. When they ran out of bottles, they threw cups. I'd been hit with plenty of cups while on the sidelines in Oakland. But the real reason we hadn't won in Oakland in our last eight trips out there had to do with the abundance of talent on the team we were facing.

Although the Raiders' pass rush was scary good, their offense was also a force to be reckoned with. They had their own talented quarterback-receiver combo in Daryle Lamonica and Fred Biletnikoff. Lamonica, who would go on to be the AFL's MVP, had such a cannon arm that it earned him the nickname "the Mad Bomber." Any time he and Joe met, boy, it promised to be a shootout at the O.K. Corral.

In this contest, it was Joe and I who struck first, connecting on a 28-yard touchdown pass on the opening drive. Then, in the second quarter, Joe scooped up a fumble on the 1-yard line. He dove headfirst into the mouth of the defense. Touchdown. We went into halftime up 14–10 as Namath's quick release and my sprinter's speed frustrated their charging pass rushers.

The tide started to turn against us in the third quarter. That's when Ike Lassiter, a 6'5", 270-pound defender, hammered Namath, forcing him to throw an interception. In the second half, the Raiders scored 21 unanswered points to take a 31–14 lead. Then, early in the fourth quarter, Namath scrambled out of the pocket, making him vulnerable to a big hit. Davidson was bearing down on him. As Namath went out of bounds, Davidson came in and hit him, full force. Joe's helmet went flying off his head. With him lying there face-down on the turf, I thought, *He's killed him.* But Namath struggled to get to his feet and staggered, shell-shocked, over to the wrong sideline. The team doctor quickly examined him. There was no way he could keep playing. But Joe wouldn't listen. We couldn't believe it. Namath was slowly walking back to the huddle.

On the next play, Joe hit Pete Lammons for a nine-yard gain. The Raiders kept getting their shots in at us, but we fought back each time. Namath hit Sauer for a 24-yard touchdown, cutting the lead to 10. But even when Oakland scored again, all but putting the game out of reach, we kept fighting.

"I don't know how much more the guy can take," Dan Birdwell said after the game. "One time he looked right at me and grinned and said something, but he could have been talking a foreign language.... It was like he was punchy or something."

With time running out, Namath found me in the end zone for the final touchdown of the game. We had lost 38–29, all but ending any hope at the playoffs. But when we walked off that field, we did it with our heads held high.

Our locker room was full of tired, battered bodies. George Sauer and I had accounted for almost every reception that day—Sauer finished with 7 catches for 146 yards and one touchdown, and I caught 12 passes for 159 yards and two touchdowns. By season's end, we wound up ranked No. 1 and No. 2 in receiving. It would be the only time in AFL history in which two players from the same team owned the two top spots.

As for Joe, he greeted the reporters with a wide grin, his right jaw swollen up like a beach ball. The reporters asked when it happened. "This morning," answered Namath. "I bit into a real tough steak for breakfast."

I went back to my hotel room and got some much-needed shuteye. Meanwhile, I'm sure Joe was downstairs at the bar having a grand old time, carrying on as if the Raiders had barely grazed him when they in fact had nearly put him in the ER. I'm sure if I came down, I'd find Joe enjoying himself, all the same. He'd be turned around on a barstool, a glass of scotch in his hand, surrounded by good friends, pretty ladies, and other well-wishers hoping for an autograph. He would probably buy a round for the bar. Somebody in the crowd would probably raise his glass. "To Joe!"

"To Joe!" everybody would repeat back.

Joe would raise his glass. "To Ben Davidson!" And then laugh heartily through his busted-up mouth.

And by then, I'd be sleeping peacefully, dreaming of spotting a flock of colorful birds while I wandered through the snowy woodlands of a Texas winter.

• • •

When the X-rays came back on Joe's face, they revealed a fractured right cheekbone. Houston eliminated us from the postseason a day before our season finale against the San Diego Chargers. The press deemed it a meaningless game. But it wasn't a meaningless game to us Jets players who had battled through a season of adversity. It wasn't meaningless to Namath, who had a broken jaw and was still suiting up. It wasn't meaningless to the Jets' Lone Star Receivers, who had pulled off one of the best seasons of any receiving group in AFL history, even when our running game all but evaporated by midseason due to injuries. It wasn't meaningless to our defense, guys like Larry Grantham, who had been gutting it out in the bloody trenches since 1960.

On December 24, Joe and I put on one last show that season. Of the four touchdowns Joe threw that day, three of them went to me. We connected on a 13-yard touchdown pass in the first quarter, then a 26-yard touchdown strike in the second quarter, and a 36-yard score in the third quarter. Joe ended up throwing for 343 yards and four touchdowns—all with a fractured jaw, a busted thumb, a hurt ankle, and two bum knees. While he became the first quarterback to pass for more than 4,000 yards in a season, what pleased me most about our 42–31 win was that he hadn't thrown one interception. Sure, he still had a little work to do...but Joseph was learning.

By season's end, everybody in New York had an opinion about Joe. To impatient fans, he threw too many interceptions. To the critics in the press room, he stayed out at the bars too late. But as for me and the other 39 players in the locker room, we saw a young man who had taken one heck of a beating that year and didn't say a word about it; a guy who wasn't afraid to go toe-to-toe against anybody, no matter how big the stick a person carried; a guy who refused to throw in the towel even after taking more blows than seemed humanly possible. Maybe it's because I've lived my whole life not far from the Alamo, but a guy like that, someone who never gives up on himself or his team no matter how great the odds are stacked against him—well, that's the kind of guy I'm proud to follow into battle, whether it's on Sunday or any other day of the week.

It turned out I wasn't alone. At the end of training camp the following year, the team called a final players-only meeting. An announcement was made: the team had chosen Joe to be their offensive captain. We were sending him a message. We had all the weapons—a great offense, a great defense—so it was time he stepped up. It was time for him to lead us to a championship.

Our first game of the 1968 season just days away, the team had rallied around Joe, but we were having a serious issue with our coach. While Joe had always negotiated his salary directly with Sonny Werblin, probably over glasses of Johnnie Walker at P.J. Clarke's, the rest of us poor souls had to hammer out our playing contracts with Weeb, who was just about the cheapest *sonofagun* you'll ever meet. On the eve of our huge season opener against the Kansas City Chiefs, five of our best veterans—Verlon Biggs, George Sauer, Matt Snell, defensive captain Johnny Sample, and I—still hadn't signed on the dotted line. It was unbelievable.

Of course, I wasn't going to let that nonsense sidetrack me from my goal, which was to topple one of the AFL's most successful franchises from its high perch. Under legendary coach Hank Stram, they always had outstanding ballclubs. It was the Chiefs who had made it to the first AFL-NFL World Championship Game (later to be renamed the Super Bowl) in January 1967. Although they ultimately lost to Vince Lombardi and his mighty Green Bay Packers, I believe that had more to do with the greatness of the coach they faced than anything else. I knew all too well that they swept us in 1967, blowing us out both games that season.

But as we walked onto the field of Municipal Stadium on that sunny fall afternoon, the largest sports crowd in Kansas City history showering us with boos, we felt this time was different. We had never had such a balanced attack before—an excellent running game, an explosive passing offense and, at long last, the final ingredient: one of the best defenses in the league.

The game started with Joe delivering a perfect arcing spiral to me, which I caught in full stride. Here's the call from Merle Harmon on WABC Radio in New York: "Namath back to throw, dropping way back, looking and throwing long for Maynard, he's out there at the 20, 15, 10, 5...touchdown! He got behind Goldie Sellers by a step. Joe Namath went for the bomb on second and inches, a bit of a surprise element possibly."

Then, we teamed up for a 30-yard pass play late in the second quarter to extend our lead to 17–3.

"Now it is second down and 10 on the Kansas City 30 with 1:55 left to play in the first half...Namath calls it for New York, drops back to pass, looking, throwing for Maynard at the 5 and...he's got it! He's in! Touchdown!"

In the second half, the Chiefs returned an 80-yard punt return, and after the great Jan Stenerud had kicked his fourth field goal of the game, our lead had dwindled to a measly single point. With the score 20–19 and with six minutes left on the game clock, our offense took over, backed up deep. It was simple. *Keep the chains moving so that the Chiefs don't get it back with great field position.*

After two sideline passes to Sauer, we were down to one last chance to maintain possession, which was to get a first down on the next play. We pick up the first and Kansas City probably doesn't have enough time to get the ball back. If we fall short, Stenerud will likely get a chance to come in and coldly put the dagger in our heart.

Here's the call: "Crowd trying to spur that defense on now with third down and 11 on the New York 4. Sauer wide to the left, Maynard wide to the right... Namath back in the end zone to throw, throws slant-in to Maynard at the 15! Don spinning and going to the 20, brought down at the 20-yard line. And the Jets got out of the hole."

The short quick-in. Classic timing route. A play we had been working on together since that first day of training camp in 1965. I broke off the line of scrimmage. *One one thousand.* I cut across the middle, getting a half-step on the cornerback. *Two one thousand.* Streaking at full speed...I turn...the ball should be there...and it is! I turn it upfield and get enough yards for the first down. After that, Namath made a series of critical third downs to keep the drive alive, and, in fact, we used up the remaining time on the clock. And Jan Stenerud and his kicking foot stayed on the sideline.

"That last drive by Namath was fabulous," said the Chiefs' legendary coach Hank Stram after the game. "I felt there was no way they could go from their 4 and maintain possession to the end of the game. I'd have given 100-to-1 odds."

Kicking off the season the way we did, beating a very good Kansas City team (who would end up losing only two more games that season), made all the difference in the world. What's more, Namath had shown in that final drive that he could be trusted to steer the ship smartly and that he understood what it meant to trust his team to help him make the plays to win the game. And his progress as a quarterback was my boon as a receiver. I wound up with 203 receiving yards on eight carries in that big victory—the best single day I had ever had as a pro.

After besting Boston 47–31, we took a plane to Buffalo. The Bills had lost their first- and second-string quarterbacks, and we came into the game favored by 19 points. Sharing the good mood of his players, Weeb convinced the pilot to fly us over Niagara Falls so that we could see it out our windows.

It would be the last good sight we would get to see that trip. Under pressure all day from the Bills' pass rushers, Namath threw five interceptions, three of which were returned for Buffalo touchdowns. We lost 37–35 despite the fact our defense surrendered only one touchdown. Buffalo wouldn't win another game that season.

We left Buffalo embarrassed. *Bad game. Shake it off.* Two weeks later, we hosted Denver, a 20-point underdog. We stormed out to a seven-point lead as Namath threw a long bomb that I caught and sprinted 60 yards to set up a touchdown. Just when it looked like we would cruise to an easy victory, Namath veered the offense right off the cliff. Like a bad movie you've seen before, Namath threw five interceptions against the Broncos, and we lost 21-13. The Shea crowd really got on Joe after that one.

By now, the defense was also giving it to Joe during practice, nobody more than Gerry Philbin. The team was in a film session the week after the Buffalo game, preparing for our upcoming game. Philbin shouted, "Hey, Joe, remember, this week we're wearing green." There wasn't much humor about the way he said it, either. Namath just kind of turned his head back a little to Philbin. He didn't say a word.

By the time we came out to practice after Joe's second five-interception game, the rest of the defense had joined Philbin in picking on Joe. That whole week at practice, every time he threw a bad pass or an interception, somebody on the defense would call out, "Hey, Joe, we're wearing green this week."

I'm sure Joe wondered how he could have possibly thrown 10 interceptions in two games, especially after his amazing clutch performance in the opener against Kansas City. I wasn't worried about Joe. I knew he wasn't going to let Gerry Philbin—or anybody else for that matter—get under his skin or lose one iota of confidence over a negative comment. That's just the way he was; he took everything in stride. He was a grown man. He didn't need a pep talk. Clive Rush, Joe, the other receivers, and I just went through the game film together until we saw what went wrong and then figured out how to fix it.

The next Tuesday, at practice, veteran defender Verlon Biggs showed up unshaven and said he had an announcement to make to the players. While Biggs was a great teammate, he wasn't much for giving speeches. He told us he wasn't going to shave until the team had clinched the Eastern Division title—and that was all he had to say. It was kind of funny. When I came in with my long hair and sideburns in 1958, I was singled out as the lone rule breaker. But there I was, 10 years later, watching as my teammates, most of them under 25 years old, one by one stood up and said they also refused to obey the league's rules on appearance. It wasn't a political protest, like so many taking place across the nation. Rather, it was a show of solidarity. No matter what happened in the rest of the season, we were in it together. Of course, if Joe was going to participate, he was going to do it in style. He grew a Pancho Villa moustache. For some reason, everybody else called it a Fu Manchu. *Fu Manchu? What the heck was that?* I'd never been to China.

After that, we got back some of the great team chemistry that we had felt after we knocked off the Chiefs in Week 1. More important, Joe was a different quarterback from that point forward. He was finally heeding the words of us veterans: *Don't try to force good things. Good things will happen exactly when you don't force them. Meanwhile, let our great defense and our great running game win the game for us.* He rediscovered the confidence he had shown in his teammates in that Chiefs game, rather than make things happen on his own. This new, team-oriented approach translated into four straight victories. At the same time, the fans and sportswriters were wondering what was wrong with Namath, who hadn't thrown one touchdown during any of our wins. The answer, of course, was *nothing.* Namath had been smart with the ball, allowing our great running game and excellent defense to shine like never before.

The number of Namath-to-Maynard long bombs might have decreased as Joe stopped trying to dictate events through his own great talent, but our team was getting better as a whole. I guarantee you that we four guys from Texas had no problem going six straight games without catching a touchdown pass. Why should we? We won every one of those contests. Now we were really having fun. Opposing defenses could no longer focus on just shutting down our high-powered passing game. In fact, they could line up against us any way they wanted. It really didn't matter. We were going to run our same offense, and good luck to them stopping it.

What helped Namath so much was that he had so many options to go to. It wasn't like those lean years when I was pretty much the only big threat. With some of those 25 quarterbacks I played with before Namath, I might have felt it necessary to use more trickery to get open. But when you had a guy like Namath throwing the ball and a complement of All-Pro receivers around you in Bake Turner, Pete Lammons, and George Sauer, you didn't really worry about trying to fool the defensive back.

He didn't need to force it to one guy with the game on line. He could sit back, relax, and calmly hit the open receiver. And that's how it was with us. Bake led the team in receiving one year, another year it was Sauer, and then another year it was me. I probably owe half my touchdowns to big tight end Pete Lammons, because all those years that we ran the square-out he'd disturb the linebacker or the safety on his side of the field just long enough to spring me loose, and then I was off to the races. By Lammons doing his job perfectly, the safety couldn't drop off and nail me or make the interception.

In mid-November, we boarded a plane to face our biggest challenge yet—a rematch with the Oakland Raiders. On account of the bad weather, the pilot couldn't get the plane to the ramp after we touched down. We were told we would have to exit the plain right there in the middle of the tarmac. Meanwhile, airport personnel had pushed up makeshift ramps to one side of the plane. Forty guys, some weighing more than 280 pounds, made their way down these little ramps in the freezing cold of night. Once we made it down to the ground, we were told to grab our bags and walk back to the terminal, a good distance from the plane. As soon as we got to the terminal, we got rides to a nearby hotel called the Edgewater.

Downstairs, in the hotel's restaurant, a bunch of the players were sitting around, eating their dinner, looking out the window at the swimming pool. Now, there's always one guy who's got some comment to make. I don't recall exactly who it was on that occasion, but one of the players said, "Hey, somebody ought to go jump in the swimming pool." Yeah, right. Nobody was going out swimming, not that night with the temperature so low.

"Man, I'll make you a deal," I said. "I'll go jump into the pool. I'll even go off the high board, clothes and all."

There was some laughter in the room, and then one of the guys spoke: "I'll donate $5 to see that!"

Then another guy interjected, "I'll put in $2."

"I'll tell you what," I said, as my teammates began throwing their dollar bills in a pile on the table. "I'll even jump off wearing my green Jets blazer."

I waited until everybody had finished putting their money in, and then I said, "Put a little extra in the pot, guys. Not only will I jump off the high board, I'll do a gainer. For y'all who don't know what a gainer is, that's when you run out there frontward and do a backward flip."

Well, before you know it, guys start tossing more bills onto the table and the pile had grown higher still. Then I took off my boots, gathered all the loose bills in my arms, and stuffed them in my boots along with my other valuables. I went outside and climbed the ladder as the rest of the team looked on through the window.

Of course, what they didn't know was that I could swim and dive really well. Once I got to the top of the ladder, I stepped onto the high board. At that height, it was even colder and windier. On three, I ran down the board in my nice green Jets blazer, flipped backward into the air, and fell through the night sky. The cold water hit me all at once—a worse shock to the system than any linebacker could ever deliver, that's for sure. But as debilitating as the hypothermia-inducing water was, that wasn't my biggest obstacle in getting out of the pool. That green Jets blazer I had on was made out of heavy wool. The moment it got soaked with water it weighed five times more. I felt like my upper body was suddenly wrapped in metal chains. Forget about swimming gracefully to the edge—now I was in a full doggy-paddle, struggling with all my might to keep from sinking. Gee whiz, I nearly drowned.

When I finally managed to get out of the water, I was frozen to the bone. Without stopping, I scurried over to my boots, pinched them up between my thumb and fingers, and got the heck out of there. I rushed up to my room. My roommate, Bake Turner, was reclining on his bed when I burst in, drenched and shivering.

"Well, Maynard," he said. "How much did you make?"

"I don't know. Let's see." So I turned over my cowboy boots and shook them over the bed. The crumpled dollar bills fell out and we counted up the loot. I'd raked in $75. All in all it worked out really well, minus the almost-drowning part.

The next day, at the team meeting, Weeb scolded us for the swimming pool incident, calling our behavior both silly and stupid. He especially chewed me out.

The game turned into another knock-down, drag-out brawl between two very talented teams. There was lots of scoring and what seemed like just as many fights. Of course, I wasn't about to participate in any bench-clearing brawl. At one point, I grabbed Mathis on the shoulder to keep him from running onto the field to join the fracas. "Where you going, T-Bird?" I said. "We got the best seat in the house right here."

The lead see-sawed back and forth through the first three quarters with the Raiders taking a 22–19 lead into the final 15 minutes.

"Well, we were backed up on our own 1-yard line," recalled Namath. "*Our own 1-yard line.* But Don had this wonderful knack of being able to go after the football, being able to leap up and get it at its highest point. Even though we were on our own 1-yard line, I decided to go ahead and throw the bomb. I called a goal pattern and then I laid it out there with all the confidence in the world that Don would somehow come down with the football. Well, he did—for a 51-yard gain. Just like that."

Yeah, just like that.

"So now we're on the 49-yard line," continued Namath. "When we came back to the huddle I said, 'Hey, Don, how you feeling?' He said, 'Shoot, Joe, I'm just fine.' I said, 'You think you can do that again?' He said, 'Hey, you go ahead and lay it on out there. I'll go get it.'

"I called the same play. Goal pattern to Don. Then, I just reared back and flung the ball as high and hard as I could downfield. As the spiral floated down, Don adjusted his route just enough to leap up after it, pull it down, and step into the end zone for a touchdown. Two plays for 99 yards, and neither one of those passes were good. He just made the plays."

I was never going to be the biggest or strongest receiver. I knew that. I was the same undersized 175-pound receiver in 1968 that I was as a rookie. Heck, I might never look or act the way that an elite receiver should. And there were times during a season when I might have done some strange things—whether it's jumping in a frozen pool, or running routes blindfolded in practice or insisting that I wear No. 13—but I made that comment to let Weeb know one thing. Nobody was more serious about playing the game of football than I was. Nobody was more dedicated to becoming better at his position, each and every year, through rigorous study and grueling workouts. Nobody put more effort into keeping his body in top shape. And that's why, in the 10 years since I played my first down in the pros, nobody had caught me from behind. Well, maybe just once. There was a guy in Denver, I think.

Jim Turner added a field goal to give us a 29–22 lead over the Raiders. We had the game all but sewn up. And I was on my way to completing the best game of my career, catching 10 passes for 228 yards. Finally, after labeling me the biggest fumbler in history and an NFL reject, the New York press would have to acknowledge my great performance!

What happened next would go down in sports lore. Lamonica hooked up with Charles Smith on a 20-yard pass. A face-mask penalty put the ball on our 43-yard line. Moments later, Lamonica hit Smith again—this time for a touchdown. The Jets fumbled the ensuing kickoff, the Raiders recovered on our 2-yard line, and they punched it in. Two touchdowns. Nine seconds. 43–32 Raiders. The game became known as the "Heidi Bowl," because the network cut away to the movie *Heidi* with about a minute left on the clock. Of course, we had no idea that the network had been flooded with angry calls. After all, we were at the game. *We were in the game.*

We got back home around 3:00 AM, so most of us didn't know what had happened until they woke up the next morning. Weeb's wife called him and said congratulations. He said, "What for? We lost the game." Well, she and everybody else in New York who was watching the game had missed the improbable ending. I'm sure when people picked up the newspaper the next day and read that the Jets had lost, they quickly scanned the column to find out if that was a misprint. It blew everyone's mind. How's that possible? Well, it was just one of those things.

After the shocking finale, I made sure to come over to Weeb. I said, "I guess that swimming pool deal wasn't a big thing, now was it?"

No Breeze in Windy Shea

WHEN YOU HAVE A QUARTERBACK who can rifle the ball 70 yards on the fly and still hit the receiver on a dime, you might be tempted to tell him to let 'er rip on every play. Bombs away! The problem is, any quarterback who relies on his talent to force big plays down the field is going to run into trouble sooner or later—even if he's lucky enough to possess a spectacular arm like Namath's. The long bomb can be a devastating weapon, to be sure, but the secret's knowing exactly how and when to take your shot. Aggressiveness is a good trait but, then again, so is being smart and under control. If the deep pass is there, by all means, don't hesitate to pull the trigger on it. But you have to let things play out and trust that if the big play isn't there for you to make, it be will down the road.

I knew that if Joe learned to read the defense and stay patient in the pocket, then during the course of the game he'd spot a weakness in the coverage that he could exploit. Or it might be something one of the coaches sees—maybe Weeb or Clive tells him that he can work the delay draw against their blitz. Or maybe a receiver makes a quick comment to Joe just before we get into the huddle. But ultimately, he alone has to make the call. And the rest of us have to do our job by running our routes precisely and not cheating to get open. As I said, we only had one busted pass play in nine years.

If Joe likes what he sees—maybe I've got one-on-one coverage down the sideline—then he'll turn it loose downfield. But if it looks like a bad bet, he'll want to check the ball down, maybe hand it off to Boozer or Snell, rather than try to force it in there. That kind of self-control is harder than it might seem, especially when you have the talent to make every throw, no matter how difficult. And the thing is, he'd probably been making incredible plays with his arm his whole life, from middle school all the way through college. But in the pros, it's a whole other world. The defenders are quicker and smarter, and they'll make you pay for too much confidence on your part, just as surely as they will for too much uncertainty. But if you've done your work in practice and paid attention at team meetings and studied the game film—basically if you've done everything humanly possible to prepare yourself for the big day—then you don't have to worry about making a mistake when it matters most. As each moment arises in the game, you'll have a clear vision of how to react. And if you trust that your teammates will also know how to react to every situation, no matter how critical, then you will succeed most of the time. After all, it's a game, and in every game there's an element of unpredictability. You don't really know what's going to happen until you play it.

Which brings me to three days before 1969. On that frigid December afternoon, we faced our longtime nemesis, the Oakland Raiders, with a few important things to settle. One, the AFL Championship, and two, a spot in the Super Bowl.

On account of the bad weather, we left our homes in Long Beach earlier than usual and headed to the stadium in shared cars. I don't recall the temperature that day, but it was cold, as cold as could be.

A little while later, Marilyn arrived at the stadium, gathering in the private upstairs dining room with the other wives. Just before game time, they took their seats on the 40-yard line. The Jets' front office had arranged for the player's wives to sit there throughout the season.

Of the 16 married players who lived out at the Azore Apartments in Long Beach, I'd say that all of us had our wives at the game. Most of our kids were home with babysitters or kinfolk, watching the contest on TV. The wives of the guys who lived year-round in New York—like Al Atkinson, Ralph Baker, Emerson Boozer, and Matt Snell—were all there too. The stage was set.

I had also come in early that day to get treatment on my hamstring, which I had strained a couple weeks earlier in a game against Cincinnati. In anticipation of this playoff game, I didn't even suit up for our regular-season finale against the Dolphins. I could have probably played, but we'd already wrapped up our division. I wanted to let the hamstring heal as much as possible for the biggest game in the history of our franchise.

By game day, my hamstring wasn't bothering me too much. But wanting to be careful, I came in early, loosened up in the whirlpool, and then had the trainer rub down both my legs. When I came out for pregame warm-ups, I learned fast that I needed to take shorter strides to avoid putting too much pressure on my sore leg.

To combat the frigid temperatures, most of the guys wore flannel shirts under their jerseys. But I've always found, even walking around in the cold as a kid, flannels cling to your body. I'd always end up getting too hot or, as soon as I stood still, too cold. So I tried wearing a nylon windbreaker during workouts in the cold and I couldn't believe how well it kept me warm and dry—and it was so light that you hardly even knew you had it on. And of course, the less you have to carry on your body, the quicker you can move around. Also, with the thinner material on your arms, you have more feel for the ball. While those big linemen would be perspiring in their heavy flannel, I'd be warm and dry in my breathable nylon. Shoot, it worked great whether you were out hunting rabbits *or* running pass plays.

I was also probably one of the only guys who wore cut-off sleeves. I just hated long sleeves—the same way I hated jerseys that came all the way up to your neck—which is why I became the first person to wear a V-neck jersey in the pros. If you look at photos from that AFL Championship, you'll also see I was the only guy who had a white dickie on; I wore it around my neck almost like a scarf.

It was cold and windy, but more than that, it was gusty. "The wind at Shea Stadium can create illusions," wrote *Sports Illustrated's* Edwin Shrake, describing the conditions in 1968. "It blows in from the outfield, whirls erratically inside the bowl, curls around the knees and down the coat collars of people in their seats, rouses little dust devils from the infield dirt and can make a thrown football dance like Joe Namath on a night out." Who knows, it could have been gusting up to 50 miles per hour, but in which direction depended on chance. Let's say that straight through the uprights is 12:00. If the wind was really gusting, our field-goal kicker, Jim Turner, might have to line up to kick the ball at 10:00 and let the gusting wind catch it and push it back across the middle. But five minutes later, the wind might have suddenly shifted, and now he's aiming the ball at 2:00, figuring the wind will push it back to the inside so it goes straight through the goal post at 12:00.

The ground wasn't completely frozen, but it was hard and slick. The wind that blew in from the open end of the stadium had stripped a lot of the grass off the field, making the surface more slippery. And you have to remember, we shared Shea with the New York Mets, so the outfield area was grass but the infield part was dirt—frozen, bumpy dirt. Strangely enough, the field also sloped down to the outfield.

Then there was the tarp issue. For some reason, it covered only the field itself. So any of the water that collected in the out-of-bound area of the field ran down under the tarp, making the sidelines and edges of the field wet, muddy, and slippery.

I had learned from playing for the Giants—who famously wore tennis shoes instead of cleats on frozen Yankee Stadium field to propel them to a victory over the slipping and sliding Bears in the 1956 NFL Championship Game—that knowing which equipment will work best in a particular situation can give you an edge over your competition.

On the day of the game, players on both teams had changed over to shoes with longer cleats for better traction on the wet and muddy field. But unlike them, I screwed only two long cleats into the heel of my custom-made white Pumas with the extra number of cleats. When I made my cut to the left or the right, I would plant my heel whereas most other receivers would plant their whole foot. That way I could keep my balance as I made the quick break but without losing any of the speed I gained with the shorter cleats. Of course, the main thing I did to keep from slipping was to take shorter, more upright steps. That way I was always in control, even when I made a sharp cut.

With this the make-or-break game of our season, it was no surprise to see the entire stadium plum full of loud, cheering Jets fans. I'm not sure of the exact attendance, but I do know that it was the largest crowd to ever see an AFL Championship Game. And you can be sure, everybody there was bundled up in fur coats or plenty of other warm layers.

I couldn't help but think back to that first week in the Polo Grounds. The field wasn't even mowed. It was covered in weeds; it looked like a cow pasture. Thinking about where the team had come from to where we were now—playing in the biggest game of the season in front of some 60,000 people—left me with an admiration for those who had fought to get us there.

I'm sure my friends and family were watching the game back home in Texas. If I remember, the game was nationally televised on NBC on a Sunday and I don't believe there was any other game on at the same time. (And I can assure you, they weren't going to switch this Jets/Raiders game before it was over.) I know my parents in Odessa were tuned in, as were a lot of my old college pals, many of whom had returned home and become high school football coaches, including my buddy Corbell. We still kept in touch. It was harder for us to find the time to talk on the phone, but we'd write letters back and forth, as we had done for so many years.

To the few of us old veterans who had survived in the league since its establishment a decade earlier—Larry Grantham, Bill Mathis, me, and even Curley Johnson, who'd come in a little later but was still part of the old Titans—this game had special significance. Nobody with the Jets/Titans organization had been there longer than I had, and while I'd fought in my fair share of big games since 1960, this one was easily the biggest of my career. But regardless, it didn't matter how long any of us had been there, if you were wearing a green jersey, then it was the most important game of your life. Win, you're in the Super Bowl. Lose, you go home with nothing.

At the same time, we knew we had an uphill battle on our hands. The Raiders had given us a hard time in every game we ever played against them. As tough a challenge as their defense posed, their offense was not to be taken lightly. As a matter of fact, they came into the title game with the league's top-rated offense. They just seemed to have our number, winning five of our last six meetings, the last one being their improbable comeback in the Heidi Bowl. All the controversy that followed that game was like gasoline on a bonfire, intensifying our rivalry and creating a buzz around our championship rematch.

For the AFL title game, Weeb lined up the offense in a double wing formation. Basically, Boozer and Lammons, who normally played in the slot, were sent out wide. Then, vice versa, Sauer and I moved in from the wide out position into the slot. Boy, did that leave Oakland scratching their heads! For one, now they had no choice but to stop Sauer and me using one-on-one coverage. Although they had the best corner unit in the league, led by big, ferocious Willie Brown, we pretty much dared them to try to stop Sauer and me with single coverage. Good luck on that.

The Raiders, unfamiliar with our offensive formation, were forced to cover me one-on-one with rookie defensive back George Atkinson, who I had burned for 228 yards on 10 catches just a month earlier in the infamous Heidi Bowl. That said, Atkinson was a fast and promising defender, even setting the Raiders' single-game record for punt-return yardage, gaining 205 yards on Buffalo in 1968.

I know this goes against what you might hear other people say, but I never did like to play against rookies. The problem is that when you're running your normal route, you don't know what he's going to do. He may make a mistake and through dumb luck end up looking like a hero by intercepting the pass. He doesn't do what he was supposed to do under their coverage, and as a result of making a mistake, he might come out smelling like a rose. When you play against a veteran, you've watched him and played against him long enough to know what he's going to do, depending on his team's coverage. But I usually made sure never to let the rookie get close enough to me. That way, even if he guessed right, it wouldn't matter. It's kind of like the pro poker players, many of whom say they don't like playing against the amateur players because you can't depend on them to make the logical move. Instead, amateurs might do something that makes no sense but through sheer luck it works out for them.

Finally, the game began. We received the ball first, our offense moved the ball down the field in a methodical, some might even say boring, manner. Even though Namath had a rocket for an arm—his spiral was so tight and low and he put so much zip on the ball that it could cut through a stormy sky like a sword—he didn't want to tempt fate by throwing too many deep bombs in those kind of conditions. The wind didn't have much effect on short patterns. On a quick slant, Joe could put the ball right on my hip. It was only on the deep pass, when you had to put more air under the ball, that you put yourself at serious risk. Our strategy was to attack the Raiders with our great running game, throwing in some short, precise pass patterns, which is exactly what we did on our first drive.

Matt Snell's long run up the middle put us deep into Raiders territory. On the key play of the drive, I ran a square-out to the left side of the end zone. Like I said, I knew that the turf in that corner of the field was soggier than you could ever imagine, not to mention sloping a bit. I wasn't sure if Atkinson knew that, but I was about to find out. I ran him back into the end zone, taking shorter strides as I streaked across the muddy, rolling terrain of the baseball infield. In a flash, I planted my heel in the turf and broke hard across to the inside. As Atkinson tried to break with me, he slipped and fell. I'd already beaten him anyway, whether he had slipped or not, but now I was wide open in the end zone. Namath delivered a bullet and I caught it. Touchdown. Jets 7–0.

The name of the game is to score first. That way you put the pressure on the opponent's offense to respond. But even after Jim Turner's field goal at the end of the first quarter gave us a 10–0 lead, we didn't get comfortable. We'd played the Raiders enough times to know they weren't going down easy. Sure enough, at the start of the second quarter, Lamonica and Biletnikoff had hooked up on a 29-yard touchdown strike.

Meanwhile, the Raiders defense was starting to land what that Saints defensive coordinator recently coined "remember me" hits. They even managed to give Joe a dislocated finger. Not that I was aware of it at the time. For one, guys on the same football team don't share injuries with each other. You won't know most things that happen to a teammate in the game until after it's ended. The linemen are right in the middle of the action so they might have seen what happened to Joe, but I'm spread out 20 yards away. At any rate, the trainer popped Joe's ring finger back into its socket.

I remember once Larry Grantham had a bone sticking out of his finger during a game. He ran over quickly to the sideline, got it taped to his other finger, and was back out there for the next play. And he was the guy who gave the defensive hand signals.

We went into halftime leading 13–10. Inside the locker room, we went over a few things on the blackboard—what was working and what wasn't. Everybody was wound up, knowing what was out there to be won. Before we headed back out on the field, I said, "Hey, the first half doesn't even count. We've got to win this one to get into the Super Bowl. Let's get after it."

Despite not catching a ton of passes in the first half, I was carefully scouting Atkinson, looking for anything I could use against him later in the game. Even when I knew the play was a handoff to Snell or Boozer, I would run hard down the field like I was going out for a pass just to see how Atkinson would react. I could see he was having a hard time maintaining his footing on the wet and muddy field. Meanwhile, I don't remember slipping one time in that game. Why, he was struggling with two good legs while I was in perfect control even with a bad hamstring. When you have the right shoes, plus when you've been around as long as I had, nothing, not even the worst turf in the world, can kill your speed.

I also noticed that he would cheat up toward the line of scrimmage ever so slightly, anticipating that it was going to be a run play. Once I felt like I knew what he would do on that particular play, I knew how I could beat him. On the sideline, I went up to Joe and said, "Hey, I got a deep one when you need it."

The game had become all-out war, with both teams going after each other like nobody's business. I'm sure the noise of the crowd was something else, but to be honest, my mind was so focused on what I needed to be doing on each play that I wasn't even aware of the crowd. Packed house or empty house, it made no difference. I still had to do the exact same job.

I do remember a couple of times in that game, maybe during a short timeout when Joe was over talking to Weeb, standing there on the field with the offense and looking at that huge crowd surrounding me, all of them cheering, and thinking, *Gee whiz, what am I doing here?* That moment might have only lasted for a few seconds, but in those few seconds I stood there struck with amazement. And there was my wife, Marilyn, watching in the stands, who used to watch me play on Kidd Field in El Paso. And now she was here watching me play in the biggest game of the season, of my career, of my life.

We were in a situation much like the first drive. I was lined up in the slot on the left side. I made my break and got five yards behind Atkinson. I was wide open in the end zone when Joe threw me the ball—only a gust of wind caught it before it could reach me. Atkinson made the interception. Matter of fact, I had him beat so bad that when he intercepted the ball I was too far past him to come back and make the tackle—and I'm the fastest guy on the field. Joe actually made the tackle on him at the Jets 5-yard line. I was 30 yards back down the field, so I didn't see Joe knock him out of bounds. But apparently, Atkinson said, "That shows you the great ballplayer that Joe was. He's not bashful about getting in there and making a hit on a guy." He couldn't fake out Joe, who was running on two bum knees. Joe laid him out and saved the touchdown—at least temporarily.

Unfortunately, the Raiders got in for the score to take the lead with eight minutes left. *We got time left. But we got to get the touchdown back.* That's all any of us were thinking.

Normally, when the guys join together in the huddle, they might exchange a word or two with each other. But the moment Joe leaned his head in, the huddle automatically became quiet. Nobody said a word. They just listened. Once in a while, a guy might crack a joke in the huddle. Of course, it depended if we were ahead in the ballgame or behind. If you're behind, the mood in the huddle is usually dead serious. You can hear a pin drop. But occasionally, if you're ahead there might be a comment. Maybe a lineman slipped on some of that funky turf in Shea, landing on his butt and completely missing his block. He might say, "Let's try that one again."

If I had something to say to Joe, it was always before we all put our heads into the huddle. That way you don't distract him when he's trying to call the play. For example, I might say to Joe, "Hey, my guy's cheating his route if you need a long one." Or Joe would ask me, "How's the quick slant look on your side?" And I'd say, "Fine, it's okay." And then he might ask George Sauer, "How does the quick slant look on your side?" And he'd let him know the situation over on his half of the field. Ultimately, Joe is going to read the defensive coverage and go to whoever is most wide open—whether it's me on the left side, George Sauer on the right side, or Pete Lammons over the middle. And maybe with the exception of that one interception (which was really on account of the wind) Joe had been doing a masterful job of doing just that.

There's no better example of Joe's outstanding maturation over three short years than what happened in the next minute following that Raiders touchdown. We went out on the field and huddled up.

Recalled Namath for this book, "'All right, look,' I said to the guys inside the huddle, 'I'm going to call two plays. If the defense is laying back, we're going to the quick-out again. If not, I want maximum protection for Don to get deep. Because we're going for it.'"

On the first two plays, Joe threw two safe, quick outs to George Sauer, the second one good for a 12-yard first down. "The defense was laying back. Why, I'll never know. Why Willie Brown laid off anybody," Namath continued.

At that point, the defense was convinced that Joe was going to keep working the ball down the field to Sauer.

"We got back in the huddle," Namath continued. "I said, 'Be alert, guys. I may check to 60 G.'"

The 60 G is the goal route to me. Or to put it in laymen's terms, the deep bomb. The G tells the running backs Boozer and Snell to stay in and block. It's what we called maximum protection. You have as many guys back there blocking as you can so that Joe has enough time to throw the long one. The linemen knew they had to protect him a little longer to give him the extra time to throw me the pass.

Now, earlier in the game, right after we had fallen behind 23–20, I had seen Joe on the sideline with his head hung down.

Recalled Namath, "I am sitting on the bench feeling mighty low because old Joe just threw the interception that set up the score. Don comes over to me, leans over, and pats me on the shoulder.

"'I'll tell you what,' Don said to me. 'Anytime you want it, I'll get a step on my man, and you let me have it.' Well, boy, he said that with such confidence it made me feel better."

Up to that point, Joe hadn't thrown a long one to me all game long. Not once. Now, on third down, the Raiders assumed we were going to try to pick up just enough yards to keep the chains moving.

"Sure enough," said Namath. "As we walked up to the line of scrimmage, George Atkinson climbed up on Don."

I saw Atkinson was only a few yards off the line of scrimmage. I heard Joe call the audible. We were going for it.

I came down at Atkinson. I didn't break my stride. I didn't give him a fake. I just slipped out to the outside and burst down the field.

At that point, I was still running at three-quarter speed. But, as it had been throughout my career, the long strides I took made everybody think I was running full speed.

"When you think he's going all out," Walt Michaels told a reporter in 1967, 10 years before becoming head coach of the New York Jets, "he turns it on. Fast, slow, fast, slow. Then he makes his move. I tell the guys in our secondary during practice to keep going all-out and never believe him."

One reason I never ran all out on a long bomb was so that I could adjust to the ball that Joe had thrown. For example, if Joe threw me the ball with the wind at his back, it might carry two yards farther than it should have, but you never know, at the last moment, the wind might bring it back my way. So I'd adjust on the fly, speeding up or slowing down to make the catch.

Even though I had a couple of steps on Atkinson, I still needed to catch Joe's 70-yard spiral.

"I dropped back and threw the ball as far and as hard as I could," said Namath.

I looked back over my inside shoulder, and what do you know, here comes the ball. I think I'm going to catch in stride and keep right on going to the end zone. Then all of a sudden, as the ball started arcing downward through the grey sky, the wind takes, it and sends it sideways. Now, I've had to fade to the outside to make sure I caught the ball on my left shoulder before—but in all my life—high school, college, and a decade in the pros—I'd never seen the ball turn completely sideways like that.

When I originally looked back for the ball, I had been expecting it to come down on my left shoulder, or 10:00. All of a sudden it was coming down at 12:00. I could see from the flight of the ball, that it was going to overshoot me by a couple of yards. That's when I got on my horse and went after it. I had caught up to the pass but, at the same time, I was running nearly parallel to the yard marker at full speed. And the problem is, the ball was moving faster to the right than I was able to fade out toward the sideline. As the ball touched my fingertips, it was now at 2:00. I grasped the ball over my head, only I was still running sideways. I couldn't straighten out the steering wheel. I had no choice but to cradle the ball and hold on for the ride. The momentum sent me crashing out of bounds at the 6-yard line.

To recap, not only did I have to catch the long bomb in the gusting wind, but I was also running on one good leg, the sidelines were wet and muddy, the ball was on the wrong shoulder, and the field was sloping uphill slightly. We ran that play only once that day. One time. Well, let's just say I'm glad for that—I might just have missed it a second time.

I remember that first day I worked on the goal route with Joe on the practice field of Peekskill Academy. I told him the key was to put the ball on the correct shoulder. Now, I'm not saying that Joe purposely threw it to the wrong shoulder in the key moment of the game. If the wind hadn't interfered with the flight path of the ball, it would have come down perfectly on my inside shoulder and, as I already had three steps on Atkinson, I would have caught it in full stride and run it in for a touchdown. I guess the point is, you can practice doing something a million times over, but sometimes in life the unexpected happens in the big moment—in this case, a sudden gust of wind. You just have to make a turn in a direction you never expected to go.

"Don made one of the greatest catches of all time," said Namath. "And if you ever get the chance to see it on film, you'll understand what I'm talking about."

So we had first down at the Raiders 6-yard line. In the huddle, Joe called the pass play to me on the right side.

"We had first-and-goal for the AFC Championship," said Namath. "I figured the Raiders were going to count on a running play, and I was going to outsmart them and call a play action pass.

As Joe came to the line of scrimmage, he read it was a blitz.

"I was wrong. The Raiders were a little smarter than I thought. A lot smarter, actually," said Namath.

Joe snapped the ball, faked it to Snell, but before he could plant and fire the ball to Sauer, he slipped on the muddy infield. As he regained his balance, he looked to his second option, Bill Mathis. But he was covered in the flat.

"I came back to big boy Pete Lammons, and he was covered," said Namath. "About that time, I saw that unmistakable No. 13 streaking across the end zone."

As the fourth receiver, I had run a delayed route where I sprinted out to the post. Atkinson was like a shadow on my back. I was deep in the end zone when I suddenly curled back around. As I came back hard toward the goal line, I saw the ball coming at me about thigh high.

"Boy, I threw that thing as hard as I could, as fast as I could," said Namath.

I mean, Joe really drilled it at me. He threw an absolute bullet.

"It was a little off line, down low, and Don slid down there and cradled the ball."

He stuck it so hard in my midsection that I couldn't keep from catching it. And that ended up being the winning touchdown. "And we all went on to the Super Bowl and y'all know the history behind that," said Namath. Later, when I was coaching, I'd use this to make the point that you can never slack off on the job, even if you're the last option in the world because you just might wind up being the guy who has to make the big play. Sure enough, that's what happened to me. On that play, I looked up and—*Gee whiz, here comes the ball.*

Going through the tunnel to Shea Stadium and into the dressing room was a blur. Everybody was going crazy and dousing each other with champagne, congratulating each other. The press was milling around trying to interview the players. Nobody was in too big of a hurry to leave.

Grantham came over to me with a big grin. "Come on, Maynard, you have to drink some champagne *now!*"

Alcohol had never touched my lips before. I said to him, "I'll tell you what, if we win the Super Bowl, I'll take a sip of champagne."

In the background, I could see Joe celebrating, having a good time, soaking in the moment.

It's like I had told him on the first day of camp: "I'm going to make you a better quarterback, and you're going to make me a better receiver."

As it turned out, I was wrong. He made *all of us* better.

Across the chaotic scene, Joe called out to me, "Are you ready for Baltimore?"

"I always come ready," I shouted back.

After the game, all the Jets players and their wives went down to Joe's restaurant, Bachelors III, to celebrate our victory. Marilyn and I arrived with another couple. As we walked in and gave our coats to the coat-check person, she handed me back the ticket for my coat and, lo and behold, it's No. 43, which was also George Atkinson's jersey number. I made the comment to Larry Grantham and Bill Baird and Bake Turner, who happened to be standing there, "Well, I'll be! I've had his number all day." And they just died laughing.

The next morning, I woke up with some extra soreness in my hamstring, but it didn't bother me none. I did my 31 sit-ups, and when I finished, I laid back for a second, staring up with a big smile. We'd gotten even with the Raiders for the Heidi Bowl. We had won the game that counted the most.

Next stop: Miami.

No Champagne

BACK IN 1968, PEOPLE DIDN'T TALK about a million dollars unless you were talking about the government's debt. Well, following our win in the AFL Championship Game, a reporter described my big reception in that game as "a million-dollar catch." Then one day, just for fun, I sat down and figured out how much all our individual shares for winning the Super Bowl would add up to (like I told my shop students, you never know when your math skills will come in handy). Sure enough, it came out to $1 million. I thought to myself, *Gee whiz, if we win the Super Bowl, then it really would be a million-dollar catch.*

But wouldn't you know it, my million-dollar catch didn't make the next week's cover of *Sports Illustrated*. Gracing the front of the magazine instead was a color shot of Baltimore halfback Tom Matte diving across the goal line for his third touchdown in the Colts' 34–0 whooping of the Cleveland Browns in the NFL Championship Game. I suppose the photographer didn't have a good angle (from the sidelines of a game he hadn't attended) to capture my twisting 52-yard catch, catapulting us to the Super Bowl. That was okay. My brother, Thurman, said he saw it on television. That was good enough for me.

Weeb had allowed us to bring our wives with us to the big game—he was really good about doing things like that for us. Since win or lose, the Super Bowl was the last game of the season, Marilyn and I decided to drive down to Miami from New York City, and Bill Baird and his wife came along with us. The plan was for Marilyn and I to continue on to El Paso after the game, turning the last leg of the trip into a vacation. We planned to stop along the way to visit old friends, some of whom I hadn't seen for many years, going as far back as high school. We also planned to stop in Dallas to see my brother and his family.

By then, I had traded in my '55 Ford coupe for a new '67 Ford, upgrading from two doors to four. I installed a propane conversion system in that car, the same I had in every other car I ever drove, ensuring my continued 30 percent savings on fuel costs—not to mention that it would run three times longer than a regular car. I guess you could call it the El Paso Flame Burner II.

About halfway down to Miami, a car ahead of us lost control and crashed. I immediately swerved over to the other lane and managed to barely skirt by the accident. Boy, I'll tell you, I've made a lot of quick moves in my football career, but I don't think any of them were as fast as that one. That's another reason I never sped anywhere in my life—not if I wasn't wearing a pair of cleats.

We arrived in Miami 10 days before the big game. Despite knocking off an extremely tough Raiders squad, the experts listed us 19-point underdogs against the Colts. Shoot, even Vince Lombardi's Packers hadn't been favored by that large a margin in the first two Super Bowls. How did that make us feel? Well, you know, in a way it didn't really matter to us.

We checked into the hotel where the rest of the Jets players and their wives were staying. Normally, I'd be assigned a room with Bake Turner, but my roommate that week was my wife. Bake was a world-class guitar player who had jammed with the likes of Charley Pride and Willie Nelson—but I still considered the situation an upgrade.

We spent that first week in Miami doing more sunbathing than body punishing. I'd never been to Miami before, so it was great to see a couple of the sights with Marilyn, hit a few nice restaurants, and relax a little on the sandy beach. Some guys took their wives to cabaret shows or other kinds of entertainment. Who knows what those single guys on the team were up to. I assume they found enough nightly diversions to occupy their time in the Sunshine State.

The following Tuesday, Weeb put in the curfew, and that was it. For the rest of our trip, everyone's focus was 100 percent on getting ready for the game.

Bed check was at 10:00, and no player, not Joe or anybody else for that matter, missed it. Like I said, you could take at least half of the stories about Joe's playboy lifestyle and throw them right in the trashcan. Sure, he had a white llama rug in his penthouse, but it was usually covered with canisters of game film that he brought home to watch on his personal projector.

And it wasn't just Joe who did that. Larry Grantham, our defensive leader, also used to take film home with him in Long Beach to study. Even the most dominating offensive line—and the Colts' unit was right up there—has some kind of vulnerability. As a linebacker, Grantham could be giving up as much as 40 pounds against the Colts' offensive guards, but a tough veteran like that is going to pore over game film looking for that one small equalizer. It might be as simple as lining up a half a yard closer or a half a yard to the left. Whatever it was, Grantham would find it.

Great talent will take you great places, but it's those who possess that superhuman dedication to their pursuit who can do the impossible. You couldn't find a group of more dedicated guys than those Jets who fought that day in 1969 in Miami. No matter what anybody says, you'll never feel like an 19-point underdog in life, not when you're as prepared as we were to take on the Colts.

Every night when we got back to the hotel, we all met downstairs in the dining room, where snacks were set up. There would be turkey and ham and peanut butter, whatever you wanted. A guy might have a sandwich there or take one to his room or maybe grab himself a cold beer or a soda pop. The nice thing about it was that you had 35 guys, all with very different personalities, different likes and dislikes, and different ways they liked to spend their free time, but at the end of the day, none of that mattered. Whatever had transpired at practice—maybe some linebacker gave a little extra shove on a guard, or maybe a coach punished a player by making him run extra laps—was done and over with it. At the end of the day, it's water under the bridge. About half an hour or so later, we'd all make our way up to our rooms. And with that, our day ended just as surely as it would start tomorrow: as a team. A team with one color on our jerseys, one purpose in our hearts, and one apple cart to seriously upset.

Thursday night before the game, Joe went to some prestigious awards banquet in town. He hadn't wanted to go without me and his other teammates, but Weeb and the front-office people convinced him to accept the invitation, especially because he was the night's featured award recipient. Some fella in the back of the room, who might've had a few too many drinks, shouted something to Joe about how the Jets had no shot at the Super Bowl. It was nothing that Joe or the rest of us hadn't heard over and over again since arriving in Miami. I guess Joe had heard enough, because he told the guy, "We're going to win Sunday, I'll guarantee you."

Believe me, when Joe said what he did, he had no idea anybody would even notice. It was just an off-the-cuff response to some heckler. "Well, when you have a group of guys work together and

244

try hard and have success," said Namath. "When someone comes in and tells them they can't do something, there's a level of anger that gets going. That's all it was. I was angry to hear that B.S. again. It wasn't planned."

Planned or not, the next day Joe's comment was splashed across the front page of the *Miami Herald*. From there, the rest of the news-hounds picked up on the scent and boy, did they run with it.

When the team came out for practice the next day, none of the players were even aware of what he had said. I doubt any of us had even read the newspaper. But Weeb was a guy who always read the newspaper, and when he walked onto the field he was beside him-self. He said, "Joseph, how could you say something like that?" We all kind of looked at each other, wondering what he had said to get Weeb so hot under the collar.

Coach felt Namath had given the Colts all the ammunition in the world. Weeb looked sick. Some of the other offensive guys and I started poking fun at him, "Ah, come on, Weeb. You don't have to worry about that. You take care of the press. We'll take care of the ballgame."

We knew Joe hadn't tried to make headlines. He just said it in the heat of the moment—responding to a week's worth of insults geared toward our team having no chance. Besides, a lot of us had been feeling that same frustration all week long. We just hadn't announced it to the whole dang universe. But Joe landing smack in the middle of the spotlight wasn't anything new to us. That's how it had been all year long. Heck, for as long as he'd been there. When "Broadway Joe" sneezed, it was front-page news in New York. A lot of us on the Jets felt the same way: *Hey, better him than us.*

Now that I think about it, Dave "Haystack" Herman might have complained a little to Weeb about Joe's comment. The reason for his concern stemmed from the fact that our offensive coordinator,

Chuck Knox (who would later become coach of the Rams), moved him over from guard to tackle where he'd be matched up against Bubba Smith. Bubba, the Colts' most fearsome pass rusher, had at least 30 pounds on Haystack. He was so big and strong and fast, lining up against him would be like trying to stop a grizzly bear. To Haystack's way of thinking, Joe had just poked Bubba the Bear in his thick side with a sharp stick.

"Guarantee. Easy for you to say that," Haystack said, half-kiddingly to Joe at practice. "You don't have to stop Bubba Smith!" We were all snickering. To this day, I always laugh when I hear about guys putting the things their opponents say about them on the team bulletin board to get themselves fired up. Maybe you do that in high school or college, but we're professionals. If you need a pep talk to get cranked up to do your job, you're in the wrong business. Heck, the best incentive you could ever give us was the $15,000 winner's share for the Super Bowl. That was just an unbelievable bonus. Nowadays, players make more in a single regular-season game than they do for winning the Super Bowl.

More than anything, the uproar over what some folks saw as a foolhardy boast against an unbeatable Colts team showed the gap between the public's mind-set and ours. Out there, we were 19-point underdogs. Inside our practice facility, cut off from the rest of the world, we were trying to guard against overconfidence.

Sure, we'd seen how the Colts had steamrolled through a very tough NFL schedule, producing a 13–1 record. We'd seen how, in the conference championship, they manhandled the Browns, who happened to be the one team to defeat them during the regular season. We were aware they had the NFL's No. 1 defense, setting a single-season record for fewest points allowed, and that their offense had outscored their opponents by a margin of 402 to 144 points.

What's more, the Colts had talent, experience, and depth at practically every position. In Earl Morrall, they had a wily veteran quarterback and recent winner of the NFL's Player of the Year award. In Bubba Smith, they had one of the most dominating defensive ends in the game. And if you think handling Bubba sounds like a challenge, try bringing down their All-Pro tight end John Mackey, a 225-pound freak of nature whose raw strength was matched by his terrific speed. So, yeah, we understood why a lot of people in the media didn't give us a chance. But if you asked if we came to Miami thinking we could beat them I would have said, "If we play good, then yes, sir, we feel we could win the ballgame."

Most folks tended to disagree. After all, in their minds, the NFL was the superior league. It was one thing to beat the Raiders; it was a whole other thing to knock off the mighty Baltimore Colts. That view on the matter was only supported more by the fact that the Green Bay Packers had rolled to easy victories against AFL teams in the first two title matches. As far as I was concerned, *that* had everything to do with Vince Lombardi. But the way most folks saw it, the Packers' victories in the '66 and '67 seasons proved that the AFL wasn't in the same class as the NFL—and it might never be.

You have to understand that when the league had started 10 years before, it was made up of players who hadn't made it in the NFL for one reason or the other. Maybe they were considered too small or too slow or too old. In my case, I felt that it was one guy who didn't like the fact I wore cowboy boots, had sideburns, and took long strides. Nobody was playing in the AFL back then to knock off the NFL, we were all playing for a paycheck. We were playing for the enjoyment you got from being part of a close-knit unit, for the rush we got from battling in the trenches, and for the thrill of winning.

The AFL's growth in 10 years went far beyond what anybody could have imagined. By 1968 the league was going toe-to-toe with the NFL for top talent as well as TV ratings. A feeling permeated the league, from the front office down to the players and fans, that we no longer had to take a backseat to the NFL. We weren't about to start flapping our gums about it to the press, though. We had too much respect for the Baltimore Colts and all they had accomplished over the years, going back to that epic 1958 NFL Championship.

To be truthful, it wasn't just the media who were convinced the Colts were going to clean our clock. Even a couple of my old college pals told me they were thinking of taking the Colts to win. "That's okay by me," I told this one friend. "But make sure you don't bet more than you can afford to lose."

To a man, we all felt like we didn't have to bow down to any team. What did the Colts have that we didn't have? *They had a great ground game.* Well, our rushing attack of Matt Snell, Emerson Boozer, and Bill Mathis wasn't too shabby either. Matter of fact, it was world-class. *They had a super passing game.* Why, we had as great a passing game as there will ever be in football. To this day, we're the only team to send a quarterback and all three of his receivers to the same All-Star Game. *They had the top-ranked defense in their league.* Well, we had the top-ranked defense in ours. Down the line, offense, defense, passing game, running game, kicking game, special teams...our guys were going to match up well against any team in the country. We didn't need to convince anybody that we could play with Baltimore. They'd find out come game time.

Our confidence kept growing as the game got closer, and that had plenty to do with all that darn game film that Weeb made us sit through all week long in Miami. Under league rules, the two teams had to exchange game film a short time before actual combat. The coaches and players for each unit—offense and defense—would sit in a dark room together, analyzing the black-and-white game film displayed on the projector screen. In the week prior, Weeb made us watch the film over and over. Finally, Lammons said, "Weeb, if you don't stop showing us these films, we're going to get overconfident!" And Lammons didn't just say it once. He said it every day that we were stuck there for hours watching that stinking old film. And that wasn't just the way Pete felt; he was speaking for all the guys on our offense.

I was more confident going into that game than any other game I had played in my career. Not just because you couldn't find a group of hungrier ballplayers than we were, but because I knew that Joe and I didn't need to score 100 points for us to win. Our great defense was going to win the game for us.

I honestly couldn't have cared less about what Joe did or didn't guarantee. I had other concerns. During the first week of practices in Miami, I was moving around free as a breeze. Of course, I'd always thrived running in that kind of hot weather. I grew up playing football in West Texas, so it can't get too hot for me. I was at practice that Thursday, getting loosened up real well. When it came to warming up, I was a perfectionist, always had been. I ran out for a couple of deep passes, just to stretch out the limbs, and I felt a sharp pain race up my hamstring. It felt like somebody had stuck me with an ice pick.

I knew I had done something to my leg, so I went to see the team's doctor, Doc Nicholas. He assured me that I hadn't torn anything. He explained to me that the sharp pain was from scar tissue that had built up around the hamstring muscle tearing loose. Underneath, the muscle had healed completely. From my study of kinesiology in college, I knew that what Doc had told me might possibly be the case. He told me to try to stay off of it until game day. I was able to jog lightly on Friday, but that was about all I did in practice. Doc Nicholas decided to give me a lidocaine shot 24 hours before the game to help relax the muscle. I *hate* needles. And gee whiz, the shot hurt more than the pain in my leg.

League rules stated that teams had to report any player injuries prior to the game. The Colts, now aware of my sore leg, were uncertain if I was going to be able to play, or if I did play, how effective I'd be. I didn't know either, having not tested my leg since Thursday. But one thing was for sure: there was no way I was going to sit out the biggest game in Jets history.

Naturally, Marilyn was concerned about my injury, especially when she saw me lying beside her in the hotel bed, a heating pad wrapped around my leg, the big game just hours away. But she'd been around football her whole life. She was a high school majorette when I met her. She had watched practically every game I played at Texas Western. She knew that football players had no choice but to play with injuries. That's just the way it was. Also, she trusted the fact that I knew my body well and wouldn't compete if I thought I'd be doing serious harm to myself. Besides, if I got out there and couldn't go all out, well, I'd just tell my buddy Bake Turner that he was going to have to carry the load that day. I had all the faith in the world in him—in all my teammates.

Our hotel rooms had been assigned by jersey number. Joe was No. 12 and I was No. 13, so we were in adjoining rooms. We came up with a system: if one guy needed the other guy for some reason, he knocked on the wall. Well, the night before the ballgame, I was lying in bed in the dark, trying to get some shut-eye, a task made more difficult by the ungainly heating pad wrapped around my leg. All of a sudden, I heard a knock on the wall.

"What do you want?" I called out through the thin wall.

"I want to show you something," Joe's voice echoed from the other side.

"No, man. It's late."

There was a long pause.

"I need you to come over here," said Joe.

At that point, Marilyn said, "You better go over there and see what he wants."

I pulled back the covers in an irritated swoop of my hand. I got up and stepped lightly to the door, the heating pad still affixed to my thigh. I moseyed on down the hall—a good five or six inches— and knocked on Joe's door. Joe opened the door and led me inside without saying a word. As I followed him in, I saw a projector set up in the middle of the room, throwing a focused light beam across the room and onto the wall, a makeshift movie screen.

"Hey, watch this," Joe said, turning on the projector. Grainy flickering images of an old Colts game suddenly appeared on the blank wall. As the film ran, I watched the Colts players set up in their defensive coverage.

"When they do this," said Joe, "I'm going to check off. And we're going for a long one."

"All right, Joe," I said. "You just call it, and I'll run it. Now, I'm going to bed."

I don't know how much longer Joe stayed up watching film. As for me, I got back into bed, closed my eyes, and went to sleep. I didn't give it a second thought.

On game day, the Jets players boarded a bus to take us from the hotel to the Orange Bowl. On the ride over, those of us on the offense told the defense, "Hey, we're gonna score a bunch on these guys." The defensive players said back to us, "Well, they ain't gonna score on us." There was a lot of back and forth like that as we made our way to the stadium. I remember Grantham blurted out, "We're going to intercept three or four balls." All I added to the discussion was one thing, which I'd learned from working in the cotton field with my dad and from playing college ball under Mike Brumbelow at Texas Western and from being a pupil of the great Vince Lombardi and then my hero Sammy Baugh once I got to the pros. What I told those 39 teammates of mine as kickoff approached was this: "We don't make mistakes, we'll win."

• • •

After all the preparation, all of the anticipation, game time finally came. It was about the third series of the game, and Joe called our play in the huddle. Then, as he walked up to the line of scrimmage he looked over at the Colts defense. He saw that they were lined up in the formation that he had keyed on—the same formation he'd shown me on film the night before in his room. He told me he was changing the play. He said, "We're going for it." I knew right then what he was planning to do. I said to him, "All right, I'll be there."

Nobody had beaten the Colts defense with a long pass all year, not that anybody had bothered to tell Joe or me. Frankly, I doubt either of us would have cared, had we known. We were going to run our play; it was up to them to stop us.

Sure enough, Joe checked off at the line of scrimmage. As soon as he snapped the ball, I was gone like Jesse Owens down the sideline.

In an instant, Joe took two shuffle steps back in the pocket, planted his back foot and cocked his arm. Before the pass rush could get to him, he fired a rocket across the sky.

My adrenaline kicked in as I sprinted down the field in long, controlled strides. No fakes, no nothing. Pure speed. I beat the first defender by a good five yards—and then I was loooooong gone. There was no way he was going to catch me. The safety came over to help chase me down, but by then he wasn't even in the picture.

I glanced back, wide open, to see the blistering spiral Joe had fired some 50 yards away, hissing through the sky toward me. With an extra burst of speed, I dove through the air trying to make the grab. The ball went about an inch past my outstretched fingertips, and I rolled hard to the turf. In our whole career, I don't think Joe and I missed on more than two long passes. And that might have been the only one ever for which I had to stretch out completely and actually leave my feet.

Even though the pass was incomplete, I guarantee you one thing: we scared them on that play. They knew that if Joe had thrown it a half an inch shorter, I would have been long gone for a touchdown. I hadn't just beaten their defensive backs, known to be among the very best in the league—I had beat them good. You could see the look of shock on their faces. *Evidently, Maynard isn't hurt at all.*

Because I had smoked their defensive backs so convincingly, from that point on in the game, Baltimore's attitude became, *they aren't going to burn us deep again.* They went to a zone coverage, setting up two, sometimes three, corners on my side of the field to guard against the deep one. I'd set up real wide. When the corners shifted over my way, Joe could snap the ball, knowing he'd have room to rifle the ball to the short side of the field. Meanwhile, I went down yonder, taking two or three guys with me, and freed up the other guys to catch the underneath pass all day long. As I told Joe early on, "You don't have to throw it to me. You aren't going to hurt my feelings."

Running out as wide as possible, with the corners following me out there, Joe was able to march the offense down the field with a mix of quick darts to the receivers and handoffs to Snell and Boozer. Fourteen yards to Sauer on the sideline hook. Back to Sauer for 11 more. Then a short pass to Snell, who ran it up the middle for 12 more. Our game plan threw everybody for a loop. The Colts sideline, the Miami Bowl spectators, the Jets fans watching the game back in New York and Jersey, Howard Cosell—pretty much everybody and his cousin—was asking the same thing: *When is Namath going to start airing it out?*

We came out for the second half with a narrow 7–0 lead, and to everybody's amazement, Joe hadn't thrown me the deep bomb since that one on the third series of the game. On our second series of the third quarter, Joe checked off. It was the go route. I sprinted down the sideline and *boom*, I got loose behind the defense, same as before. Namath launched a rocket. I was wide open in the back of the end zone as the ball sailed toward me. I reached out my arms. I caught the ball...just out of bounds. We're talking, maybe the width of your four fingers out of bounds.

But the fact we got behind them so bad—again—convinced them to stay within their zone coverage in the second half. Joe made that throw just to let the Colts know, *If you're thinking of relaxing on Maynard, I'm going to make you pay.*

Joe didn't really do anything different on that play than he'd been doing all season. He read the defense, called the right play, released the ball quick, and, of course, he had the incredible arm strength to reach me 50 yards downfield. It was just a hair over-thrown. But the ability to call for the go route at the perfect moment not only shows you what an innate feel he had for the game but how hard he prepared himself mentally for each contest. The same was true for every single player on our team.

In the third quarter, coach Don Shula benched Earl Morrall and brought in a new quarterback. Ten years earlier, when I was just a rookie, I had watched Unitas lead his team to an epic victory in the Greatest Game Ever Played. I couldn't help but feel a slight knot in my throat seeing the greatest gunslinger of his era take off his cape and walk onto the field. Shoot, some of our wide-eyed corners knew about him only from the tales they had read as a kid. And now they were suddenly being asked to stop the legend, Johnny U. I get the feeling their insides were rattling a little bit, too.

Unitas had been a winner all his life. He was, to many of us, the ultimate winner. A champion's champion. And I don't care how many miles he'd logged or how much wear and tear he had on his once-atomic arm—any time Johnny Unitas took the field, you ought to be concerned. He would attack you with everything he had. And even if he'd lost a little of the zip on his passes, the one thing he hadn't lost was his calm mastery of the game.

When Unitas came into the game in the second half, it gave the Colts offense a real shot in the arm. As the quarter progressed, his play-calling was sharp, his throws pinpoint accurate, and his killer instinct intact. As for his arm strength, I'll tell you what, there was still a little thunder left in that bat. At the same time, he compensated for his reduced power by throwing the ball a half a count quicker and working the play fake to perfection.

In the face of this final onslaught from a once-great captain in his twilight, the Jets defense stood tall, and in the fourth quarter, we remained ahead 16-0. But Unitas wasn't done yet. With his uncanny timing and patented patience, he put together an impressive drive that ended with the Colts completing their first score of the game. All of a sudden, our lead had been narrowed to just nine points.

If there was a time for our offense to panic, this was it. Unitas was catching fire, and the memory of the Raiders' devastating 14-point comeback in the infamous Heidi Bowl lurked in the shadows. Joe forced a pass into tight coverage, it was intercepted, and we let the game slip away. Well, all that *could* have happened, but it didn't.

Everybody had assumed that the only way we could win is if Namath threw for 400 yards. But in that key moment in the fourth quarter, with the Colts coming back on us, we decided more or less teamwise to keep going to our running game. We played carefully. At the same time, we knew we could go to our dynamite passing attack if we needed to. As it turned out, I don't think Namath attempted a single pass in the fourth quarter. He didn't need to. The Colts scoring took nothing away from the way our defense was hanging tough. Their play in the fourth was no less outstanding than it had been all game long. And the fact that Joe didn't have to make one more throw the rest of the game said more about the great performance of our running backs and that of our defense than anything else.

The funny thing is that Namath had done the same thing to the Colts in Super Bowl III that I'd watched Unitas do to my Giants team 10 years before in the 1958 Championship Game. In the first quarter of that game, Unitas threw a deep bomb to Lenny Moore that resulted in a long completion. It had put such a fright in the Giants defense that Tom Landry assigned two guys to guard against Moore beating them on a long one. What that did was create an opening for Unitas to go to Raymond Berry on short sideline passes, on which he killed New York all day long. It is the reason the Colts offense managed to have success against the NFL's best defense in that historic game.

As much as some people like to praise the revolutionary events of that game, of that time, of that generation, it's easy to undervalue those things that endure because they are good and solid and make sense. If not for that little extra bit of preparation on Joe's part the night before that game, who knows if we would have pulled off the victory.

I think Joe and I—and you could throw Unitas and Mantle and Huff in there, too—grew up with similar values. It didn't matter what you did—football, school, picking cotton, shoveling coal—you did it with purpose and you did it to the best of your ability. Growing up, you played the games you liked to play. I ran track in high school; Joe played basketball. The possibility of playing football for a living doesn't enter your mind until later—in your sophomore, junior, or senior year of high school. It's not like it is today, where people start preparing for a pro career from an early age. That change, of course, has a lot to do with the money these young men stand to make now.

In all fairness to every quarterback who's ever played the game, and I've seen some unbelievable ones—Slingin' Sammy Baugh, Sid Luckman, Notre Dame's legendary Johnny Lujack, Bart Starr, and, of course, the great Johnny Unitas—I will say this: Joe was as good as anybody who ever played the game. And with respect to all of his 400-yard passing days, he was never better than he was in Super Bowl III with the stakes at their absolute highest.

Somewhere down the line, I got a photo that someone took toward the end of Super Bowl III. It's an unbelievable shot. Eleven guys in Jets uniforms are walking up to the ball, which is in the shadows of the end zone, about to try and run down the clock with some 80 yards of real estate in front of us. The players are shot from behind, and you can read the number and name on the back of each guy's jersey as we were walking up to the line of scrimmage.

There we were, in this once-in-a-lifetime moment, about to march down the field and seal the biggest game of our lives. But when you look at that picture, you also just see 11 regular guys going back to work; giving it everything they had, one last push; and making sure the job got done.

Well, we got the job done.

Sometimes when you come out of a situation in which there's been an unreal amount of pressure on you, your reaction can almost seem strangely low-key. It can take time for the realization of what you've just pulled off to sink in. It took me a full week before it really hit me. Hey, the Jets beat the Colts in the Super Bowl—*and I'll be, we're the ones who did it!*

After the game, we drove to Jacksonville for the All-Star Game. I'll never forget that. Among those representing the Jets were Namath, Sauer, Lammons, and me; there were 11 Jets in all who played in that game. It was the first time in history that the receivers plus the quarterback to start an All-Star Game all came from one team.

When we came into the dressing room, we were greeted by the other AFL players as if they also had the Jets insignia on their helmets. Seeing their happy, even joyous, reactions, it dawned on me that to these players—and to every player or coach or employee who had ever been involved in the AFL—that our upset over the Colts wasn't just as a victory for us, but also a victory for them. I suppose they had a right to feel that way. As much as we were a part of the league as a whole, the rest of the league was part of us. If the AFL had folded in those early years, we all would have folded together. But instead, we survived, then thrived, and ultimately captured the Super Bowl. Without a doubt, it was a win for every one of us.

Did I think that our win proved the AFL had become equal in talent with the NFL? Probably not, but here's why. While we had some great stars, like Joe and George Blanda and Len Dawson, we weren't as talented all the way down to our 11th player. The NFL simply had more experienced players than we did. At the same time, I would put our best AFL teams up against their best teams any day of the week. It was no fluke that we beat the Colts in '68, even though some said so. The next year, when the Kansas City Chiefs went out and defeated the Minnesota Vikings in Super Bowl IV, that put all of that nonsense to rest.

Of course, the longer you played in the AFL, the stronger your loyalty was to the league and the more personally you felt the rivalry with the NFL. Many of us had been discarded by the NFL only to wind up in the AFL, happy just to have a job. For many of us veterans, there was a part of us that had never forgotten that feeling of rejection, of being told we weren't good enough. Our victory in Super Bowl III showed them that we had made it, despite what they had said. And we had done it without compromising who we were as individuals or stifling our quirks or conforming to their notion of how a football player should look and act. We never surrendered any of the wild and carefree exuberance that we had for the game as kids, whether it was throwing the pigskin around in the vacant gin lot or out back behind some rowhouses. I didn't always care for the politics that sometimes went on behind the scenes of pro teams, but I can truly say that there wasn't a day on this earth that I didn't love the game.

Over the entire history of pro football, there have been a couple of singular events that set off a boom of new interest and excitement in the sport. I marvel that I was lucky enough to be involved in three of them—the '58 NFL Championship, Super Bowl III, and the Heidi Bowl. The buzz that accompanied each of those thrillers, not just in the press but in barbershops and beer halls, led to greater exposure of the league, followed by sold-out stadiums and waterfalls of money from the advertising world.

Whole regions of the country that had never given one toot about football were suddenly rearranging their Sundays to root on their team, whether from their downstairs den or the upper sections of Shea. Cities like Denver, Kansas City, San Diego, and Oakland went from being football wastelands to pigskin meccas. And it's in part because of our upset in Miami that the Super Bowl is now the biggest yearly sporting event in the world. It's so big, in fact, that as soon as it's over, everybody starts working towards the next one a year later, from the teams planning for the draft to the organizers lining up new sponsors.

It's funny. Prior to the final game of the '68 season against the Miami Dolphins, Weeb asked me, *how's the leg?* I told him it was coming along pretty good. Then he asked if I wanted to play. I said, "Well, we've already wrapped up the division and I might get out there in the game and instinct takes over and I could hurt my leg again. I want to make sure I'm as healthy as I can be for the game against Oakland with a shot at the Super Bowl at stake." So I didn't even suit up for that game. Bake Turner filled in for me and ended up gaining 157 receiving yards on seven catches. As a result of giving up my spot in that game, I lost the league's receiving title to Lance Allworth by just 15 yards.

Later, one of the guys on the team said, "Hey, Maynard, if you had played that last game you would have finished the season as the league's top receiver in total yards instead of Lance Allworth."

"Yep," I said, "I traded 15 yards of credibility for $15,000."

After we won, I never razzed my friends who had picked the Colts. I just hoped they'd listened to my advice about not betting the ranch on the other guys.

As soon as time expired, I always got off the field as quickly as I could. I never did stick around to shake hands with the guys on the other team. In fact, a couple of times when we were playing on the road in front of a hostile crowd I ran off the field faster than I did on my routes. You never know, occasionally a couple of fans from the opposing team who had a few too many beers might decide to express their displeasure by chucking one at your head. If you look closely at that famous clip of Joe jogging off the field, flashing the No. 1 sign over his head, he's still got his helmet on. Well, that's because every time there's a winner, there's a loser. And some of the folks in the camp aren't always coming up to pat you on the back.

Some would prefer to fling a bottle and put your eye out. When that happens, a helmet is always a good thing to have on your head.

After Super Bowl III, I felt amazing. We won it. It's over with. We don't have to go out and play it again. Now it's time to sit back and relax, and in my case, have an extra glass of iced tea. Not that when we got back to the locker room, the guys didn't try to get me to toast our win with a glass of champagne.

The only people allowed in the locker room during those first minutes of celebration were the players and coaches. Guys were hugging each other, shaking hands, and slapping each other on the back. It's probably one of the most exciting and memorable couple of minutes you'll ever share with people you know—all the appreciation you have for each one of your teammates that might have never been expressed through the years explodes forth in that moment.

The unity of that team was incredible. Some of us had been playing together since the franchise's first season in 1960. We had about 13 Texans on that championship squad, and we were all the best of friends. We got better and better each year. First, the running game came around, then our defense showed up. The final piece of the puzzle came with the arrival of this rookie quarterback who had all the talent in the world. But nobody knew for sure if he could handle being thrust into the spotlight and if he could grow up as quickly as we were asking him to. If you think about it, it's kind of amazing that in three years' time this young kid emerged as the leader that we needed him to be in order for our team to fulfill the mission we'd set out for: a Super Bowl victory.

Larry Grantham came up to me amid the raucous scene, holding a bottle of champagne like it was the Super Bowl trophy itself. "All right, Maynard," he said. "You said you would drink some champagne if we won. Well, here you go."

"Well," I drawled. "I decided I'm going to put it off for another year. But if we do it again next year and, well, I'll have two glasses."

Sure, I got some guff from Grantham and the other guys, but they honored my wishes. And, at the same time, maybe they took what I said to them as a challenge. (Of course, we never did get back to the Super Bowl. In fact, no Jets team has made it to the big game since our win in Miami in 1969.)

Usually, at that juncture, one of the coaches announced to the roomful of players who was going to be awarded the game ball. But on that day, game balls were given to everybody on the team. Then the press came in and that shared moment in time was broken and was never to be recaptured.

One lone press guy came up to talk to me. I'll never forget the first thing he asked. "So how do you feel that you didn't catch any balls in the Super Bowl?"

I looked over at Namath. A brightly lit figure standing among a throng of reporters fought for position around him. He was wearing his big, carefree smile. Now that I think about it, wherever I turned, I saw a player, dressed in white and green, exhausted, sweaty, and wearing a smile as wide as the Rio Grande.

How did I feel about catching zero passes in the Super Bowl?

I felt like a million bucks.

The Real Super Bowl Is Today

WE HAD BEATEN THE COLTS—fair and square—in Miami. But we knew that to remove any doubt that the AFL was every bit equal to the NFL, if we were really going to turn the world upside down, we had one more game to play and one last team to beat.

Seven months had gone by since we had captured the Super Bowl. But when we returned to New York for the 1969 regular season, many people said that we weren't even the top dogs in our own city. "New York was a Giants town," they said. "Always had been, always will be." We were always going to be the little guys.

"Right now, they are the champions of the world," wrote the *New York Times'* George Vescey. "Does that make them the champions of New York?"

The issue would be settled on August 17, 1969. On that hot and rain-soaked day, 70,874 people showed up to the Yale Bowl in New Haven, Connecticut, to witness the first-ever meeting between our teams. At that same time, Camille, a Category 5 hurricane, was approaching landfall in Mississippi. The Woodstock Music Festival was in its third and final day.

In our locker room prior to kickoff, Weeb announced that our three original Titans—Larry Grantham, Bill Mathis, and I—would be co-captains for the day. I thought that was a really nice gesture on

Weeb's part. He knew—heck, the whole team knew—how we'd been rejected by the NFL almost 10 years earlier. We had been trying to prove ourselves ever since. This was our chance at a bit of personal redemption.

I turned to my teammates. "That down yonder in Miami is over," I said. "We won. But look here—if we don't beat the Giants today they will call it a 'fluke.' They'll say we lucked out. They'll come up with any darn excuse they can think up. The real Super Bowl is going to be today."

I'll tell you this—every player on that team, from the veterans to the rookies, was fired up and ready to take the field that Sunday.

I don't imagine that there was anybody who wanted us to win that afternoon any more than I did. That's because, on the opposite side of the field, stood the very same man who had cut me from the Giants as a rookie way back in 1959. The man who had told me I didn't belong in New York City because I looked strange. That I didn't belong on the Giants because I ran strange. That I didn't belong in the NFL because I wasn't good enough. Allie Sherman.

I was bound and determined that this was going to be the game of my career—of my life! As I was warming up on the sidelines before the game, some fan up in the stands who appeared to have had a bit too much too drink hollered down to me, "Hey, Maynard! Go home! You're too old and you're too slow." I thought to myself, *Gee whiz, what did I ever do to this guy?*

We went out there and we put up 24 unanswered points on their defense in just 17 minutes. At one point, I caught a long one from Namath on the 20-yard line, right over by where that fan had been heckling me. If I remember correctly, it was about a 70-yard catch.

We went into halftime with a 24–0 lead, but there was no way Weeb was going to pull us starters for the start of the second half. We wouldn't have let him even if he wanted to pull us.

"I guess you can call this the wrap-up of the merger," Pete Rozelle had declared during halftime.

I went out there in the second half and caught another long pass down that same sideline, this one probably around the 35-yard line. After that, I didn't hear that guy make a peep.

We emerged with a resounding 37–14 win. We had really stuck it to them, and it felt great. Namath played a masterful game, completing 14 of 16 passes for 188 yards and three touchdowns. When asked after the game when he thought the Jets were in command, Namath answered, "The first time we got the ball." If somebody else made that comment, you'd call them boastful, but with Namath, it came out as fact.

I was standing on the sideline with five minutes left in the game when I heard a bunch of Giants fans singing, "Goodbye, Allie." Well, I turned around, faced the stands, and I started leading the crowd in song! Suddenly, the whole crowd was singing it—"Goodbye, Allie"—as the game went on. It was one funny sight. But it was also a great moment of personal vindication for me. I had beaten the man who had nearly devastated my career 10 years earlier. Well, I might have been an NFL reject in 1958, but today I'm a winner. At that moment, I was probably the happiest guy in the world.

The next day all of the coaches and players watched the game film. At one point, the cameraman had caught me over on the sidelines, facing the stands and waving my hands like a conductor. Somebody called out, "What it the world were you doing, Maynard?"

"Well, I was just sending Allie Sherman home," I replied. My teammates got a real kick out of that.

Two weeks after we embarrassed the Giants at the Yale Bowl, Giants owner Wellington Mara fired Allie Sherman. *Goodbye, Allie.*

As for all those stubborn NFL loyalists—those who declared our victory over the Colts a fluke, those in the country who were opposed to change, those who were opposed to giving the AFL equal status—the show we put on against the Giants settled the matter once and for all.

A few months later, the New York Mets won their first World Series. I think both Mets and Jets fans felt alike. *Finally, we've arrived.* I can't speak for the Mets players, but those of us who played for the White and Green felt we could walk a little taller, hold our heads up a little higher. We wore big smiles around the city for a long time after our win in the Yale Bowl.

Unfortunately, despite all the great talent on that Super Bowl squad, we never made it back to that championship game.

Always the competitor, Namath suffered a devastating knee injury in 1971 when he attempted to tackle 230-pound Detroit Lions linebacker Mike Lucci. When I heard the news that Namath was done for the season, I cried.

The Jets have yet to return to the Super Bowl.

Years later, when I finally got to meet Lamar Hunt in person, I thanked him for founding the league and for giving me a job. Later, he sent me a personal letter to let me know how much my words had meant to him. To this day, it's one of my most cherished mementos.

My appreciation for the city of New York and its great people has only grown with each passing year. New York was good to me, and I think I was good to it. All in all, everything worked out real well.

Seventeen years—and 10,000 yards—after my career began, I retired from pro football. I settled back down in El Paso, Texas, where I've lived happily for the past 56 years.

Well, Mom and Dad, it looks like I can finally stop moving.

Co-author's Note

MODESTY PREVENTS DON MAYNARD from listing off his accolades, but I'm afforded no such limitation. Quite simply, Don is one of a kind and a trailblazer in football history.

Many know that he was the first New York Titan, but that was simply the first of a series of firsts in Don's career. He was also the first wide receiver—in the NFL or AFL—to gain 10,000 yards. He was the first player with more than 50 100-yard receiving games in his career. He had more than 50 catches and 1,000 receiving yards in five different seasons. At the time of his retirement, he led football in pass receptions (633) and receiving yards (11,834).

He was also an innovator in football equipment. He, with the help of longtime Jets equipment manager Bill Hampton, made many innovations, some of them now the standard of the sport. Don was the first player to wear a V-neck jersey, a mesh jersey, white-colored cleats, short "soccer style" spikes, cheek pads inside the helmet in place of a chin strap, an added elastic belt to his pants to accommodate standing in stance on the line of scrimmage, and special socks that went above the knee to protect from grass burns and infield dirt. Put simply, Don's mind was always working. He was always looking for that extra edge to make himself a better competitor.

He was inducted to the Pro Football Hall of Fame in 1987 and is a member of the halls of fame for the American Football League,

Texas Sports, UTEP (formerly Texas Western), New York City & State Athletic, El Paso & Big Country Athletic, and Blue-Gray All-Star Football Classic.

He is a member of the All-Time AFL team and was a Pro Bowl player in 1966, 1968, 1969, and 1970.

Don has also been an All-Star in his work off the field, doing charity work for many organizations, including the American Heart Association, the American Cancer Society, the March of Dimes, and Boy Scouts of America. He is the founder of the NFL Cancer Research golf tournament and the NFL Charity Nationwide Golf Tournament.

After all those years instructing his teammates on smart budgeting, he opened a financial consulting firm. He has also worked in sales, marketing, public relations, coaching, education, and, of course, plumbing.

Acknowledgments

Thank you to all of the people—classmates, students, teachers—who have inspired me through the years. To Lamar Hunt, for founding the AFL, and to the other owners who supported the league in its beginning. To the great teammates who I played with and against. And to all the great fans at home (and few on the road), thank you.

—D.M.

I would like to thank my family. My parents, David and Karen; my sister, Courtney; our Lil' Lady, my Nana Ruth; and all my uncles, aunts, and cousins. I would also like to thank Katy Sprinkel, my editor at Triumph Books; Adam Motin, who continues to be a great supporter; Bill Ames; and Tom Bast. Sarah Mendelsohn and Amy Hutchinson provided their invaluable help transcribing interviews. As always, my gratitude to Allen St. John, Kyle Smith, Carla Rhodes, Emily McCombs, Chris Mohney, Chris Spags, John Brooks and Courtney O'Brien Brooks, Nick McGlynn, Dana Sterling, Constantine Valhouli, and the great Bonnie. A heartfelt thanks to Joe Namath for sharing his time and wisdom with me. Finally, to Don Maynard, it was an honor working with you. As you might say, I tip my hat to you, sir.

—M.S.